Marketing for Managers

A Practical Approach

Second edition

The answers to all the questions
you were afraid to ask

LF Pitt

JUTA

Pilot edition published 1997
First Edition 1998
Second Edition 2002

© Juta & Co, Ltd
PO Box 24309, Lansdowne 7779

ISBN 0 7021 5933 6

Cover design: Cath Crookes
Typesetting and design: AN dtp Services, Cape Town
Digital Imposition and Imagesetting by Syreline Process
Printed by Creda Communications, Eliot Avenue, Eppindust II, Cape Town

Pascale, RT & Athos, AG. 1981. *The Art of Japanese Management: Applications for American Executives.* New York, NY: Simon and Schuster.

Peppers, D & Rogers, M. 1993. *The One-to-One Future: Building Relationships One Customer at a Time.* New York, NY: Currency Doubleday.

Peppers, D & Rogers, M. 1995. A new marketing paradigm: Share of customer, not market share. *Planning Review,* 23 (March–April): 14–18.

Prahalad, CV & Hamel, G. 1990. The core competence of the corporation. *Harvard Business Review,* May-June: 79–91.

Quinn, lB. 1992. *Intelligent Enterprise.* New York, NY: Free Press.

Rappaport, A. 1987. *Creating Shareholder Value: The New Standard for Business Performance.* New York, NY: Free Press.

Rayport, IF & Sviokla, II. 1994. Managing in the marketspace. *Harvard Business Review,* November–December: 141–150.

Revans, RW. 1971. *Developing Effective Managers: A New Approach to Business Education.* New York, NY: Praeger.

Reicheld, FF. 1993. Loyalty-based management. *Harvard Business Review,* March–April: 64–72.

Sainsbury, D. Quoted in Dillon, RI. 1988. The family custom. *Hermes,* Summer 22–27 New York, NY: Columbia Business school.

Shapiro, BP. 1994. Tectonic changes in the world of marketing. In Duffy, PB (ed). *The Relevance of a Decade.* Boston, MA: Harvard Business School Press.

Sheff, D. 1995. The virgin billionaire. *Playboy,* February: 114–136.

Simmonds, K. 1986. Marketing as innovation: The eighth paradigm. *Journal of Management Studies,* 23(5) (September): 479–500.

Slater, SF & Narver, IC. 1991. *Becoming more market oriented: An exploratory study of the programmatic and market-back approaches.* Cambridge, MA: Marketing Science Institute Report No. 91: 128.

Stalk, C, Evans, P & Shulman, LE. 1992. Competing on capabilities: The new rules of corporate strategy. *Harvard Business Review,* March–April: 57–69.

Taco Bell Corp (Harvard Business School Case 9-692-058). Boston, MA: Harvard Business School Publishing.

Tichy, NM & Devanna, MA. 1986. *The Transformational Leader.* New York, NY: John Wiley and Sons.

Townsend, R. 1970. *Up the Organization.* New York, NY: Knopf.

Tushman, M & Romanelli, E. 1985. Organizational evolution: A metamorphosis model of convergence and reorientation. In Cummings, L & Stow, B (eds). *Research in Organizational Behavior Vol. 7.* Greenwich, CT: JAI Press.

Weilbacher, WM. 1993. *Brand Management.* Lincolnwood, IL: NTC Business Books.

Preface to the second edition

Much has happened since the publication of the first edition of this title. I have once again moved institutions, and this time continents, and so my life has changed in many ways. I have continued working with existing collaborators and found new ones.

Marketing has also changed, as it will no doubt continue to do. This second edition represents the most recent work that I have done with both existing and new colleagues, and presents to readers some of the most important developments in the marketing environment.

The first important change is that there is a new first chapter. For many years, I have believed that we often define marketing and have marketing strategy before we even consider why we need it. Chapter 1, constructed with Pierre Berthon and Mike Ewing, presents a framework for managing competitive advantage as a process. Importantly, the most significant changes occurring in marketing have to do with our evaluations of the outcomes of that process.

Chapter 4 is also new. It represents the thinking of my friends Pierre Berthon and Mac Hulbert, and myself. For many years, we have questioned whether the prevalent marketing line of 'give customers what they want and you will be successful' is universally true. We have published a number of papers on the topic, and this chapter distils these in a way we have found appealing to practicing managers.

Marketing is about the management of relationships, and can be broadened to management of relationships with stakeholders other than customers. Until recently, the problem with this has been that the complexity of the process makes it very difficult for individual marketing executives. Technology has come to the rescue, and these issues are explored in the new Chapter 13, which reflects work done with my colleagues Nigel de Bussy, Rick Watson and Mike Ewing.

The first edition of this work was one of the first texts to include the Internet and the World Wide Web as weapons in the marketer's arsenal. However, it is surprising to look back on this chapter and to see how much has become passé – we simply accept in 2002 the things that were so amazing in 1996. The danger of including such a chapter is that the content can quickly date. Therefore, rather than prescribing in this chapter, I have attempted to provide a framework for thinking about the impact of technology on marketing and strategy.

Two sources have influenced my thinking in this new edition. First, there have been the numerous colleagues who have offered comment and helped shape my thinking. Some have already been mentioned; others include Rian van der Merwe, Julie Napoli and Marie Murgolo-Poore. My department head, Ram Ramaseshan, makes this a great place to work and think, and he helps to keep bureaucrats out of whatever hair I have left. In South Africa, I have enjoyed great relationships with colleagues at schools such as Unisa, GIBS and Pretoria – especially Arien Strasheim, Nic Binedell, Melanie Prinsloo, Flip du Plessis and Yolanda Jordaan. Second, there have been the readers and users of the book – students, executive and short-course participants. I have been encouraged by their favourable comments and hope that this second edition lives up to their expectations.

Leyland Pitt
Perth, Australia, April 2002

Contents

About the author

Leyland Pitt is Professor of Marketing at the School of Marketing, Curtin University of Technology, Australia, and adjunct Professor of Marketing at Kingston Business School, UK, the University of Vienna, and Ecole Nationale Ponts et Chaussees in Paris. He has taught marketing and electronic commerce in MBA and executive programmes at schools such as Warwick Business School, London Business School, the Graduate School of Business at Columbia University, and the Graham School of Continuing Studies at the University of Chicago. In South Africa, he taught at the University of Cape Town's Graduate School of Business, Unisa's School of Business Leadership, and the Gordon Institute of Business Science.

His particular areas of interest in research and teaching involve marketing and electronic media, the staging of consumer experiences, and marketing strategy. An author of over 100 papers in scholarly journals, his work has appeared in publications such as *California Management Review, Sloan Management Review, Journal of the Academy of Marketing Science, Journal of Business Research, Journal of Advertising Research, Communications of the ACM*, and *MIS Quarterly* (for which he also served as Associate Editor). He is also a winner of the award for the best paper in the *Journal of International Marketing.* He has conducted in-house management development programmes for leading organisations throughout the world, including British Airways, Hong Kong and Shanghai Banking Corporation, Volkswagen, Volvo, Royal Metropolitan Police Service, Armstrong World Industries, Economist, and Lloyds TSB. He has also been the recipient of a number of awards for teaching excellence, including the MBA teacher of the year at Henley, MBA teacher of the year (two years running) at Copenhagen Business School, and he was on the Dean's List at the School of Business Administration, Simon Fraser University, Vancouver, Canada.

Juta & Co Ltd

Introduction

Low cost and differentiation are mutually inclusive

Customer equity

From CLTV to customer equity

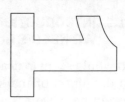

Before marketing

1.1 INTRODUCTION: COMPETITIVE RATIONALITY (OR, WHY WE NEED STRATEGY)[1]

It would seem logical that a book on marketing should begin with a definition of marketing, then look at marketing strategy and examine the marketing concept. This book doesn't. Instead, we begin by looking at something far more fundamental: Why organisations need marketing and, especially, why they need marketing strategy. Only by doing this, will we become truly convinced of the need for marketing and understand it as the powerful relationship building function that it is.

One of the few markets in the world in which there is currently little evidence of oversupply is organ donation for transplantation. Unlike other industries, such as air travel, rental cars, hotel accommodation, personal computers, detergents, vehicle manufacturing and motor car tyres (where there is evidence of over-capacity of as much as 40%), the demand for human body parts for transplantation, such as corneas, kidneys, livers, hearts and lungs, tragically and significantly exceeds availability. Attempts by health authorities and charities to convince individuals to carry volunteer donor cards that can be referenced in the event of their death have only proven moderately successful. Potential donors either do not wish to be reminded of their mortality or the walls of indifference are too high to scale. Recently, Novartis (the result of a merger between two major pharmaceutical firms, Ciba-Geigy and Sandoz) has made significant progress in breeding pigs with genetically compatible body parts, which may be transplantable into humans, with minimal danger of tissue rejection. There are indications of progress being made on similar initiatives by other players in biotechnology. In the not-too-distant future, a patient seeking a transplant may have a choice of suppliers of organs for transplantation. Like most markets, the market for organs may then be faced with over-supply; indeed, it

---

[1] Based on Pitt, LF, Ewing, MT & Berthon, P. 2000. Turning Competitive Advantage into Customer Equity. *Business Horizons*, September/October, pages 11–18.

is difficult to think of many industries in the world where this situation does not, or at least will not, exist.

The scenario sketched above serves as a good setting in which to introduce what Peter Dickson (1992) has called the cycle of 'competitive rationality'. Over-supply in a market has one fundamental effect: it creates customer choice. Customers are free to choose from the offerings of various suppliers in a market, all driven by a desire to use excess capacity to generate revenues and reduce costs. As Dickson points out, customers who are faced with a choice become sophisticated very rapidly. They seek value and, in doing so, become adept at price comparisons, seeking benefits at every turn and frequently playing off one supplier against another. In their attempts to deal with these ever more fickle, demanding customers, firms try every trick in the book. They try to develop new products or services; they price differently; they strive to deliver the product or service in ways the customer hasn't seen before; or, they endeavour to communicate with customers in hitherto unexpected ways. In short, they attempt to innovate. This does not necessarily mean that they engage in what has been entered into the popular vernacular as 'rocket science' or 'brain surgery' – frequently this innovation is little more than another leaf of lettuce on the hamburger (Morris, M, 1998). Firms attempt almost anything to drag the jaded customer out of a state of bored indifference.

However, the problem in most markets is that innovation leads rapidly to imitation. No one remembers the name of the first life assurance company to offer premium discounts to non-smokers; within a few weeks, the entire industry was doing it. Moreover, to complete the relentless cycle of competitive rationality, imitation leads to more over-supply. Obviously not every firm faces this situation all the time and, indeed, markets themselves 'go round'. However, it is important to realise that, while a particular firm or market might not currently face an over-supply situation, it is merely in another phase of the cycle. Moreover, the cycle is inexorable. Choices are three-fold: get off the cycle and exit the market (so what next?); start an entirely new cycle (difficult for all but a few players and probably not sustainable in the long term); or, keep up with the cycle.

In this chapter, we propose that, in order to keep up with the cycle of competitive rationality, firms need to manage a process of competitive advantage. Competitive advantage is not, we believe, something static – that a firm either has or does not – but rather, like competitive rationality, a cyclical process that can be continually managed. While this approach doesn't represent new thinking in the management and marketing literature, we contend that two important changes have recently occurred in the process. First, the notion of distinct positions of competition has become obsolete. Second, the outcomes of these positions are also outmoded; a single, all-encompassing consequence will be the focus of most organisations in the future. These two changes will be the foci of this chapter.

1.1.1 Managing competitive advantage as a process

In an award-winning article, Day & Wensley (1988) alerted us to the management of competitive advantage as a process, rather than something static, or fixed, and hinted that the aspiration of 'sustainable' competitive advantage was probably a pipedream for most firms. Their model of the process of competitive advantage is shown in Figure 1.1.

Figure 1.1: Process model of competitive advantage (Day & Wensley, 1988)

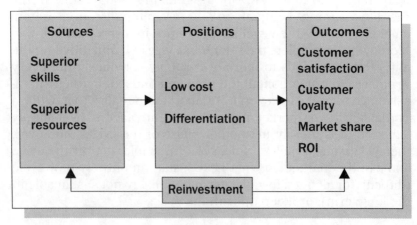

According to Day & Wensley (1988), there are only two sources of competitive advantage for a firm: it either has superior skills or superior resources – and hopefully, both. 'Superior skills' is a catchphrase for greater resources in terms of human talent, expertise, abilities or competencies. 'Superior resources' implies greater stocks of financial and other capital, better productive capacity, better location, access to supply and the like. These sources of competitive advantage are used to achieve one of two positions of advantage or ways of competing. Following Michael Porter (1985), the authors identify two generic competitive strategies – low cost or differentiation. Supposedly, the low-cost competitor is able to produce and deliver the product or service at the lowest cost, with the advantages of margin and pricing flexibility that this confers. For competitors who are unable to achieve the low-cost position, the only other course of action is to differentiate. In other words, these competitors must make the product or service bigger, smaller, faster, more colourful, better quality, offer superior service, or offer a bigger range than other suppliers. These producers must differentiate their offerings in ways that customers value and are prepared to pay for, in order to compete successfully at best and survive at least. Porter (1985) implies that the two strategies are mutually exclusive and that to attempt to be a low-cost differentiator is to court the disaster of being stuck in the middle: increased costs without real differentiation. While that might have been true for the late 1970s and early 1980s, developments such as flexible manufacturing technologies have made these choices less clear-cut (Hill & Jones, 1998). It may not only be desirable to strive after both positions, but in many situations, also the key to survival and success.

According to Day & Wensley (1988), when a firm exploits either of the two generic strategies with some success, the outcomes will be evident in a number of variables. The performance of a successful competitor will manifest itself in financial productivity, measured by a return on investment (ROI) – or, for that matter, ROCE, ROA, RONA, or any of a number of financial acronyms. The successful competitor's performance will also manifest in the form of increased market share or, at the very least, maintenance thereof. There are two other outcomes of achieving a position of competitive advantage. One is customer satisfaction. A firm that offers customers the benefits of a differentiated offering, or passes on some of the savings achieved by lower cost will satisfy customers. The other is customer loyalty. Satisfied customers tend to remain loyal to firms that fulfil them and, given the choice, refrain from patronising competitors.

Most managers give more attention to the outcomes of market share and financial productivity for two reasons: these outcomes tend to be easier to measure and managers are typically rewarded for improved results. Managers are inclined to agree that customer satisfaction and loyalty are important and that (as loosely implied in the sequence of Figure 1.1) they lead to market share and ROI (or other measures). However, they will likewise contend that these concepts are more vague and difficult to measure. To an extent, they are right. While attempts by consumer psychologists and marketing researchers to improve the measurement of customer satisfaction (Anderson, Fornell & Lehmann, 1994) and service quality (Parasuraman, Zeithaml & Berry, 1985; 1988) have been laudable, we should not forget that what they are trying to achieve is daunting. They are attempting to 'get inside the heads' of customers and assess complex human processes, such as satisfaction, using lamentably inadequate tools, such as five- and seven-point scales. Customers are required to express enigmatic feelings, impressions and emotions by circling points on ordinal scales to which marketers attribute interval characteristics.

What makes market share and financial productivity measures appealing as outcomes of a position of competitive advantage, is the fact that they are 'hard' – they are expressed in numbers that can easily be calculated, compared and tracked. The problem, however, is that they are historical – a good way of tracking the past, but a rather inadequate indication of the future. While customers may be capricious at times, they are not so fickle as to be satisfied today and dissatisfied with the same offering tomorrow, or switch loyalty midstream. Indeed, most customers are probably more tolerant of marketers' shortcomings than the latter would give them credit for, and only downgrade ratings or shift allegiances as the result of gross dereliction by supplier firms. Again, the problem with most measures of customer satisfaction and loyalty is that they are soft and impression-based. They are, however, about the future.

The logic of the model presented in Figure 1.1 is that the astute firm will reinvest the financial outcomes of competitive advantage in the sources of competitive advantage, namely superior skills and/or superior resources. This activity closes the loop in the model and suggests that managing for competitive advantage is a process that is continually renewed, revived and refreshed. Certainly, a strategist's skills may be distinguished by his or her knowledge of the sources of competitive advantage in which to invest, what position(s) to adopt, and the ability to determine the outcome of the process effectively. We argue that the process is changing in two significant ways:

- low cost and differentiation are no longer separate, but entangled by necessity; and

- the four outcome variables in the process have outlived their usefulness. In future, they will be replaced by one overarching outcome variable that will direct all of marketing strategy and most of corporate strategy.

These changes are the result of the most dramatic force affecting marketing today: information technology.

1.2 LOW COST AND DIFFERENTIATION ARE MUTUALLY INCLUSIVE

Michael Porter (1985) implied that a firm could not follow two generic strategies simultaneously because, in attempting to do so, it would become unfocused. Our observation of some successful firms in a variety of industries seems to suggest the opposite. Indeed, one may query whether it is possible to compete without attempting to be both low cost and well differentiated. In all likelihood, this change has come about because the impact of information technology (Porter & Millar, 1985). Information technology is enabling and driving firms to do both. Two well-publicised examples of firms in different industries appear to reinforce our contention.

The Internet bookstore Amazon.com has received much attention. The firm offers low book prices – often as much as 40% less – on a huge range (in excess of four-million titles), because it doesn't actually own much inventory. Instead, it uses technology to communicate rapidly and inexpensively with both suppliers and forwarding companies. What the firm provides to its customers is extremely well differentiated – after all, any bookstore can sell books. Rather, Amazon.com sells 'information about books' using a very powerful database search facility. The firm also customises its offerings to the individual. Customers receive e-mail updates on books of their preference and are alerted to best matches with their previous purchases each time they log-on to the web site.

Dell Computer is one of the success stories of electronic commerce (Serwer, 1998), with estimates of sales off its web site needing to be updated daily. In February 1998, these were estimated to be in excess of $4 million each day.[2] The company has been a sterling performer through the latter half of the 1990s, and much of its recent achievement has been attributed to its trading over the Internet. Using Dell's web site, a customer is able to customise a computer by specifying (by clicking on a range of options) attributes such as processor speed, RAM size, hard drive, CD ROM, and modem type and speed. A handy calculator instantly updates customers on the cost, so that they can adjust their budgets accordingly. Once the customer is satisfied with the specified package, he or she can place an order and pay

---

[2] On 29 September 1998, Dell's Head of Internet Marketing, UK, Joanne Grey confirmed this while addressing delegates at a seminar at Henley Management College, and informed that latest sales off the site were $7 million a day (with European sales accounting for $7 million weekly).

online. Only then does Dell make up the machine, which is delivered to the customer just over a week later. Even more importantly, Dell only places orders for items such as monitors from Sony, or hard drives from Seagate, once the customer's order is confirmed. The PC industry leader Compaq's current rate of stock turn is 12 times per year; Dell's is 30. This may seem like an attractive accounting performance or a simple lowering of cost, until one realises the tremendous strategic advantage it gives Dell. When Intel launches a new, faster processor, Compaq effectively has to sell six weeks' of old stock before they are able to launch machines with the new chip; Dell only have to sell ten days' worth (Magretta, 1998).

Both Amazon.com and Dell do more than just differentiate products or services, as both Porter (1980) and Day & Wensley (1988) suggest they should. They take differentiation to the extreme and 'differentiate customers' (Peppers & Rogers, 1993). However, both business models operate at extremely low cost; in the absence of real cost data, we would contend among the lowest in their respective industries.

1.3 CUSTOMER EQUITY: THE SINGLE OUTCOME OF A PROCESS OF COMPETITIVE ADVANTAGE

While the two sets of outcomes in the Day & Wensley model presented in Figure 1.1 have their own particular strengths, each has its limitations. In summary, the outcomes of ROI and market share are hard but historical, and the outcomes of customer satisfaction and customer loyalty are future-oriented but soft. Ideally, what is needed is a single outcome that is both hard (a number that can be expressed financially) and future- (customer-) oriented. We propose that customer lifetime value (CLTV), which leads to customer equity, is that single appropriate outcome.

Traditional accounting systems have viewed customers as sources of revenue. Increasingly, firms are beginning to use their accounting systems to view customers as assets, and basing their decisions on customers much as they would base their decisions on investments. We define CLTV as the net present value (NPV) of the profit a firm stands to realise on the average new customer during a given number of years. This is illustrated in the spreadsheet in Figure 1.2.

Figure 1.2: A simple spreadsheet for the calculation of CLTV

Revenue	YEAR 1	YEAR 2	YEAR 3	YEAR 4	YEAR 5
Customers	1 000	400	180	90	50
Retention Rate	40.00%	45.00%	50.00%	55.00%	60.00%
Ave Ann Sales	150	150	150	150	150
Total Revenue	150 000	60 000	27 000	13 500	7 425
Costs					
Cost %	50.00%	50.00%	50.00%	50.00%	50.00%
Total Costs	75 000	30 000	13 500	6 750	3 713
Profits					
Gross Profit	75 000	30 000	13 500	6 750	3 713
Discount Rate	1.00	1.20	1.44	1.73	2.07
NPV Profit	75 000.00	25 000.00	9 375.00	3 906.25	1 790.36
Cum NPV Profit	75 000	100 000	109 375	113 281	115 072
CL TV	75.00	100.00	109.38	113.28	115.07

This elementary spreadsheet might be typical of a firm marketing a magazine subscription. If we assume the firm sells 1 000 new subscriptions in Year 1 at $150 each, the calculation of net revenue and net costs at 50% of revenue are simple procedures. A further important issue is retention: How many customers at the beginning of the year are still subscribers at the end of the year? What we have done in Figure 1.2 is to assume a retention rate of 40% at the end of Year 1, and then increase this gradually over the five-year period. Thus, 400 customers are still subscribers at the beginning of Year 2, 180 at the beginning of Year 3, and so on. The revenues and the costs for a year are functions of the number of customers at the beginning of that year.

Calculating gross profit is then a simple subtraction procedure, and what follows is perhaps the only, albeit slightly, complex calculation of the procedure. As in all investments, the returns for a customer five years from now are not worth what they are today. Therefore, we need to discount gross profit. The discount rate selected for Figure 1.2 is 20%. This figure is discretionary and will vary from firm to firm. Some may choose a premium bank rate, others an internal rate of return, and still others some minimum rate of investment acceptability. This is not critical to our discussion because the principles remain the same. This discount rate is used to calculate the net present value (NPV) of the cumulative gross profit over the years. The final calculation is a simple one: What is the CLTV of a customer who was put on the books in Year 1? The answer is the NPV of the cumulative gross profit for the year divided by the number of customers in Year 1 (in this case 1 000). Thus, the CLTV of one of these customers in Year 4 would be $113.28, and in Year 5 $115.07, and so on.

An obvious application of this type of spreadsheet is its use in calculating 'What can be done to increase CLTV?'[3] The decision-maker can change variables such as price, costs, discount rate, the number of years an individual will be a customer and, of course, the retention rate, to determine the effects these will have on CLTV. Generally, it is worth considering what can be done from a marketing strategy perspective to maximise CLTV. It is also critical to realise that, while calculating 'average' CLTVs can be useful and insightful, it is possible, and in many cases imperative to calculate the CLTV of a named, individual customer on a customer database.

In summary, we can increase CLTV by:

1. Increasing lifetime – either by increasing retention rate or customer life (i.e. the number of years a customer remains a customer).

2. Increasing sales to or because of a customer, either by increasing the firm's share of the customer's purchases, or by increasing the customer's referral rate (the number of times they refer others to the firm's products and services).

3. Cutting the costs of serving a customer.

Each of these tactics will now be expanded upon.

---

[3] Similar spreadsheets can be downloaded from www.1to1.com

1.3.1 Increasing customer lifetime

Customer lifetime can be increased in two ways – either by reducing the probability that the customer will defect (Reicheld & Sasser, 1990) or, conversely, increasing retention; or by increasing the life of a customer. These alternatives incorporate the outcomes of customer satisfaction and loyalty shown in Figure 1.1, for they rely substantially on keeping satisfied customers loyal, or as loyal as possible. There is a vast range of industries focusing on customer retention and loyalty, ranging from airline frequent-flyer schemes through to supermarket loyalty card programmes. Even Coca-Cola has an established loyalty programme (Morris, B.1998). Many reward customers simply by discounting, or offering free products or services (such as airlines offering free flights, and telephone companies discounting frequent calls to friends and family members). Increasingly, firms are realising that all customers are not created equal, and that more individualised strategies will be more effective at retaining customers. Frequent flyers who fly thousands of miles annually are unlikely to be motivated by the reward of even more flying. Smarter airlines are now rewarding these customers for their loyalty by making their flying a more rewarding experience: the use of lounges at all times, upgrades, first call on standby tickets, etc.

Extending customer life (Page, Pitt & Berthon, 1996), by increasing the number of years the customer will be a customer, can also enhance the lifetime of a customer. All products and services tend to have a 'natural life' for a customer. For example, the life of a customer for a financial service such as a home mortgage can be very long (around 25 years), whereas the life of a customer for a product such as teenage fashion clothing can be much shorter (just a few years). In the case of business-to-business markets, the life of a customer can be very long indeed, and may exceed the physical longevity of the individual actors, as two firms trade with each other for over a hundred years. Recently, there have been some excellent examples of firms extending the life of a customer by adapting marketing strategy.

Kimberley Clark, manufacturers of Huggies disposable diapers (nappies) were subject to the limitations imposed by the fact that the 'life' of a Huggies customer (the baby) was on average 18 months, before the baby became toilet-trained. Market research revealed a considerable degree of guilt feeling among parents. Mothers and fathers feel guilty when friends and family comment that little Johnny or Mary 'is still in nappies' and, simultaneously, feel guilty at rushing a small child who might not be 'ready for pants'. Consequently, Huggies introduced 'trainer pants', which fit like real pants, but are disposable and have all the absorbency of a conventional diaper. No more guilty feelings for parents. More importantly, Huggies have increased the life of a customer by about six months (before they finally wear real pants).

Effectively, this is a 33% average increase in customer life (and doing 'what-ifs?' on a spreadsheet such as Figure 1.2 would demonstrate the effect of this strategy on CLTV).

An alternative strategy would be to ask how the customer's life could start earlier. The Danish toy marketer Lego makes building blocks that, on average, are played with by children between the ages of four and eight. Thus, the customer life is about four years. Recently, the company has embarked on strategies that start customer life earlier and extend it for longer. The company launched Duplo (essentially bigger Lego blocks) that can be played with by children as young as two, thus adding two years to customer life. At the other end of the customer life spectrum, the company launched Technical Lego, an intricate set of construction blocks and fittings for older children (or what some cynics call 'Lego for Dads'). It is uncertain how many years of life this strategy has added to the Lego customer, but it is not inconceivable to suggest that it may have doubled.

1.3.2 Increasing sales to or because of a customer

Two strategies can be followed to increase sales as a way of boosting CLTV. These involve increasing the share of sales to an individual customer and/or managing that customer in order to get him or her to refer others to the firm's products or services.

The first entails answering the question: 'What else can the customer obtain from me that creates value for him or her?' In many ways, this suggests that market share means a lot less than 'share of customer'. Whereas market-share-marketers are concerned about increasing their share of an overall market, customer-share-marketers care more about getting deeper into the individual customer's shopping basket, credit card, purse, wallet or handbag. The difference in logic between share of market and share of customer thinking is illustrated in Figure 1.3. Share of market is predicated on economies of scale and strives to sell as many of one product to as many customers as possible. Share of customer thinking, however, relies on economies of scope, and asks what other products or services can be sold to a customer. According to the market share model, a marketer of a product like laundry bleach seeks to grow the business by finding more customers to whom he or she can sell the same laundry bleach. A share of customer marketer thinks of all the laundry bleach a particular customer will purchase over a lifetime, and determines to increase and maximise his or her share of those purchases. Even more importantly, this marketer continually examines other products and services the customer will need and want, and strategises how to deliver these.

Figure 1.3: Market share thinking v Customer share thinking

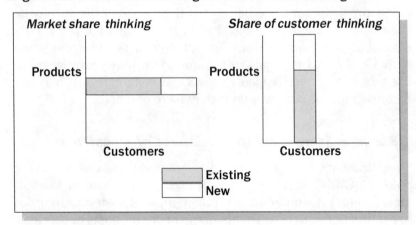

Encouraging existing customers to recommend the firm's products and services to friends, family and colleagues can also increase sales. Obviously, customers who are satisfied and loyal will be more motivated to do this (Bone, 1992; Morin, 1983). Marketers will increasingly endeavour to identify customers who recommend and reward them for their referrals. However, many may go beyond this and actively encourage word of mouth by 'managing the memories' of loyal customers. Individuals tell stories mostly about the things they remember best, so it follows that, if managers do not allow customers to forget their firms, they will tell stories about them. This is particularly true for service firms or in instances where service constitutes a significant part of the offer. Because services are intangible, customers frequently rely on the testimony of others (word of mouth) more than in the case of products (Zeithaml, 1981). In the case of a product, the customer actually has 'something to show for it', whereas with services there is usually just a memory. Smart services marketers realise that these memories can be managed to their advantage – firstly, to increase word of mouth, and secondly, to bring back past customers by reminding them just how good/pleasant/worthwhile (or whatever) the service was.

1.3.3 Cutting the costs of serving a customer

The more the costs of serving customers can be reduced, the greater the profit margin on that customer (which can be capitalised into the future). Whereas all avenues for reducing the costs of serving customers should be explored, the synergistic link between reducing serving costs and customer retention is paramount. In simple terms, loyal customers are less expensive to serve. This is because the firm understands them better, and they understand the firm and its procedures.

In many environments, it is also possible to reduce costs by getting the customer to perform some of the work of service delivery, or what Downes & Mui (1998) call 'outsourcing to the customer'. Surprisingly, customers frequently prefer this as it gives them greater control over the service delivery process. In the past, this approach was most apparent in service firms, but with recent technology, it is also being followed in product manufacturing and retailing situations. This enables both process and product innovation (performing a process better and developing new product or service concepts). Recent examples involving the use of technology, especially the Internet, abound. As a process innovation, a number of airlines encourage frequent flyer club members to access membership and mileage details over the Internet. For example, British Airways Executive Club members can access mileage earned, details of recent transactions, and even determine where these miles will take them to by logging-on to the British Airways web site (http://www.british-airways.com). In the long term, the airline will be able to cut considerable costs out of the process of serving customers – no need to mail out bi-monthly status reports to millions of club members, and a huge reduction in telephone inquiries that need to be answered by real people.

As a product innovation, the Internet site Musicmaker (http://www.musicmaker.com) enables customers to compile their own selection of songs or music items on a web site, then presses the CD and delivers it to the customer. While the innovation is one that many customers enjoy, the firm also reduces the costs of serving its customers by getting them to do the compilation and does not have the burden of huge stocks of pre-recorded CDs.

1.4 FROM CLTV TO CUSTOMER EQUITY

Whereas the competitive advantage process model of Day & Wensley (1988) offers a powerful and useful tool for the management of organisations, it has become somewhat dated in two ways. First, the two generic strategies are no longer mutually exclusive but jointly indispensable. Second, the outcomes originally identified are obsolete and can be replaced effectively by a single measure. To a large extent, both of these shifts have been driven by information technology. CLTV becomes the definitive criterion for assessing the outcome of a process of competitive advantage.

It is important to note that the spreadsheet presented in Figure 1.2 involves the CLTVs of 'average customers'. However, nothing precludes the firm from recognising that all customers are individual and might have unique CLTVs. Daily we see around us the attempts of marketers to capture data that will enable them to get closer to calculating the CLTV of an individual customer – loyalty cards, warranty registration schemes, customer databases and the like. If these CLTVs were then summed, we would have the total value of the firm's customer base, or what Blattberg & Deighton (1996) call customer equity. These authors argue that marketing should be managed by the customer equity criterion. Thus, any marketing decision should be evaluated on whether or not it increases customer equity. For example, when thinking about customer acquisition and retention, the decision should be based on where the next marketing dollar (or pound, or yen, or whatever) would be better spent – on getting new customers or keeping existing ones. The answer is, whichever of the two strategies has the greatest effect on customer equity. Similarly, if we are going to manage for customer equity, there are major implications for how we organise marketing in organisations. Whereas in the past many firms favoured a brand/product management structure, and structured themselves along these lines, nowadays there is a strong argument for the implementation of a customer portfolio management system (Berthon, Hulbert & Pitt, 1997). Rather than structure the firm along product or brand lines, where the performance evaluated is that of the past (typically market share), the firm's customer base is allocated to portfolios of customers, each of which is distinctly managed. The performance of a customer portfolio manager is evaluated on the basis of his or her ability to increase the value of the portfolio. This is a future-based measure, for the value of the portfolio is essentially its customer equity, which, in turn, represents the CLTVs of all the customers that make up the portfolio.

There are other issues in the Blattberg & Deighton (1996) article for managers to consider. Rather than allocating marketing and advertising budgets according to such variables as media selection and spend, or territories, or even customer markets, managers may wish to split the budget between customer acquisition and customer retention activities. Customer equity becomes the basis upon which this decision can be made. The authors go on to make the somewhat radical suggestion that firms may even wish to consider organising themselves along the lines of acquisition and retention, and evaluating the performance of these divisions on their ability to contribute towards customer equity.

1.5 Conclusion

The relentless cycle of competitive rationality implies that a sustainable competitive advantage is an illusion at best, and that executives should rather strive to manage a process of competitive advantage. This requires adopting positions of advantage, assessing the outcomes of the process, and skilfully reinvesting the financial outcomes into the skills and resources that enable the firm to compete. Increasingly, the positions of competition or generic strategies are becoming mutually inextricable, while simultaneously, it is becoming feasible to monitor only one outcome of the process, namely customer lifetime value (which leads to customer equity). The focus in this chapter has been on the unification of generic strategies, and more particularly on customer equity as an outcome of the process of competitive advantage. We have proposed that advances in information technology will accelerate these developments, and there is ample evidence in the business environment that the acceleration process will continue.

References

Anderson, E, Fornell, C & Lehmann, DR. 1994. Customer satisfaction, market share, and profitability. *Journal of Marketing*, 58 (July): 53–66.

Berthon, PR, Hulbert, JM & Pitt, LF. 1997. Brands, brand managers, and the management of brands: Where to next? *Commentary Report No. 97–122*, November. Cambridge, MA: Marketing Science Institute.

Blattberg, RC & Deighton, J. 1996. Manage marketing by the customer equity test. *Harvard Business Review*, July–August, 136–144.

Bone, PF. 1992 Determinants of word-of-mouth communications during product consumption in Sherry, JF & Sternthal, B. (eds). *Advances in Consumer Research*, 19, 579–583.

Day, GS & Wensley, R. 1988. Assessing advantage: A framework for diagnosing competitive superiority. *Journal of Marketing*, 52 (April): 1–20.

Dickson, PR. 1992. Toward a general theory of competitive rationality. *Journal of Marketing*, 56 (January): 69–83.

Downes, L & Mui, C. 1998. *Unleashing the Killer App.* Boston MA: Harvard Business School Press.

Hill, CWL & Jones, GR. 1998. *Strategic Management: An Integrated Approach*. Boston, MA: Houghton Mifflin.

Magretta, J. 1998. The power of virtual integration: An interview with Dell Computer's Michael Dell. *Harvard Business Review*, 76 (2): 73–84.

Morin, SP. 1983 Influentials advising their friends to sell lots of high-tech gadgetry. *The Wall Street Journal*, 28 February: 30.

Morris, B. 1998. Doug is it. *Fortune*, 25 May: 34–42.

Morris, MH. 1998. *Entrepreneurial Intensity: Sustainable Advantages for Individuals, Organizations and Societies*. Westport, Connecticut: Quorum Books.

Page, MJ, Pitt, LF & Berthon, PR. 1996. Analysing customer defections: predicting the effects on corporate performance. *Long Range Planning*, 29, 6 (December): 821–834.

Parasuraman, A, Zeithaml, VA & Berry, LL. 1985. A conceptual model of service quality and its implications for future research. *Journal of Marketing*, 49 (April): 41–50.

Parasuraman, A, Zeithaml, VA & Berry, LL. 1988. SERVQUAL: a multiple-item scale for measuring customer perceptions of service quality. *Journal of Retailing*, 64 (Spring): 12–40.

Peppers, D & Rogers, M. 1993. *The One-to-One Future: Building Relationships One Customer at a Time*, New York, NY: Century Doubleday.

Porter, ME. 1985. *Competitive Advantage: Creating and Sustaining Superior Performance*, New York, NY: Free Press.

Porter, ME & Millar, V.1985. How information gives you competitive advantage. *Harvard Business Review*, July-August: 1–14.

Reicheld, FF & Sasser, WE. 1990. Zero defections: quality comes to services. *Harvard Business Review*, Sepember-October: 301–307.

Serwer, A. 1998. Michael Dell rocks. *Fortune*, 11 May, 27–34.

Zeithaml, VA. 1981. How consumer evaluation processes differ between goods and services. In Donnelly, JH & George, WR (eds) *Marketing of Services*, Chicago, IL: American Marketing Association.

Introduction: What is marketing?

The marketing concept

Customer orientation: Is the customer always right?

Goal orientation

The systems approach

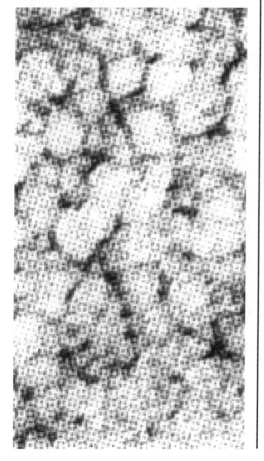

Marketing and the marketing concept

2.1 INTRODUCTION: WHAT IS MARKETING?

What is marketing? Over the years scholars and practitioners have developed a number of formal definitions of marketing. Marketing has been defined as an economic function, as an activity which is broadly based within profit-making businesses, and as an overall philosophy of management. As an economic process, marketing consists of those activities which conduct goods and services from producers to consumers. As a business activity, marketing comprises those actions designed to develop products, price them, place them effectively in market places, and promote them to customer markets in such a way that the organisation realises a profit. More recently marketing has been viewed as a broader range of activities which have to do with the effectiveness of the exchange process. In this sense marketing is as much at home in nonprofit settings as it is in those organisations which have profit as their major objective.

If we were to ask the average person on the street what marketing was, we could expect many different answers. Many people might tell us that marketing is synonymous with selling, or is very much the same thing as advertising. They might also say that marketing is concerned primarily with products. Some might have been exposed to forms of market research, by being invited or perhaps pressurised to participate in surveys. Indeed, some respondents might have an altogether less positive view of marketing and may see it as an activity designed to persuade gullible customers to buy products that they don't need, don't want and can't afford.

Perhaps the best general perspective that we could gain on marketing would be to examine a series of situations. If in many Western countries, one were to turn on one's television set on a Sunday morning at around 11:00, what could one reasonably expect to see? The likelihood of finding some kind of church service or religious programme would be very high. A church or religious organisation would be actively engaging an audience with its message, or a television evangelist would be interacting with his or her audience. The question can be asked: How does this benefit the viewers? Our streetside respondents in the previous paragraph might answer that issues such as involvement, commitment to a belief or to a cause would be reasons for this engagement. The cynics among them might suggest that the viewers are enjoying the benefit of convenience, in not having to leave home to attend a church service on a Sunday. Some might respond that there is nothing in it for the viewers, while, at the opposite extreme, others might say that salvation awaits the participants. How, on the other hand, does the purveyor of the message stand to gain? Again the cynics might argue that the motive is purely financial: large amounts of money are sent to the religious organisation or evangelist by many possibly gullible followers. Of course, financial gain is not to be ignored, but this might not be the primary objective of the organisation. It could also be argued that the organisation is encouraging participation in its work, offering the broader religious community a spiritual service, or commitment to a worthwhile cause.

Let us suggest a second scenario. If an individual is charged with a serious crime, what would his or her recourse be? Most people would say to get hold of a good lawyer. The questions are different in each instance. How does this benefit the alleged criminal? With the assistance of a competent lawyer, the accused may get a lighter sentence, and may escape further prosecution. What are the benefits for the lawyer? Obviously the lawyer receives money. But providers of legal services often work on a client's behalf even if there is little financial reward. They derive their reward from work satisfaction and an enhanced reputation.

A third scenario is worth considering. Nowadays we are inundated with requests to donate money towards environmental causes: save the dolphins, save the rhinos, save the environment, save the rain forests and save the world. How does the donor benefit? Making a donation gives the donor an opportunity to express his commitment to a worthy cause and to help save the environment and its creatures for his (or her) personal benefit and for posterity. How does the recipient organisation benefit? It receives the financial resources to pursue good works and to achieve worthwhile environmental objectives.

Do any of these activities involve marketing? The answer is yes, even though the terms *advertising, selling* or *market research* have not been used in the examples quoted. Two of the above organisations are nonprofit businesses, and in none of the examples was a tangible product being sold. Yet the activities in the examples are classified as 'marketing'. Why? It does not take much to realise that the examples have at least one thing in common — in all three cases, both parties to the marketing benefit from the activity. With this as a starting point, we can begin to develop a definition of marketing: marketing has to do with the management of *mutually beneficial activities*. What are these activities? One could say that the activities are exchanges or transactions. Only five years ago most managers, academics and students of marketing would have been quite content with this description. However, it is flawed because an exchange or transaction implies a one-off event, typified in PT Barnum's famous dictum, 'a sucker is born every day'. Unfortunately, suckers — new undiscovered customers — are in short supply in the 1990s. We therefore need a more suitable description of marketing for the 1990s. Perhaps a better definition is that marketing has to do with the management of *mutually beneficial relationships.* Why is this so? For many organisations the emphasis has shifted away from a search for new customers towards retaining existing customers. The main reason for this is that in most manufacturing and service organisations in the 1990s supply, or the ability to supply, exceeds demand quite substantially. It has become necessary for organisations to build and maintain their relationships with existing customers.

What is a relationship? Formal sociological, anthropological or psychological definitions aside, one can probably safely assume that most readers participate in relationships. Perhaps we should consider what characterises relationships. A relationship is something that takes place over time, for mutual benefit, and that has such attributes as commitment and trust. Most people in relationships do not reconsider the relationship anew each day. For example, most marriage partners do not ask themselves daily whether they should continue their relationship.

(Granted, even in the happiest of marriages partners do on occasion ask themselves this question, but not every day!) Marketing relationships are no different: while no marketing relationships are perfect, suppliers and consumers realise that there is mutual gain to be derived from the relationship. The trend in both academic and practical marketing circles is to talk of *relationship marketing*. In this text, therefore, when we refer to marketing, we mean the management of mutually beneficial relationships, even if this definition is not yet accepted by all — organisations and customers.

2.2 THE MARKETING CONCEPT

Marketing academics and practitioners can take pride in the fact that marketing, unlike other functional areas of business, has a philosophy. This philosophy is known as the *marketing concept*. While it cannot be said to answer all questions, the marketing concept is unique to marketing in the same way that marketing is unique as opposed to other functions within the firm. There is really no such thing as a production concept or a finance concept. (The Chicago School of Finance has an approach to finance characterised by the hypothesis of efficient markets, but this does not constitute a philosophy that is useful for the running and managing of a business.) The marketing concept is indeed a philosophy: it proposes a way of *managing* organisations.

What is the marketing concept? Very simply, the marketing concept rests on three basic tenets. These are customer orientation, goal orientation and a systems approach. This is shown in the diagram in Figure 2.1. We will discuss each of these three tenets in turn. Primarily, however, most people identify with the marketing concept in terms of customer orientation.

2.2.1 Customer orientation: Is the customer always right?

Observers and consumers of popular management literature of the 1980s will have been exposed to the notion of customer orientation in its various forms. The phrases 'close to the

Figure 2.1: The three tenets of the marketing concept

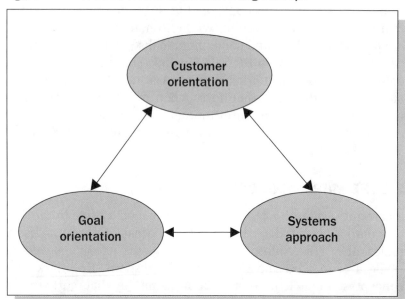

customer', 'market orientation' and the 'customer is always right' appear with monotonous regularity. However customer orientation simply means that the organisation strives to identify the needs and wants of customers and to satisfy these in order to achieve its objectives. Obviously an organisation could have other orientations. The organisation could be product oriented, believing that as long as it produces the very best product or service, the world will beat a path to its door. Another orientation that an organisation could adopt is that of production orientation. This view suggests that as long as the organisation can produce enough of the products or services for which there is a demand, it will be successful. In a world where production exceeds demand, this philosophy is not so easy to apply! A fourth orientation that an organisation could apply is a sales orientation. A sales orientation implies that as long as the organisation tells the market loudly and for long enough about its products and services, customers will purchase them. This may be true in the short term, but in the long term customers will not return if the products that they have been induced to purchase do not satisfy their needs.

Customer orientation means that the organisation strives to identify the needs and wants of customers and to produce the products or services that will satisfy these needs and wants. In reality this has wider implications: every activity of every person, department and function within the organisation strives to serve the customer, and the organisation as a whole is structured to achieve this.

Does this then mean that the customer is always right? A number of authors, critics and speakers in the areas of management and marketing are fond of the phrase 'the customer is always right'. Indeed, many successful organisations have been built on the notion of customer sovereignty. For example, LL Bean, the leading North American mail order retailer, has two simple rules tacked to the walls of the office of every manager and employee within the organisation: *Rule number 1:* The customer is always right. *Rule number 2:* If the customer is wrong, refer to rule number 1. Certainly, this philosophy has not done the performance of LL Bean any harm, and the company's policy of replacing products for customers, no matter how unreasonable the request, is legendary. However, not all organisations agree that the customer is always right. Within the airline industry in recent years there have been several examples of organisations which do not believe that the customer is always right. The first of these is the very successful Virgin Atlantic, founded and managed by Richard Branson. In a recent interview Branson suggested that the customer was indeed not the most important individual to Virgin Atlantic. Rather, he suggested, to Virgin Atlantic the most important individual was the employee. If the organisation looked after the interests of its employees, employees would treat customers likewise, to the ultimate benefit of shareholders. In many organisations, he implied, the opposite order applied: managers cared most about the needs and requirements of shareholders, and in order to achieve profits paid some attention to customers, so that the employee came a distant third. Herb Kelleher, president of South West Airlines, puts forward a similar view. South West Airlines is the only major airline to have achieved profitability *every year* for the last 25 years. It has made money doing what conventional wisdom in the airline industry would suggest is impossible: operating short-haul flights at budget rates. Kelleher not only believes that the customer is not always right, but that this is one of the most damaging and damning lies of marketing! 'The customer is frequently a drunk or a drug addict, and abuses my staff. My job as chief executive is to make sure that this kind of customer never flies with us again', says Kelleher.

So who is correct? Is it LL Bean, whose view is that the customer is always right, or do we side with Branson and Kelleher and disagree? Marketers would probably value a decision tool which would help them decide when their customers were right, and it is possible to provide such a tool. In many organisations managers have in fact discovered the rudiments of such a device by focusing on how the business is defined. This is illustrated below.

Most marketers would agree that McDonald's, the fast-food hamburger chain, is a highly successful marketing organisation. While not all of us like the products that McDonald's markets even the most outspoken critic of the food must commend the marketing successes that McDonald's has achieved over the past 40 years. The organisation operates almost 15 000 franchised and company-owned outlets in over 100 countries throughout the world, serving billions of customers every day. Now picture the following situation: I walk into a McDonald's (anywhere in the world) and begin a friendly conversation with the person behind the counter. I remark on the weather, and comment on the sports results or recent political events. What is the response? The reaction would be something along the lines of 'Hi, may I take your order please?' So, no friendly chat from the person behind the counter. Somewhat taken aback I place my order: two Big Macs, two french fries and two soft drinks. The assistant quickly gets my order and tells me that I owe, for instance, R16.98. I proffer an American Express credit card. Firmly but politely I am told that McDonald's accepts cash only. I pay the amount requested, am thanked for my custom and told to 'Have a nice day'. In the space of a few minutes I have been wrong twice — and this while dealing with an organisation that most marketing critics would agree is a highly successful marketing organisation. What happened to the notion of the customer being right? What is the secret of McDonald's success? Some would say McDonald's has successfully taught customers how they should do business with the company: its customers know how they are to behave. What is the truth? The answer lies in McDonald's definition of its business.

McDonald's defines its business very simply: *QSCV*. What does this acronym stand for? It is not too difficult to guess that Q stands for QUALITY. Gourmets and culinary experts might shudder at this. However, McDonald's has a particular definition of quality. McDonald's defines quality in terms of consistency. The food served by McDonald's restaurants all over the world always looks and tastes the same. This is very important to travellers and people who want to know what they will be getting regardless of where they are. Wherever McDonald's is situated in the world — in Stockholm, Sydney, Johannesburg or Cape Town, Singapore or Seattle — McDonald's food always looks and tastes the same. In many cities in which McDonald's operates it is not safe to drink the water but McDonald's products are always consistent in quality.

The S is for SERVICE. How does McDonald's define service? Not in terms of friendliness and chattiness; hence the assistant's reluctance to indulge in pleasant conversation. To McDonald's service means speed: the ability of customers to obtain the products that they order in a very short space of time, normally under 60 seconds. So why would the assistant not participate in pleasantries? Because by doing so the customer behind me in the line might have to wait for longer than usual, and this is unacceptable to McDonald's. If the customer were then to complain that the service was not fast enough, he or she would indeed be *right*.

The C is explained if one considers McDonald's major target market: children, normally in the age group 7 to 17. The parents of these children are concerned about one thing when their children consume fast food, and that is CLEANLINESS. When next in McDonald's observe that someone is always cleaning, even when nothing appears dirty. McDonald's continually reinforces its message of cleanliness. If, therefore, you were to visit a McDonald's that did not live up to acceptable standards of cleanliness and you were to complain, you would be *right.*

V is for VALUE. McDonald's is in the business of offering a lot of food for very little money. In fact, *The Economist* has calculated that the relative prices of McDonald's products (usually the Big Mac) in different parts of the world are a more reliable gauge of the cost of living than all the economics statistics produced by governments, the International Monetary Fund and the World Bank put together! McDonald's is in the business of providing value. It is no coincidence that when major competitor Taco Bell sells a taco in the US for 49 cents, McDonald's sells a burger for the same price.

Why then did McDonald's assistant refuse my credit card? Well, first, because the action of taking a card, swiping it and waiting for approval would probably have caused the customer after me to wait unreasonably long. However, McDonald's would also have had to pass on a small but significant commission on the transaction (usually in the region of four or five percent) to the credit card company. This means that customers paying cash for their purchases would indirectly subsidise my meal! And that would mean that any customer who paid cash would not have received the basic McDonald's promise of value. Furthermore, in its efforts to provide value, McDonald's operates at very small margins on many of the products it sells. By giving away even four to five percent of this margin, McDonald's would be driving down its profits, its ability to expand and its ability to offer value for money to its millions of customers worldwide. So, if you want consistency of quality, speedy service, cleanliness, and value for money, *you are always right at McDonald's* because this is how McDonald's has defined its business.

Strategists and human resources experts frequently overlook the fact that the need to define a business originated in marketing.

In fact, the need to define the business one is in was pointed out in 1960 by Harvard Business School professor Ted Levitt. In a classic article entitled 'Marketing myopia', Levitt stated that many businesses, indeed whole industries, in the United States and other parts of the world had failed because they had not adequately defined the business they were in. Too many businesses defined themselves in terms of what they did or made, rather than in terms of the customer needs that they satisfied. So, for example, Levitt pointed out that the great railroad companies were doomed by their insistence that they were in the railroad business rather than in the business of moving goods and people, that is, transportation. Likewise, the great film studios ran into trouble because they continued to define themselves as being in the movie business. When exposed to competition as presented by professional sport, theme parks and television, they attempted to deal with the problem by making more movies and making them more extravagantly, instead of defining themselves as being in the entertainment business and gearing themselves to this. My favourite definition of a business is that by Charles Revson of Revlon Cosmetics. When asked what business he was in, Mr Revson replied: 'In the factories we make cosmetics. But in the drugstores we sell hope.' If one defines the business one is in carefully and effectively, being able to answer when the customer is right or wrong is quite simple. The customer is indeed always right, depending on how one has defined the business one is in!

Where would one look for the business definition of most of the organisations we know and work in? The answer should be easy: in the mission statement. Indeed, that is where one would expect to find the definition of the business. However, a perusal of the mission statements of many of the leading organisations in the world today might leave one somewhat disillusioned. Mission statements have been exploited by corporate do-gooders to such an extent that they offer very little in the way of strategic guidance, let alone a definition of the business. Many mission statements proclaim all sorts of good and honourable sentiments such as being a responsible corporate citizen, a responsible employer, a believer in people, a caretaker of the environment or a seeker of corporate value. They often go on for many pages without ever defining what business the firm is in! It is time for marketers to bring marketing into the mission statement in such a way that the mission statement reflects the business the organisation is in. By knowing what business they are in, marketers and managers in general will more easily be able to judge whether the customer is right or wrong. If the customer wants what you have defined your business as giving, the customer is indeed always right. If the customer wants what your business has not been defined as providing, then this customer should probably not be a customer.

In recent years we have seen that truly effective marketing organisations go beyond identifying and satisfying the needs and wants of customers. Indeed, effective organisations of the eighties and nineties have had an almost uncanny ability to anticipate customers' needs and wants. Thus, for example, Akio Morita of Sony ignored advice from employees and market researchers that the world would not want or use the Sony Walkman. 'By the time we launch it, the world will be ready for it,' was Morita's opinion. This reminds me of a quote attributed to the great Canadian ice hockey player, Wayne Gretsky. When a sports commentator asked what made him so successful (noting also that Gretsky was not all that effective with a hockey stick, not very fast on ice and not even a wonderful skater), Gretsky answered, 'I skate to where the puck is going to be!' This seems to be what marketing organisations gearing themselves to the twenty-first century will have to develop: the ability to anticipate where the customer will be. Authorities such as Carpenter and Nakomoto suggest that this ability is closely associated with what strategists call 'first-mover advantage'. They argue that first-mover advantage is created when the marketer defines the evoked set that the customer will use to evaluate all future offerings within a particular product category.

2.2.2 Goal orientation

Goal orientation is the second tenet of the marketing concept. It recognises that all organisations must have goals. However, the business must realise that its goals must be reached through being customer oriented.

2.2.3 The systems approach

The third tenet of the marketing concept is an integrated marketing approach, often referred to as a systems approach. This means that marketing efforts and activities do not happen in isolation, but as an integrated and holistic set of activities which must be performed systematically if the organisation is to be successful. Much of the focus in this text is on an integrated approach to marketing strategy.

2.3 CONCLUSION

In this chapter we have discussed what marketing is and how it is viewed. Rather than attempt to develop a formal, 'textbook' definition of marketing, we referred to it as an activity which has to do with the management of mutually beneficial relationships. We also referred to a philosophy of business known as the marketing concept, in which marketing is seen as resting on three cornerstones, namely, customer orientation, goal orientation and an integrated or systems approach to marketing. However, marketing should not be viewed as a panacea for all organisational ills. People unfamiliar with marketing expect it to influence customers to do things they would normally not do. Practitioners of marketing have learnt over the years that marketing cannot persuade customers to do things that they would not do under normal circumstances. Rather, it is a judicious way of finding out what customers want or hopefully will want in the future.

References

Levitt, Theodore. 1960. Marketing myopia. *Harvard Business Review,* July–August, 45–46.

Appendix

MARKET ORIENTATION: UNDERSTANDING IT, MEASURING IT, MANAGING IT

Market orientation, that is, the requirement for an organisation to focus on the needs of customers in guiding its strategies, has been the focus of marketing education and training efforts for many years. Presumably, the market-oriented organisation will be more successful, whatever that means. Yet there has been little evidence that this is indeed so. For something supposedly as important as market orientation, there have been few serious attempts to measure the construct, and even less effort expended on significantly linking it to performance criteria such as profitability, growth and market share. In short, does it really pay an organisation to be market oriented? In recent years, spurred primarily by the work of Ajay Kohli of the University of Texas and Bernie Jaworski of the University of Arizona, there has been a revival of interest in market orientation and what it involves.

The market-oriented firm is one that successfully applies the marketing concept. The term *market oriented* is to be preferred to *marketing oriented* because this highlights its organisation-wide application, as opposed to something only marketing departments do. One view is that the marketing concept can be defined in three ways: as a philosophy, as a concept, and as currently implemented. Much of the confusion over the years in defining marketing and in the understanding of the marketing concept results from a failure to make the distinction between marketing as a culture, marketing as a strategy, and marketing as a tactic. We will here look at marketing as a philosophy and marketing as it is implemented.

Market orientation as a philosophy

There is a broad agreement that market orientation as a philosophy consists of three core aspects. These are as follows.

- **Customer orientation.** This requires an understanding of the psychological and social factors that determine the customer's actions. Such an understanding enables the marketer to ask the market-research questions that make it possibly to identify core needs, and this in turn will give clear direction to basic research. By identifying the basic customer needs that they serve and defining their business accordingly, organisations will avoid what Ted Levitt terms marketing myopia.

- **Integration of effort.** This enables the firm to provide the value to meet customer needs. It involves coordinating endeavours in terms of the elements of the marketing mix for each product or service. Moreover, because market orientation is an organisation-wide pre-scription, it is necessary that the whole firm is organised and co-ordinated to serve the customer.

- The setting of **organisational objectives** (or, in the case of business firms, profitability objectives). An adoption of the marketing concept means seeking to serve customer needs in order to meet the requirements for achieving objectives/profit. This is essential for long-term survival.

Market orientation, from the beginning, was formulated with a view to providing the organisation with long-term direction. Many managers, however, especially in Western firms, must balance this against demands for short-term performance.

Defining market orientation and developing a measure

Jaworski and Kohli have provided the following operational definition for market orientation as a construct. Their definition links the three core elements of the philosophy of market orientation with the perceptions of practising managers:

> 'Market orientation is the organisation-wide generation of market intelligence pertaining to current and future customer needs, dissemination of the intelligence across departments, and organisation-wide responsiveness to it.'

Market intelligence is based not only on 'verbalised customer opinions' but is seen as 'a broader concept' in that it includes consideration of such factors as competitors and political and legislative changes that affect customer needs and performance. The current as well as future needs of customers are considered. Recently, Jaworski and Kohli have provided researchers and practitioners with MARKOR, an instrument for measuring market orientation. This has attracted much research attention in the USA, and has also been used to measure marketing orientation in firms in countries such as the United Kingdom.

Market orientation as implementation

Here we can ask: How many companies have actually implemented the marketing concept? The answer is: Too few. Only a handful of companies really stand out as practitioners of the marketing concept.

Using MARKOR, organisations will now be able to measure and assess their level of market orientation. An even more fundamental question is already being answered: Does it make a difference? Jaworski and Kohli suggest it does. Our work in the United Kingdom, Malta and South Africa suggests that market-oriented firms are more profitable, enjoy higher levels of growth and, overall, exhibit better performance. For organisations wishing quickly to assess their level of market orientation, a user-friendly version of MARKOR appears here.

The amended MARKOR scale

MARKOR is a scale developed by Ajay Kohli and Bernie Jaworski to allow managers to assess the degree of market orientation within their organisations. An amended version of the scale is provided below. We have changed some of the items in the original scale so that all the items are now positively phrased. This has not materially changed the content of the items, and makes the scale a little easier for managers to use. However, we have not determined what the effects of our changes are on the validity and reliability of the scale, so any large-scale use of the scale should either stick to the original version, or evaluate the effects of the changes in a scientific way. The scale is especially well suited for use by groups of managers within the same organisation, in which case ratings on items should be added and averaged to get a mean score on each item.

All that is required to use the scale is that you assess your organisation on each of the statements, and indicate the extent of your agreement by circling the appropriate point on the scale. When you have completed all the items, follow the scoring instructions provided at the end of the questionnaire. There are no wrong or right answers, and the best approach is to work quickly and record first impressions.

1. In this company, we meet with customers at least once a year to find out what products or services they will need in the future.

1 2 3 4 5 6 7
I disagree strongly — I agree strongly

2. In this organisation, we do a lot of in-house market research.

1 2 3 4 5 6 7
I disagree strongly — I agree strongly

3. We rapidly detect changes in our customers' product preferences.

1 2 3 4 5 6 7
I disagree strongly — I agree strongly

4. We survey end users at least once a year to assess the quality of our products and services.

1 2 3 4 5 6 7
I disagree strongly — I agree strongly

4. We are quick to detect fundamental shifts in our industry (e.g., competition, technology, regulation).

1 2 3 4 5 6 7
I disagree strongly — I agree strongly

6. We periodically review the likely effect of changes in our business environment (e.g., regulation) on customers.

1 2 3 4 5 6 7
I disagree strongly — I agree strongly

7. We have interdepartmental meetings at least once a quarter to discuss market trends and developments.

1 2 3 4 5 6 7
I disagree strongly — I agree strongly

8. Marketing personnel in our company spend time discussing customers' future needs with other functional departments.

1 2 3 4 5 6 7
I disagree strongly — I agree strongly

9. When something important happens to a major customer or market, the whole company knows about it in a short period.

1 2 3 4 5 6 7
I disagree strongly — I agree strongly

10. Data on customer satisfaction are disseminated at all levels in this business unit on a regular basis.

1 2 3 4 5 6 7
I disagree strongly — I agree strongly

11. When one department finds out something important about competitors, it is quick to alert other departments.

1 2 3 4 5 6 7
I disagree strongly — I agree strongly

12. It only takes us a very short time to decide how to respond to our competitors' price changes.

1 2 3 4 5 6 7
I disagree strongly — I agree strongly

13. We hardly ever ignore changes in our customers' product or service needs.	1 2 3 4 5 6 7 I disagree strongly I agree strongly
14. We periodically review our product development efforts to ensure that they are in line with what customers want.	1 2 3 4 5 6 7 I disagree strongly I agree strongly
15. Several departments get together periodically to plan a response to changes taking place in our business environment.	1 2 3 4 5 6 7 I disagree strongly I agree strongly
16. If a major competitor were to launch an intensive campaign targeted at our customers, we would implement a response immediately.	1 2 3 4 5 6 7 I disagree strongly I agree strongly
17. The activities of the different departments in this company are well co-ordinated.	1 2 3 4 5 6 7 I disagree strongly I agree strongly
18. Customer complaints never fall on deaf ears in this company.	1 2 3 4 5 6 7 I disagree strongly I agree strongly
19. If we came up with a great marketing plan, we probably would be able to implement it in a timely fashion.	1 2 3 4 5 6 7 I disagree strongly I agree strongly
20. When we find that customers would like us to modify a service, the departments involved make concerted efforts to do so.	1 2 3 4 5 6 7 I disagree strongly I agree strongly

How to score MARKOR

1. Obtain an average rating for each item on the scale if the questionnaire is being completed by several people; if it is being completed by a single individual simply use the ratings for each item.
2. Sum the (average) ratings for items 1 through 6 and divide by 6; sum the (average) ratings for hems 7 through 11 and divide by 5; sum the (average) ratings for items 12 through 20 and divide by 9.
3. The three numbers you arrive at reflect the perception of the effectiveness of the organisation on the three dimensions of market orientation, namely *intelligence generation* (how well the organisation

generates intelligence), *intelligence dissemination* (how well this intelligence is disseminated throughout the organisation), and *responsiveness* (how well the organisation responds to changes in the market and in the environment). The average of items 1 through 6 is the score for intelligence generation; the average of items 7 through 11 is the score for intelligence dissemination; the average of hems 12 through 20 is the score for responsiveness.

What do the scores mean?

The lowest possible score which can be obtained on any of the above dimensions is 1, the highest is 7 — it is unlikely that many organisations will be at these extremes. Obviously the nearer to 7 the score on the particular dimension is, the better the organisation is perceived to be performing on that dimension, and vice versa. Urgent attention should be given to the dimension on which performance is least effective, and this can also be achieved by referring to those items which scored the lowest ratings.

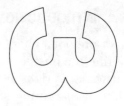

Marketing strategy: an introduction

Introduction

Defining a business

The notion of a target market

The marketing mix

The marketing environment

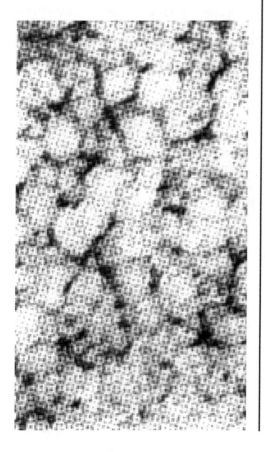

3.1 INTRODUCTION

The previous chapter highlighted the need for organisations to define the business they are in in order to distinguish when the customer is right or wrong. In this chapter we introduce the notion of marketing strategy. Marketing strategy begins with the definition of business. How does an organisation know what business it is in? What are the variables which enable us to answer this question?

3.2 DEFINING A BUSINESS

There are a number of indicators which enable us to infer the nature of an organisation's business. It is convenient to call these indicators the 'four Cs'. The first indicator of the business an organisation is in would be its competitors. The first C of our four Cs therefore refers to COMPETITORS. For example, if you knew that the competitors of company A were companies such as DHL, Federal Express, UPS and Securicor, it would not be unreasonable to assume that the company was involved in the fast parcel and mail delivery business. Secondly, knowledge of who the CUSTOMERS of an organisation are provides a high level of insight into the business of the organisation. So, for example, if you knew that the customers of company A were individuals or organisations wishing to send small packages or documents effectively, rapidly and efficiently to contacts in other parts of the country or the world, you might conclude that the company concerned was involved in the fast delivery of parcels and letters. The third indicator of the business an organisation is in are the COMPETENCES the organisation possesses. These are less obvious and may be somewhat more difficult to identify than the Cs of *competition* and *customers.* However, to be successful in the package delivery business, an organisation has to be competent in areas such as vehicle and transportation management, delivery and information systems, and have extensive communications skills. The fourth C, namely COLLABOR-ATORS, is also more difficult to quantify than are competition and customers. However, it should be obvious that no organisation can exist in isolation. All organisations, in order to reach their objectives, need to be able to collaborate, or cooperate, with individuals and other organisations. So, for example, success in the package delivery business would to a large extent depend on collaboration with suppliers (such as the suppliers of computer hardware and software, or vehicles and systems), with employees (who should be willing to work long hours, often under difficult conditions), with government on international, national and local levels (to speed up the delivery process) and even with competitors (when a system breaks down competitors can hopefully be relied on to provide a back-up service).

The contribution of the four Cs to the marketing strategy process is shown in Figure 3.1.

Figure 3.1: *Defining the business — the start of marketing strategy*

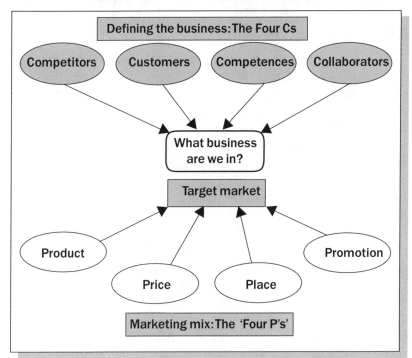

3.3 THE NOTION OF A TARGET MARKET

Once an organisation knows what business it is in and understands who its customers are, it will be able to determine and identify with greater precision the target markets it serves. From a marketing perspective this is fundamental, since marketing strategy is determined by the demarcation of the target market. A target market consists of people with certain needs and the ability and resources to satisfy those needs, or at least the willingness to transact to satisfy their needs. It is true that whenever customers are faced with a problem, an opportunity exists for an astute marketer to enter a business. Once the marketer has identified the target market (we discuss the concepts of market segmentation and target marketing in more detail in Chapter 4), the strategist is able to define the marketing mix that will best serve the needs and wants of the particular target market.

3.4 THE MARKETING MIX

Most people who have attended a marketing course, be it a one-day course or an entire PhD, remember at least one facet of marketing: the now almost clichéd 'four Ps'. The four Ps were introduced by McCarthy in the 1960s (*see* McCarthy, 1982), when he found that it was easier for his students to remember the instruments of the marketing mix by referring to them in this way. The first of the four Ps is PRODUCT: that is to say, marketers need to identify and manage all those aspects of the product (or service) that they market. This includes issues such as product name, branding, product design and features, packaging, range, quality, colour/s and size/s. We will discuss product strategy in more detail in Chapter 6. The second P of the marketing mix is PRICE. What price will the customer be charged? Here the marketer needs to understand not only the dynamics of costs and competition and their influence on price, but also the nature of customer demand, for if the customer is not prepared to pay the price for the product, then, regardless of costs or competition, the product will not be sold. Typical pricing strategy decisions are whether to charge higher-than-average or lower-than-average prices for products, what prices to charge for new products, and whether to test the limits of customer sensitivity to price by tools such as price differentiation. We will look in more detail at pricing strategy in Chapter 7. McCarthy designated PLACE as the third P of the marketing mix. Nowadays it is probably more convenient to talk of placement strategy. What we are really talking about is distribution, but the point is easier to remember in the form of a P. Distribution strategy involves the marketing decision maker in considering issues such as the movement of products and services from producer to consumer in the right quantities, at the right time, and to the right place. Attention must be given to issues such as the structure of distribution channels, the identification of intermediaries, handling conflict and power within the channel, and the motivation of individual intermediaries. In McCarthy's original formula, the fourth P of the marketing mix was PROMOTION. 'Marketing communication' might nowadays be a more appropriate term, as it involves activities as diverse as advertising, personal selling, publicity and various sales promotions efforts. Again, it is easier to remember this point as a P. A typical issue facing the marketing manager with regard to promotion involves the extent of the use of mass advertising versus more personalised techniques, such as selling. We look at marketing communication in more detail in Chapter 9.

What is marketing strategy? A simple example will illustrate why it is necessary to segment and target markets to develop a suitable marketing strategy for each of these target markets. Think of a product that most people use, such as soap. First of all, one soon realises, not everyone uses soap to wash (unfortunately!). More importantly, manufacturers of soap know that there is great variety in the demand for soap. Consequently, some soaps are marketed by emphasising their skin care properties, others are marketed on the basis of their deodorising properties, or are simply cheaper than competing brands. Another example might be toothpaste. Again, not everyone uses toothpaste. As with soap, there is great variety in the demand for toothpaste. Some consumers value its dental care properties, others its cosmetic properties, and children prefer toothpaste that tastes good and looks interesting. There are also people who do not have teeth to brush: they need a tizzy tablet to drop into a glass of water along with their dentures at night! If you think further about products that everyone uses, you might light upon a basic commodity such as water. Everyone needs water to drink, to wash in and to use in preparing food. However, a look at the shelves in a supermarket will quickly dispel the notion that water is merely a commodity. One of the great growth areas in modern marketing has been the proliferation of different brands of bottled water.

One may also assert that toilet paper is a product that everyone uses. Agreed, we all have the same basic need for this product. However, it is interesting to note that toilet paper manufacturers do not regard the world as a single, homogeneous market for toilet paper. Indeed, the toilet paper market recognises at least three (and in recent years, four) major market segments for the product.

What is the point of our discussion? We are attempting to show that marketing strategy is about putting together the right 'mix' (which is why it is called a 'marketing mix') of the four Ps for a particular target market. So what does *product strategy* look like for the 'developed world urban market', the first of the four major market segments for toilet paper? The product is very important: consumers search for qualities in the product that are meaningful to them. These qualities include pliability, strength, thickness and softness, and colour. Colour is important because the shopper usually wants the toilet paper to match the colour scheme in the bathroom. *Price* is less important to this shopper for two reasons. Firstly, toilet paper is not a 'shopping product'. Consumers do not shop for toilet paper in the same way that they might shop for clothes or computers. The consumer will not delay the purchase of toilet paper in the hope of finding a bargain! The second reason why price is relatively unimportant in the marketing strategy for this target market is because the demand for toilet paper is what economists would call inelastic. The consumer will not purchase more toilet paper in the long term simply because it has become less expensive. One can use only so much of the product at a particular time. Similarly, the consumer would not purchase significantly less of the product over time if the price of the product were to increase. Toilet paper is a basic necessity in the modern home. When one considers *placement strategy* for toilet paper, it is important to note that toilet paper is a convenience product. It is a product which the consumer must be able to purchase with the least possible inconvenience. This is reflected in the distribution strategy for toilet paper for this market. The product is to be found just about everywhere: in supermarkets, hyperstores, convenience stores, pharmacies, drug stores and small local corner shops. Where is the emphasis in *promotional strategy* for this product in this market? Advertising is the tool most frequently used, and the emphasis in the advertising message is on the properties of the particular brand. Advertising will stress the qualities that the target market values, namely pliability, softness, quality and the range of colours. Very little emphasis is placed on personal selling at the consumer level, although salespeople will call on intermediaries in the distribution channel. Limited use might also be made of promotional tools such as coupons.

A second major market segment identified by toilet paper manufacturers is what can be called the institutional market. This target market consists of governments, government departments, hospitals, schools, universities, and companies with large workforces. In this market the *product* itself is not that important. Generally the toilet paper is single ply, produced in a limited range of colours, and of lower quality than that targeted at the developed world urban market segment. Packaging is of little importance, and the rolls of toilet paper are usually simply packed in a large cardboard box. *Price,* however, is of critical importance to this market, and the supplier who is able to supply in bulk at the lowest price will probably win the order. The product is often purchased on a bidding or tender system. Therefore, the supplier who quotes the lowest price and has the most convenient delivery arrangements will have the best chance of winning the business of a large government department, university, hospital or company. *Distribution* is of minimal importance as a marketing tool, and the main distribution tasks involve logistics. Moving large quantities of relatively low-value products as efficiently and swiftly as possible is the major objective of distribution in this case. Similarly, *advertising* plays almost no role at all. There may be some reliance on a sales function if the product is not sold on tender or bid: a salesforce may call on large institutions at regular intervals to obtain orders for large quantities of the product for use in the institution.

The third market segment which toilet paper marketers have identified as important is the market in developing countries of the world. Consumers in this segment are to be found in less developed parts of the world, on continents such as Africa, South America and Asia. The marketing task here is that of changing attitudes and behaviour. Many of these consumers do not use toilet paper in the conventional sense, but are accustomed to using newspaper, leaves or corn cobs. The marketer in this case has the task of illustrating the superior capabilities of toilet paper and its advantages in terms of hygiene and sanitation over other methods. Thus less emphasis is placed on *product strategy* and *pricing strategy* than on *communication* as a way of illustrating the superior benefits of the product over the alternatives. Much of the communication effort utilises mass media advertising (particularly newspaper advertising, television and radio) to demonstrate the health and sanitation benefits of toilet paper. *Distribution* is also problematic: in less developed countries, conventional retail outlets such as supermarkets, hyperstores and pharmacies are not available. The marketer must therefore rely on small neighbourhood grocery stores or general dealer retail outlets, and frequently also on informal market outlets.

It is important to note that market segments and target markets do not remain static. Indeed, market segmentation and target marketing require creativity on the part of the marketer. The astute and entrepreneurial marketer succeeds by recognising opportunities presented by new, evolving markets and exploiting these through judicious marketing strategy. For example, in the late 1980s a number of toilet paper marketers recognised that the trend towards environmental concern was creating an opportunity. Bleached toilet paper creates a major environmental problem: the chlorides and oxides used to bleach paper are very detrimental to the physical environment. Smart toilet paper manufacturers developed a new product — unbleached toilet paper — with the emphasis on *product strategy.* This meant environmentally aware consumers could purchase an environment-friendly product which, although somewhat drab in appearance, would satisfy their desire to be environmentally responsible. Despite the fact that production costs were probably not very different, marketers of this new product were able to command above-average *margins* for it because the environmentally aware consumer was prepared to pay more for a 'green' product. Conventional distribution channels could be used so there was no requirement for radical changes in the *distribution strategy. Advertising messages* emphasised the issue of concern for the environment.

3.5 THE MARKETING ENVIRONMENT

No organisation exists in a vacuum. All organisations are part of a broader business environment characterised by innumerable variables which impact upon organisations in various ways. It is important to note, too, that these variables tend to be beyond the control of the individual manager or indeed the individual organisation. Rather, they represent a bewildering array of threats and opportunities to any particular firm. It is the fundamental task of marketing strategists to adapt their marketing strategy to the variability of the business environment.

What are the variables to which the marketer must adapt? A simple way of remembering the variables in the marketing environment is to think of the acronym PEST. PEST is not your neighbour's child: the letters of the acronym refer to the variables in the business environment that face the marketer, and to which the marketing strategy must be adapted.

The P in PEST stands for the political and legal subenvironments. Political events impact on marketing strategy. For example, Stolichnaya, the famous Russian vodka, suffered massive losses in market share in 1980, when Russia invaded Afghanistan.

Consumers vented their frustration at the behaviour of the Soviet Union by rejecting a brand which had for years been built around the fact that it was genuinely Russian. Only recently, with 'perestroika' and 'glasnost', did the brand become acceptable again.

Another major influence on marketing is legislation. Legislation may affect marketing positively or negatively but it should be obvious that marketers cannot choose to ignore or flaunt laws. Antismoking legislation, for instance, has been a major threat to marketers within the tobacco industry. However, it has created numerous marketing opportunities for service operations, ranging from airlines (for example, all Air Canada flights are nonsmoking flights) to restaurants (which may offer nonsmoking sections or be entirely nonsmoking). So, the same legislation can be interpreted by some as threatening and by others as providing opportunities. In Western Australia during the late 1980s politicians debated the pros and cons of enforcing the fencing of privately owned swimming pools. Some swimming pool marketers saw this as a threat, believing that the cost of fencing a pool would deter potential customers. Others saw it as an opportunity to enter the fencing business as well, exploiting the database of satisfied customers for whom they had built pools.

The economic environment (E) is the second variable which has a significant effect on marketing strategy. Interest rates, employment rates, the balance of payments and trends in world economic markets can impact on the individual firm.

Fluctuations in world currency markets frequently bump up or shrink importers' profits. The economic subenvironment is characterised by the availability of data on the economies of most countries. Although this makes it easy for the marketing manager to find information, his task is complicated by the need to assimilate and understand vast quantities of economic data.

The S in PEST stands for the sociocultural environment. The sociocultural environment comprises the attitudes, values and norms of a society. These attitudes and values change with time. There are many examples of changes in values and attitudes in our societies. For instance, our attitude toward the use of credit has changed fundamentally. Most of our grandparents lived by the dictum 'neither a borrower nor a lender be'. They resolutely believed that if one could not afford to pay cash for a purchase, the purchase should not be made. The way to finance a major purchase was to save until one had the target amount, after which the purchase could be made. Today's consumer takes the line that, if there is sufficient credit available on one's credit card, the purchase can be made! This has created huge opportunities for new forms of business. Companies such as Visa and Mastercard have flourished. It has also boosted the direct mail industry and international marketing. It is now possible to order a product from another country and to simply pay for it by credit card.

Another factor that altered the attitudes and values of society was the changing role of women in most parts of the world. Thirty years ago women were an insignificant part of the labour force in most countries; today they are as much part of the workforce as are men. This has been a boon for marketers of labour-saving devices, and for those specialising in prepared foods. For others it has been a serious threat. It is inconceivable to promote a sewing machine today on the grounds that it will enable a woman 'to be a good wife and responsible mother by making clothes for herself and her children'! Firstly, a woman does not have the time to make clothes for herself and her children if she is in full-time employment. Secondly, because she is in full-time employment, she can afford to buy her own clothes, and does not need to be a 'good wife' to gain her husband's approval. Thirdly, a slogan like this would be seen as very patronising and politically incorrect! How have sewing machine manufacturers coped with this trend? The answer is — with difficulty! One way of coping with this change in society's values and attitudes would be to emphasise that sewing machines offer their owners the benefit of being able to be create and wear unique garments, unlike those purchased 'off the peg' by other consumers.

It is important to note that values are culturally based and not universal. So, for example, many societies frown upon the consumption of alcohol by young children. However, this value is not universally held. In some societies it is acceptable for children as young as seven or eight years of age to consume table wine in modest quantities. In Spain, France and Italy no objection would be raised if a parent poured a small glass of wine, watered down, for a child to consume at a family meal. This is what anthropologists refer to as acculturation: the learning of a society's values or culture by its members. Children in Spain, France and Italy learn that the consumption of wine in moderation is a social activity of their society. Sometimes marketers deliberately or inadvertently fail to observe cultural values, with dire consequences. Lindeman's, a major Australian wine producer, launched a range of tetrapack wine coolers, packed like fruit juices in briquettes with plastic straws, to exploit the picnic and outdoor market. The idea was that consumers could store the flavoured wine in the refrigerator, from which it could be taken and placed in an ice-box or picnic basket for an outdoors occasion. The product was withdrawn after a very short time when consumers protested that it was readily consumed by children. Because the product was brightly packaged and resembled a soft drink or fruit juice, children looking in the refrigerator for a soft drink were consuming the wine cooler and ending up rather the worse for wear! More recently in the UK there was an outcry about alcoholic lemonades marketed under brand names such as Hooch and Two Dogs. Many were concerned that these pleasant-tasting beverages were being targeted at under-age drinkers.

The T in PEST stands for technology. If we need evidence of the tremendous impact of technology on our lives and our behaviour as consumers, we need only look at the products we use every day now that did not even exist five or ten years ago. How can the marketer deal with the issue of technology? There are no easy answers to this question. However, certain generalisations do apply. The first is that human needs do not in fact change very rapidly. Indeed, many of the needs of consumers today are the same as those experienced by our ancestors many hundreds or even thousands of years ago. One such need is the need to remember. Thousands of years ago our ancestors painted the events in their lives on the walls of caves. Today, Kodak satisfies our need to remember by selling photographic equipment and materials. The second generalisation is that technology changes. Thus new competitors have satisfied our need to remember. Cinematographic film such as that made by Kodak has been supplanted by video technology. A third generalisation is that new technology often comes from unexpected sources. Video technology did not emerge from Kodak or any of the other manufacturers of photographic equipment. Rather, it came from manufacturers of electronic goods such as Phillips, Sony and Sanyo. The technology which supplants video technology might not come from a traditional electronic goods manufacturer, but from a computer hardware or software producer such as Microsoft, IBM or Apple!

3.6 CONCLUSION

Although the variables (the PEST variables) in the environment in which marketers function change, marketers must adapt their marketing strategy to these changes. They do this by manipulating certain controllable variables — the four Ps of marketing strategy — in a way that will enable them to capitalise on changes in the business environment.

References

McCarthy, W Jerome. 1982. *Basic Marketing: A Managerial Approach.* Homewood, Illinois: Richard D Irwin.

Introduction

To serve or create?

Beyond customer orientation

Towards a theoretical framework

Understanding strategic dynamics

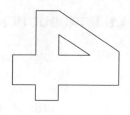

To serve or create:[1] strategic orientations

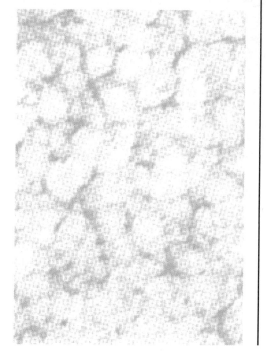

[1] Based on Berthon, PR, Hulbert, JM & Pitt, LF. 1999. To serve or create? Strategic orientation towards technology and customers. *California Management Review*, 42, 1 (Fall): 37–58, and Berthon, PR, Pitt, LF & Hulbert, JM. 1996. Structuring companies for markets. *Financial Times, (Mastering Management Series)*, 16 August, page 8.

4.1 INTRODUCTION

In the previous chapter, we briefly considered the marketing concept. In this chapter, we take a more serious look at the idea that lies at the heart of marketing. We ask the question: Is the marketing concept really as simple as finding out what customers want and giving it to them?'

In the late 1980s, NeXT was founded by Apple computer pioneer Steve Jobs, to produce a desktop computer. Technologically, NeXT's machines were years ahead of their time, incorporating hardware and software that only appeared in other computers a decade later. However, the product failed and was withdrawn from the market. Potential customers were frustrated in their efforts to find word-processing and spreadsheet applications to run on NeXT computers. Observers would say that NeXT suffered from technological myopia (Hill & Jones, 1998), as managers were so enthused by the wizardry of the product that they ignored basic market realities, and, of course, the customer. Marketers would criticise NeXT for a lack of customer orientation.

Eli Lilly's launch of Humulin, the first human equivalent of insulin, received a tepid market response (Christensen, 1997). The product had been developed in response to the requirements of leading endocrinologists and diabetes specialists, who stated that there was a large, untapped market for 100% pure insulin – not the variety extracted from pork, which had impurities that led to insulin resistance in some patients. However, the specialists tended to treat a far greater proportion of diabetics with pork insulin resistance, whereas most other physicians saw patients without resistance problems, for whom insulin extracted from pork was quite acceptable. They had no need to prescribe Humulin and the product performed poorly in the market place. Technologists would criticise Eli Lilly for paying too much attention to what customers said they wanted.

Two philosophies stand out among the various principles that guide the way in which managers think about business. A philosophy, often identified as *customer orientation*, contends that identifying the needs and wants of the target market, and delivering products and services that satisfy these is key to attaining organisational goals (Band, 1991; Day, 1990, 1994; Naumann, 1995; Webster, 1988). However, an innovation philosophy asserts that customers will prefer those products and services that generate the greatest interest, provide the greatest performance, features, quality and value for money – in short, technological superiority (Smith, 1980; Clark & Fujimoto, 1991; Kodama, 1995; Utterback, Allen, Hollomon & Sirbu, 1976). Managers in firms that enact an innovation philosophy or *innovation orientation*, devote their energy towards technological innovation – inventing and refining superior products[2]. An innovation outlook emphasises issues such as new products, innovation and discontinuous improvement. Customer orientation stresses customer service, satisfaction and focus. It is quite tempting to see these philosophies as mutually exclusive, if not conceptually opposite. This situation is sometimes exacerbated by specialists who focus on one or the other area, develop criteria of excellent practice, and claim these as panaceae for business success, although some authors have focused on the need to integrate technology and market (Gupta, Raj & Wilemon, 1986; Souder, 1987; Shanklin & Ryans, 1984). While there are few instances of firms applying one as a management philosophy to the exclusion of the other, in practice, firms vary significantly in the degree to which they emphasise one or other philosophy – an unsurprising situation given limited resources.

In this chapter, we investigate the roots of the innovation and customer philosophies in order to examine why those who adhere to a narrow conception of customer orientation and

---

[2] We use the term product in its strictest sense, covering an expanse from poetry to traditional material 'product', from teaching to technology, and from images to ideologies. Our use of the term not only encompasses traditional products and services, but also includes ideas and images, and thus the entire marketing communication process. Indeed, in its original sense the term technology resonates closely with our thinking. Technology, from the Greek *tekhnologia* meaning 'systematic treatment', and more literally *tekhne*-art + *-logia* - ratio, reason, discourse is possibly captured in the term 'systematic art'.

adherents of an innovation orientation are divided. We introduce a more inclusive model to explain the customer-orientation/technology-orientation dichotomy, the archetypes and inter-relationships of which may have important implications for all who care about organisational strategy. We use the model to explore and add insight into the evolving strategies that emerge from an ever-changing market place. The dynamics of the change process are investigated, using three well-known companies as examples.

4.2 TO SERVE OR CREATE? A RE-EXAMINATION OF CUSTOMER ORIENTATION

Since Peter Drucker stated that the sole purpose of a firm was to create and keep customers (Drucker, 1954), many managers have adopted a customer orientation philosophy. The concept evolved into the advice that, to be succcessful, organisations should attempt to ascertain customers' needs and wants, and produce the products and services to satisfy these. Its most enthusiastic proponents argue that companies should focus their very being on this, and structure themselves in such a way that everyone within them is oriented towards customers. In recent years, there have been increasing efforts to formalise definitions of customer orientation.

For example, specifically within the sales context, Saxe & Weitz (1982) developed the SOCO (Sales Orientation – Customer Orientation) scale in order to measure the extent to which sales-people are customer-oriented. More generally, customer orientation is embodied and subsumed under the idea of market orientation (Kohli & Jaworski, 1990; Narver & Slater, 1990). This latter philosophy has typically been considered to consist of three core aspects (Kohli & Jaworski, 1990; Kotler, 1991; McGee & Spiro, 1988): customer orientation, organisation-wide integration of effort, and clear objectives (in the case of business firms, profitability).

Drucker rightly receives considerable credit as a progenitor of customer orientation. Too often forgotten, however, is the fact that his was a concept of a business as a whole, and embraced more than customer orientation, as the following excerpt makes clear:

> ... if we want to know what a business is we have to start with its *purpose*. There is only one valid definition of business purpose: *to create a customer*. It is the customer who determines what a business is. For it is the customer, and he alone, who through being willing to pay for a good or service, converts economic resources into wealth, things into goods. What the business thinks it produces is not of first importance – especially not to the future of the business and its success. What the customer thinks he is buying, what he considers 'value' is decisive ... Because it is its purpose to create a customer, and business enterprise has two – and only these two – basic functions: *marketing* and *innovation* [author emphasis] (Drucker, 1954: 37–38).

Drucker's work also makes it clear that, when he discusses a function, he is thinking of the term broadly, and not identifying what some might think of as a functional department. Consider the following:

> Marketing is so basic that it cannot be considered a separate function (i.e. a separate skill or work) within the business ... it is, first, a central dimension of the entire business. It is the whole business ... seen from the customer's point of view. Concern and responsibility for marketing must, therefore, permeate all areas of the enterprise. (Drucker, 1973: 63)

> Marketing alone does not make a business enterprise ... The second function of a business, therefore, is innovation – the provision of different economic satisfactions ... In the organisation of the business enterprise innovation can no more be considered a separate function than marketing. It is not confined to engineering or research but extends across all parts of the business ... Innovation can be defined as the task of endowing human and material resources with new and greater wealth-producing capacity. (Drucker, 1973: 65–67)

Here, Drucker outlines the purpose of a business, and the emergence of today's marketing focus on customer orientation from his formulation was, in a sense, ineluctable. The marketing concept has its genesis in the focus on the customer – finding out what the customer needs, wants and values, and delivering this as expeditiously and as economically as possible. The 'how' (the product or service itself) is secondary – a simple means to the end of a satisfied customer. The quintessential focus of a business is the customer and *marketing* is the realisation of this process. However, taken alone, this is an over-simplification of Drucker's philosophy. Indeed, to focus solely on this aspect is to make an implicit assumption of the exogeneity of customer wants and needs (Carpenter, Glazer & Nakamoto, 1997). We argue that, in many cases, the implicit assumption goes further, to suppose the pre-existence of a customer.

We regard it as central that Drucker spoke of *creating* a customer, rather than *serving* a customer. This, combined with the injunction to *innovate*, suggests a less well-articulated aspect of Drucker's original vision; an aspect of business which comes *before* the customer, which enables the *creation of* the customer, and is concerned with *innovation* – the creation of innovative products and services. Reflecting on this principle soon reveals its logic. In many instances, needs, wants and even values arise when products are created. The innovation of products has the potential to engage people's minds and imaginations, thus creating customers. For example, Disney creates the fantasy that creates the customer (Fjellman, 1992). Over the longer term, innovation is a pre-requisite for *creating* customers, and a different process from attracting customers who already exist.

Much recent research has focused on only one aspect of Drucker's vision (e.g. Narver & Slater, 1990; Slater & Narver, 1995; Kohli & Jaworski, 1990; Jaworski & Kohli, 1993; Kohli, Jaworski & Kumar, 1997; Selnes, Jaworski & Kohli, 1997; Deshpande & Farley, 1998). Thus, researchers in the area of market orientation have defined the market-oriented firm as one that successfully applies the marketing concept (Kohli & Jaworski, 1990). Deshpande & Farley (1998) synthesise the work of Narver & Slater, and Kohli, Jaworski & Kumar with that of their own, to produce a combined ten-item measure of market orientation called MORTN. The items in this scale focus on serving the customer, but place little emphasis on customer creation. However, Drucker was not alone in recognising that serving customers would be insufficient to ensure long-term success. According to McKitterick of General Electric:

> A company committed to the marketing concept focuses its major innovative effort on enlarging the size of the market in which it participates by introducing new generic products and services, by promoting new applications for existing products, and by seeking out new classes of customers who heretofore have not used the existing products ... Only thinking of the customer and mere technical proficiency in marketing both turn out to be inferior hands when played against the company that couples its thought with action and actually comes to market with a successful innovation. (McKitterick, 1957)

We do not need to develop the case further, as Webster summarised the situation well when he wrote:

> Merely being 'customer oriented' in the philosophical sense was not enough, nor was marketing skill, narrowly defined; constant innovation was also necessary to deliver better value to consumers in a competitive marketplace (Webster, 1994: 10).

Drucker, McKitterick and Webster agree that customer orientation alone is insufficient to ensure prosperity over the longer term. This is a perspective supported by recent empirical research (Deshpande, Farley & Webster, 1993, 1997). Indeed, authors such as Macdonald (1995) are concerned that customer focus can create confused business processes, while Christensen & Bower's work (1996) suggests that firms may lose leadership positions by listening too carefully to customers! Certainly, it seems plausible that, while focusing on meeting the needs and wants of today's customer, the firm must simultaneously innovate to ensure the creation of new customers and means of satisfying future needs and wants, attaining what has been termed organisational ambidexterity (Duncan, 1976; Tushman & O'Reilly, 1996). To adjudge the theoretical merits of this more inclusive argument demands that we ensure the advice is not bound in time and space. To do this, we need to examine the historical and environmental context in which the concepts were developed.

4.3 BEYOND CUSTOMER ORIENTATION: THE RETURN TO INNOVATION

Initially it may seem somewhat perplexing why much of the recent literature emphasises *serving* the customer over *creating* the customer. However, if we explore the genesis and evolution of the literature on customer orientation the reasons become clearer. Indeed, there is little doubt that environmental contingency played a major role.

In one of the classic articles in marketing literature, Robert J Keith, a Director of Pillsbury suggested that the desirability or otherwise of a market orientation is at a minimum contingent upon conditions in the market environment. In describing Pillsbury's progression from a *production* orientation (producer push), to a *sales orientation* (still producer push) to a *marketing orientation* (customer pull), and ultimately to *marketing control* (where marketing permeates the entire company) Keith points out that:

> In the early days of the company, consumer orientation didn't seem so important ... no-one would question the availability of a market. (Keith, 1960: 37)

The move from marketing orientation to marketing control was a shift from short-term to long-term orientation, from marketing tactics and operations to overall business policy and strategy, all focused on the consumer. In contemporary terms, he described vividly a shift from a functional or departmental view of marketing, to a pan-company view of marketing as a total business philosophy:

> Soon it will be true that every activity of the corporation –
> from finance to sales to production – is aimed at satisfying
> the needs desire of the consumer. When that stage of develop-
> ment is reached, the marketing revolution will be complete.
> (Keith, 1960: 38)

For many years, companies found adequate solutions to their competitive problems through a well-managed functional marketing operation, typically by means of a marketing department charged with the responsibility for 'marketing' (Webster, 1994). As competitive pressures increase, a return to the original role of marketing as an organisation-wide philosophy or general management function is being contemplated (Hulbert & Pitt, 1996). Within a time-limited paradigm, serving the customer may bring competitive advantage. To a considerable extent, this is probably something that could be achieved by a marketing department alone. Over the longer term, however, the critical importance of customer creation will surely emerge. Arguably, serving customers and creating them is an organisation-wide responsibility. In a comment that some would find remarkably prescient, Keith concluded:

> There is nothing static about the marketing revolution . . . the
> old order has changed, yielding place to the new – but the
> new will have its quota of changes, too. (Keith, 1960: 38)

As the business environment, subject to the turbulence of globalisation, de-regulation, rapid technological development and unstable if not chaotic financial markets, changes it becomes even more appropriate to question whether customer orientation alone will be sufficient to ensure prosperity. In the view of several contemporary authors, the answer is 'no'. Dickson (1992), for example, suggests that aggressive competition leads to oversupply, wherein customers are offered more choices and thus become more sophisticated. Consequently, achieving effective differentiation is increasingly difficult. Marketers' attempts to serve these more sophisticated consumers spur them to incrementally innovate, which in turn leads to imitation and back once more to over-supply. Paradoxically, whereas innovation becomes essential, its advantages seem to dissipate just as rapidly. D'Aveni (1994) has taken this line of reasoning further, arguing that a new cycle of Schumpeterian discontinuous *innovation* is necessary to break the stalemate and enable a new competitive equilibrium.

4.3.1 Marketing and innovation

Unequivocal empirical evidence on the benefits of customer orientation is still under construction. Many of the studies thus far have been short-term and are therefore unable to answer the question of the long-term importance of radical innovation and R&D. Any experienced marketer is aware that markets can mislead as well as inform. For example, Ford of Europe built the Mk4 Escort around extensively 'broad' and 'deep' market research. When launched, the car was poorly received by both customers and journalists; sales volume had to be built through heavy discounting (Martin, 1996). In some of its latest ventures, such as the Puma Coupé, Ford has consciously eschewed market-research input (*Car*, 1997b). In fact, Ford has stated that it is now a product-led rather than a market- or customer-led company (Bulgin, 1997). Elsewhere, Quinn (1992: 298) describes state-of-the-art technologies, like those of Cray Research, Genentech, Hughes Electronics and Kyocera, being developed in freestanding technical units, not directly connected to formal marketing units. 'Heads of these projects often know more about the technologies than anyone in the world, including potential customers. So long as demand in the industry to which they sell is driven solely by technical performance criteria, the lab head can essentially define the characteristics of the next generation of products.' Good timing and technical performance predominate, although no doubt these project leaders possessed considerable insight into their customers' requirements.

Further, a broad stream of research suggests the central importance of innovation to good performance (Capon, Farley

& Hulbert, 1988; Capon, Farley, Lehmann & Hulbert, 1992; Deshpande, Farley & Webster, 1993, 1997).

An innovation orientation turns traditional marketing philosophy on its head. Products precede needs and create their own demand by changing the way customers behave. More generally, various authors have stressed the central importance of innovation to organisational success. For example, Schumpeter (1934) argued that innovations produced by companies were the engine of economic evolution and progress. Deming (1986) stressed that the need for internal process innovation is central to competitive position, while Nonaka & Yamanouchi (1989) argue that innovation is the lifeblood by which companies renew themselves.

Sources of innovative ideas include technology, engineering and production, inventions and patents, other firms, and management and employees (Urban & Hauser, 1980). However, irrespective of the idea source, a basic innovation orientation within the company is central for innovative ideas to root and reach fruition. This innovation orientation can be described as having two components. First, an orientation that is generative and receptive to new ideas – an attribute that Zaltman, Duncan & Holbek (1973) call 'openness to innovation'. Second, an organisational ability to implement new ideas – what Burns & Stalker (1977) call 'capacity to innovate'. Innovation orientation thus combines the elements of openness to innovation and capacity to innovate.

An additional source of ideas for new products is the customer. Von Hippel (1976, 1977) found that, in many high-tech industries, a significant percentage of innovative ideas were the results of users developing prototypes themselves. However, it is important to recognise that these are high-tech industries where the customers are either scientists or technicians. Any broad-scale survey of customers' needs and wants would fail to identify these breakthroughs. Innovations by consumers (as opposed to business-to-business customers) are likely to be isolated and, by definition, extreme 'outliers'. A generic 'customer orientation' would tend to aggregate customers' views and miss the extreme 'outliers' of customer innovation. An orientation that focuses on innovation rather than aggregate customer needs may be more likely to recognise these externally generated ideas.

To reiterate, the rationale for an innovation orientation is that technology has the potential to create markets and customers. It can do this by defining human needs, hence determining the nature of consumer demand. Breakthrough technologies, or 'killer applications', do not merely change markets or ways of doing things – they have far-reaching effects on the way society functions, and how human beings work and live (Downes & Mui, 1998). By providing customers with new products, services or processes, advancing technology invariably induces changes in their basic behaviour – 'changes that are sometimes so fundamental that before long they cannot imagine living any other way' (Pilzer, 1990: 53 – 54). Indeed, Hamel & Prahalad (1991) and D'Aveni (1994) have argued that being first to a market, combined with continual innovation, is the key to survival in a turbulent business environment. The fast pace of change in competitive market environments might be seen as additional evidence for this view.

4.3.2 Competitive arbitrage

There is ample indication that much achievement in the recent past, and perhaps even more in the future, will come from anticipating and *creating* customer wants (Carpenter & Nakamoto, 1989; Carpenter, Glazer & Nakamoto, 1994). If one embraces a population ecology perspective (e.g. Hannan & Freeman, 1977; McKelvey & Aldrich, 1983), the competitors that survive will likely be ever more proficient in conventional management practice. It appears quite likely that attempts to interpret and respond to customer wants will become so ubiquitous that the opportunity to sustain competitive advantage through such approaches may become scarce (Gatignon & Xuereb, 1997: 87). Although managers may perceive inherent risk in strategies that create and target future needs and wants, accepting such risk is likely to become central to competitive advantage. Moreover, Gatignon & Xuereb (1997) make almost exactly this point in interpreting their recent empirical results, arguing that a synthesis of technological and customer orientation is well suited to markets where uncertainty is high.

4.3.3 Changing needs and environments

The pace of change raises another set of issues with the manifest fluidity of customer needs and wants. If these continue to change rapidly, traditional customer-oriented firms will increasingly be aiming at moving targets. Given the lags inherent in even a radically re-engineered product development process, by the time a firm gets its new product to market, it will be virtually impossible to avoid betting on what customers will really desire. In the next section, we focus on these issues by developing a theoretical framework to answer the following questions:

- What are the different modes of strategy and when is each appropriate?

- Is there a 'best way' to develop the strategy and organisation in order to mesh with customers' future needs and wants?

- Could this reshaping embody the keys to marketplace success?

In exploring these questions, we focus on the customer and on innovation. We identify four modes of interaction between customer and innovation orientations, and discuss the managerial implications of each mode.

4.4 TOWARDS A THEORETICAL FRAMEWORK

The potential relationship between innovation and customers is of a two-way nature as shown in Figure 4.1.

'A' represents the flow from customers to innovative technology, which usually comprises traditional market research. It may also include informal knowledge and market observation by managers and others, novel approaches to market research such as 'spending a day in the life of the customer' (Gouillart & Sturdivant, 1994), and immersion with consumers or buyers

Figure 4.1: Innovation/Customer communication flows

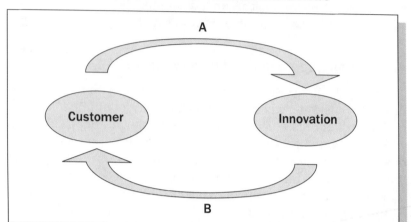

(Johanson & Nonaka, 1987). Similarly, there is a flow from innovative technology to customers (represented by the 'B'). Technological change has the potential to change people's perceptions, their expectations, and their preferences. Once commercialised, these changes may re-shape the way people live, the way society is structured, and the manner in which human beings conceptualise themselves – positively or negatively (e.g. Wiener, 1954; Mander, 1991). Saloner, quoted in a recent *Economist* argues that Silicon Valley, a hotbed of innovative companies, 'works on a "field of dreams" business plan': if you build something, customers will come' (*Economist*, 1997: S-17). While this may seem extreme, anecdotal examples of new technologies changing markets are legend. Consider, for example, the changes in working class lives with the advent of the railroad; the changes in American life style resulting from widespread automobile ownership in the mid-twentieth century; and the influence of the integrated circuit and the micro-processor on countless consumer durables, improving their convenience and functionality in ways that consumers enjoy but still do not fully understand. Thus, managers and their companies learn from the market, and the market (customers) learns from new technologies and associated products, as demonstrated by Carpenter & Nakamoto (1989) and Carpenter, Glazer & Nakamoto (1994). To a greater or lesser extent, this two-way flow or dialogue is present for every product or service in every market. However, for any one organisation, the degree of focus on innovation and/or the customer can vary substantially. By dichotomising these dimensions, we can identify four archetypal configurations for the firm (*see* Figure 4.2).

Figure 4.2: Strategic orientation archetypes

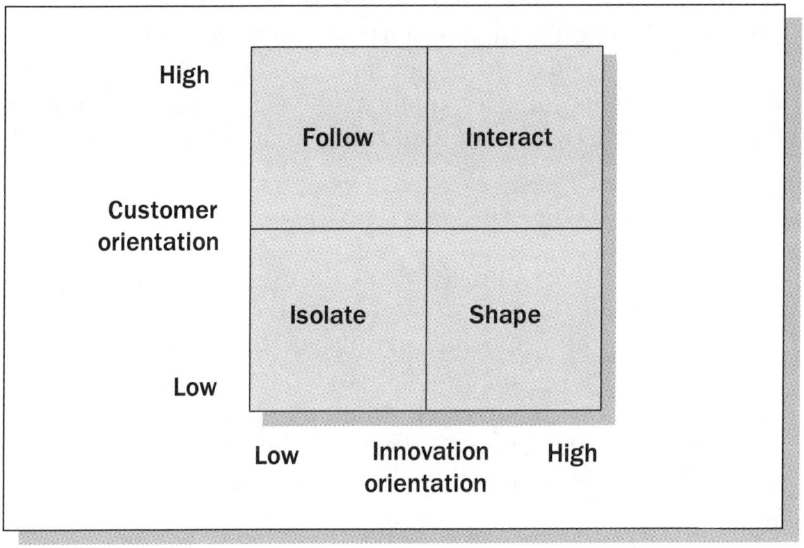

Let's explore each archetype in turn.

4.4.1 Isolate

The organisation becomes the focus of its own attention in isolate mode, for there is little or no communication between innovation and the customer. In other words, it becomes organocentric (Woodruff, 1997:139). Technology either stagnates or is developed for its own sake; it is not customer-driven. Nor is the market modified in any appreciable way by the presence of this technology. This is the classic 'isolationist' mode in which either minimal product development occurs or, when it does, is irrespective of or despite customer needs. Similarly, minimal or no market research occurs. There is no meaningful communication between product and market – they evolve or stagnate along separate paths.

In isolation mode, the organisation becomes introverted, and concerned with its internal problems and operations at the expense of both innovation and customer focus. This mode characterised the British motorcar and motor cycle industries during the late 1960s, and especially the 1970s. Limited product development was undertaken, and what was done was often tangential to market needs and preferences. Indeed, British Leyland became notorious for poor quality, low-value products, which, while innovative, were shunned rather than adopted.

4.4.2 Follow

The customer drives innovation in the follow mode. The firm relies heavily on market research – both formal or structured (using surveys) and informal or unstructured ('walking in the customer's shoes') – to establish the parameters of products and services, and to drive development. This can either be from scratch, in the case of new product development, or from an established position, where the product or service is refined. Examples of the former in the motor industry include:

- the development by Toyota of the Lexus, where they attempted to establish exactly what the market would require of a luxury saloon car before attempting to build it; and

- of the M5, or Miata, by Mazda, where engineers played the sounds of engines to potential customers, to be able to design the ideal sports car sound into the product.

In the service environment, the Courtyard concept by Marriott Hotels, where frequent business travellers were involved in conceptualising the ideal budget business accommodation (Wind, Green, Shifflet & Scarborough, 1989) is an excellent illustration.

According to the manager who sponsored this project, 'In designing the actual product, the research allowed management to focus on the items customers wanted, and we avoided focusing on things important to management but not important to the customer.'

4.4.3 Shaping

Where innovative technology rather than the customer is the focus, this is known as a shape strategy; technology shapes the market. Potential customers may not even have been aware that they needed or wanted the benefits derived from a particular technology until it became available (Pilzer, 1990: 18). Shaping suggests that technology defines human needs, and thus determines the nature of customer demand by providing new products or services that induce changes in basic behaviour. The product becomes quintessential in shaping or defining a given market. This typically occurs in two areas: in the forming of expectations and in the forming of prototypical preferences. For example, Japanese car manufacturers followed the former route in the 1970s by loading their basic products with options not normally available as standard in their competitors' cars. Customers' expectations were raised and they began to question why these options were not standard in other manufacturers' vehicles. Firms learned that they needed to distinguish between so-called qualifying and determining attributes. As competitors become better at fulfilling customers' requirements, sometimes the determinants of choice are the less important (but *determining*) attributes.

Examples of shaping prototypical preference strategy are Jeep in the USA and Land Rover in the UK, in defining the four-wheel drive utility market. These manufacturers shaped what consumer psychologists call the customers' category prototypes and disproportionately influenced the criteria against which customers evaluated other, later entrants to the market (Carpenter & Nakamoto, 1989). In subsequent studies, researchers have been able to demonstrate that even 'irrelevant' attributes may influence choice, supporting the idea that a properly executed shaping strategy can be particularly effective (Carpenter, Glazer & Nakamoto, 1994). Historical evidence that may be adduced for this argument includes order of entry studies (Urban, Carter, Gaskin & Mucha, 1986) and brand longevity data (Aaker, 1991).

The shaping strategy also manifests itself in two distinct forms: *defining* and *influencing* (although it might be argued that the latter is a delimited version of the former). The *defining* strategy is one in which entrepreneurial imagination and action combine with often-serendipitous series of events, and lead to a product defining a market. For example, in the early 1980s, Chrysler forged ahead with the original minivan concept, despite market research indicating that people were strongly negative towards the vehicle. The Chrysler minivan went on to create and define the minivan market. Similarly, in the early 1990s, Compaq gambled millions of dollars on PC network servers, despite research indicating that the market would never abandon mainframes. The PC server has now replaced the mainframe in many markets, and Compaq remains the definitive server against which others are judged (Martin, 1995).

In the *influencing* mode, products influence market expectations and trends, but do not define the market or necessarily capture it. For example, Apple's Macintosh defined what most customers wanted in a personal computer – a user-friendly tool with a graphic interface that did not require technical computing skills. It did not go on to dominate the PC market. Ironically, Apple seemed to think it might learn these lessons in the case of the Newton, its hand-held personal digital assistant, launched in 1993.

'The Newton's features were defined through one of the most thoroughly executed market research efforts in corporate history; focus groups and surveys of every type were used to determine what features consumers would want' (Christensen, 1997: 134). Yet the Newton failed dismally and was withdrawn by Apple in late 1996.

Freddie Laker's ill-fated airline venture did not delimit the air travel market. However, it did shape the expectations and perceptions of travellers about the price of trans-Atlantic travel, and opened the way for subsequent entrants. It was no coincidence that Virgin's Richard Branson wanted to name his first aircraft *Spirit of Sir Freddie* (Brown, 1994).

We suspect that the distinction we are making is, in many cases, only *ex post*, for *influencers* would often like to define. However, in some cases the *influencing* choice is undoubtedly *ex ante*, as witnessed in negotiations to attempt to influence new standards in consumer electronics, or, as Kodak has attempted with the Advantix film format for 35 mm photography. An *influencer* does not have to dominate a new standard to benefit enormously, especially if the end-use market is elastic (Brandenburger & Nalebuff, 1996).

Lest we create the impression that all shaping strategies are good and necessarily productive, it should be pointed out that many fail (Quinn, 1986). Successful shaping requires the placing of two large bets, one on technology and the other on the market.

Failure rates in developing new technology are notoriously underestimated because of a tendency to sink without trace. Failure to shape, however, is equally common for another reason – technological pioneers often have a poor understanding of market and customer learning processes. Much of the new research discussed above is based on the benefits of being first in the mind of the buyer. However, the technological bias of many innovative companies leads them to believe that being the first to perfect, to produce or even to sell and distribute is enough to win the marketplace prize. By under-investing in marketing communications (by design or default), they unwittingly cede their position to a follower. The management-consulting firm AD Little sees an ironic symmetry to this problem.

Technologists in fast-moving consumer goods companies – archetypes of marketing-dominated companies – tend to adopt a low profile and do what they are asked to do without much debate, so convinced are they that their companies, being market-oriented, must be marketing-driven.

The reverse is equally true: in technology- or engineering-driven companies, marketers often tend to follow – and sometimes mimic – their colleagues in the technical departments (from which they themselves often come). (Deschamps, 1994: 11–12).

4.4.4 Interact

True dialogue is established between the customer and technology in the interact mode. While dialogue is present over time in any marketplace, at any one time, firms are usually engaged in a monologue. The term dialogue is appropriate here because it uses the metaphor of speech to underpin the market-technology relationship, providing a spectrum ranging from 'conversation' to 'negotiation'. Li & Calantone (1998) have referred to this link between markets and new product development as 'market knowledge competence', a similar construct to what we refer to as 'interact'. Market knowledge competence has received attention in marketing and strategy literature, with authors such as Glazer (1991), Hamel & Prahalad (1994) and Sinkula (1994) considering it a key strategic asset of an organisation. The term conversation conjures up the image of a genteel two-way flow of information, ideas offered, modified and evolved. Negotiation sums up the harder image of a power play between products and markets, where there are trade-offs of values and features. Many industrial markets operate in the *negotiation-interact* mode – for example, a prospective customer may publish a bid or tender and invite potential suppliers to submit their offers before moving to the next step in the development of the product or service. In contrast, bespoke tailors have, for years, involved their customers in *conversational* dialogues about the product they will in a very real sense 'co-produce'.

History provides us various examples of the interaction mode. Many of the early car manufacturers at the upper end of the market, such as Bentley, Duesenberg, Alvis and Bugatti, co-operated with independent coachbuilders to make cars to owners' specifications. Interestingly, Rolls Royce seems to be moving once again in this direction, to distinguish itself from other high-quality car producers. It announced its return to the manufacture of the 'bespoke' automobile, promising that no two cars that left the factory would be the same – each car being exactly tailored to each individual customer's specification (*Car*, 1997a, *The Times*, 1997). Perhaps one of the best-known examples is that of Boeing's successful inclusion of eight of its most important customers as members of the 777 design team (*Flight International*, 1993).

Another perspective on the interact option is afforded by the developing emphasis on 'relationship' marketing (Heide & John, 1990; Spekman & Salmond, 1992; Morgan & Hunt, 1994). As companies learn more about their customers' preferences, subtle changes occur as the emphasis moves from responsiveness in service alone to a broader interpretation. These ideas are reflected in such concepts as mass customisation (Pine, 1993; Pine, Peppers & Rogers, 1995), 'segment of one' markets (Blattberg & Deighton, 1991), and 'one-to-one' marketing strategies (Peppers & Rogers, 1993). Ultimately, the 'market-of-one' will be matched by a 'product-of-one'. Good examples include Dell computers (Magretta, 1998), which facilitates the specification of a personal computer on a web site by a customer, and Musicmaker (www.musicmaker.com), which allows customers to create their own compilations to be pressed to CD. Levi Strauss jeans (McGarvey, 1995) also illustrates the point well. Since 1995, Levi Strauss has offered women customised pants based on their individual measurements. The Personal Pair programme was an immense success, achieving a 38% repeat purchase rate compared to the typical 10-12% rate of regular Levi Strauss customers. The company expanded the programme and, in November 1998, Personal Pair was merged into the Original Spin product, offered to both men and women. Levi Strauss now pitches customisation at the youth set, offering 49 500 different sizes and 30 styles, creating nearly 1.5 million options. Each pair of pants is created according to the customer's unique measurements and fashion sense. The orders are sent via modem to a factory where the pants are cut single-ply and shipped within two to three weeks. If a customer wants button-fly, low-cut jeans that reveal the navel and flare in the leg, or if they just want jeans that fit, Levi Strauss will deliver. Cost savings in retail inventory allow the company to sell customised pants at a competitive price (*INSIDE 1to1* Newsletter, 4 December 1998).

Recent developments on the Internet, and particularly the World Wide Web, offer some ideal opportunities to expand the interaction mode. Customers and manufacturers will be able to enter into dialogue about the design of a product or service, its delivery and modes of payment. Glazer suggests that the emergence of 'smart' markets will require the development of information-intensive strategies and 'smart' products – '... product and service offerings that adapt or respond to changes in their environment as they interact with consumers' (Glazer, 1997).

The Firefly Network (www.firefly.com) creates virtual communities of users by getting them not only to give a lot of information about themselves, but also to do a lot of the work required to create this virtual community. Customers give information about their preferences for books, music and films. Firefly then builds a profile of the customer's likes, which is continually updated as the customer provides more information – usually in the form of rating scales. This information is then correlated with other users' interests and enjoyment profiles to recommend new music, books and films. Customers also give their opinions of the films, music and books that they have seen, which are then fed back to other users. The information is not only very valuable to the customer, but a major asset to the company itself, which vends it to film producers, record companies and booksellers. The customer is not only a co-creator of their own service and enjoyment; they also produce on behalf of Firefly a very valuable and saleable information service.

4.5 UNDERSTANDING STRATEGIC DYNAMICS

Obviously there can be movement among the modes over time. For example, initially a product may be developed to meet a specific customer need (follow) or to define a market (shape).

Over time, a shaper might become a follower, lapse into isolation, or become truly interactive. There is a temptation to be normative about which mode to pursue; devout marketers might espouse a following strategy, and engineers and technologists a shaping strategy. Even an isolation strategy might have adherents. After careful thought, however, interaction would probably get the popular vote. Unfortunately, reality is seldom that simple. Dialogue and interaction may be expensive at best and irrelevant at worst. Although they may reduce risk, we can also argue that they may be less likely to consistently produce either the breakthrough product or service that characterises the successful shaper or the devotion to true customer satisfaction that good followers are able to deliver. To understand the dynamics of mode change among the archetypes, it is worth reviewing some of the factors that may inhibit or foster the change process.

It has long been recognised that organisations are in a continual state of flux (Hofer & Davoust, 1977; Hall, 1980; Miller & Friesen, 1983; Morris, Davis & Allen, 1991). Organisations change modes over time, and valuable lessons may be learned from each mode. The potentially maligned isolation mode can be a period in which a company turns its attentions inward and becomes introverted. This can be highly productive in, for example, phases of reflection, re-assessment and re-organisation – such as company mergers. A state is neither good nor bad in itself; evaluation depends on how that state is used. Among the most important factors influencing a change of state are:

- *Inertial factors*: Firms typically establish and embed approaches to technology and market deeply in their cultures, and this inertia renders them unlikely to change unless presented with a threat to their survival. Even where survival is at risk, strong constituencies such as diverse labour unions and top management may obdurately resist change.

- *Environmental factors:* It can be argued that the efficacy of a particular mode is partly contingent upon the characteristics of a specific business environment. In a very stable environment, an isolate strategy might be effective and economical. In contrast, in an environment of complex and rapidly evolving needs and wants, combined with a variety of technological alternatives, an interactionist approach might appear more appropriate.

- *Competitive factors:* Cycles of near-equilibrium and dis-equilibrium are the lifeblood of competitive markets, creating waves of discontinuity that bring ever-greater value to customers in such markets (Schumpeter, 1939; D'Aveni, 1994). According to this view, stability is a temporary illusion and market-technology dialogue will be ongoing.

4.5.1 Understanding the implications of changes of mode

As noted earlier, the typical mode change will be exogenously driven. However, to retain strategic mastery, firms must acquire the ability to proactively assert control over this process. In other words, the emergent is better if planned. In order to do this, we must understand the implications of each mode and the requirements for successful changes of mode. Possessing this knowledge may be a necessary but probably insufficient condition to ensure successful change, such are the forces of stasis that must typically be overcome (Hannan & Freeman, 1984). Figure 4.3 shows a comparison of the modes of interaction, their characteristics and four crucial competencies associated with each archetype we have discussed. By comparing the cells in the figure, it is evident that very substantial change is necessary to accommodate movement from one mode to another. This explains why large external shocks are typically necessary to bring about shifts. However, empirical research has established that, in general, planned re-orientations are more successful than crisis-driven change (Virany, Tushman & Romanelli, 1992; Tushman & O'Reilly, 1996).

Table 4.1: Modes of interaction and crucial competencies for different archetypes

Archetype: Mode	Isolate	Follow	Shape	Interact
Inter- organisational focus	The organisation focuses on itself. It is organocentric.	Each other: follow 'like competitors' through mutual benchmarking	The business environment	The business environment and self
Interaction with customer	Low and primarily transactional	High and following	Directive	High and reciprocal
Product development	Minimal/ tangential to customer needs and wants	Incremental (Kaizen)	Technology-driven/ discontinuous	Co-development
Market strategy	Maintenance	Responsive	Assertive	Collaborative
Organisational competencies/ culture	Inwardly focused/ bureaucracy	Customer service/develop-mental R&D	Technology-driven/ assertive marketing	Holographic interacting adhocracy

4.5.2 Changes of mode

When we consider that there are four modes in Figure 4.2, it is evident that 12 possible mode transitions may occur. We do not intend to explore all of these, but rather to illustrate the transitions that may occur by examining some case examples.

Boeing: The recent history of Boeing provides an excellent example of mode transition. In the times before deregulation, Boeing was a *shaper*. The major US airlines did not possess significant marketing capability and Boeing stepped into the breach by acting as an ancillary marketing department for its customers, analysing future patterns of demand and equipment needs. As the capital costs of new airframes rose, evidence of movement toward *interact* began to appear (Beeby, 1983). The 747 relied on a high degree of collaboration with PanAm, but the most dramatic example was provided by the 777, for which eight leading airlines provided employees to participate in Boeing's design teams on an ongoing basis (Quinn, 1992: 180). With its decision to drop the development of a 'super-jumbo' of 600–800 seats, Boeing appears to have settled into a *follow* mode. British Airways and Singapore Airlines expressed strong interest in the proposal, but Boeing decided to follow the rest of the airlines in saying 'no' to the project, at least for the time being.

AOL: Initially a *shaper*, America Online dominated the on-line provision of Internet services, shaping customer expectations of what an Internet provider should be. Others emulated AOL's strategy with varying degrees of success. However, complacency overtook AOL; its customer base learned and evolved in terms of expectations faster then the company realised. From a shaper position, AOL slipped back into relative *isolation*. It became increasingly out of touch with customer expectations, focusing rather on its internal objective of growth. To this end, in December 1996, AOL offered an unlimited-use fee structure. It came as quite a shock when customers started to rebel at the poor response time AOL servers were providing. Initial platitudes soon turned into panic. AOL is now primarily in a *follow* mode, with its customers dictating their requirements (*Economist*, 1997).

Microsoft: Initially in *isolate* mode, Microsoft derided the Internet, ignored the market, and did little in the way of product development in the area of a Web browser. However, seeing the exponential growth of the World Wide Web, and the explosive success of Netscape, the *shaper* of the browser software market, Microsoft was spurred into action. In a well-documented *volt face*, Microsoft moved from *isolate* to *follower*.

It developed its Explorer browser software by imitating virtually every feature of Netscape's Navigator product. Whether aggressive marketing combined with giving the product away free to anyone and everyone is enough to overtake the *shaper* Netscape remains to be seen (*Economist*, 1996), particularly in view of customer reports on Explorer, which alleged serious security defects.

4.6 CONCLUSION

The mode transitions discussed above have much in common with Schotter's (1981) perspective on economic institutions – namely that the institution's development can be inferred from the existence of an evolutionary problem, and that every evolutionary economic problem requires a social institution to solve it. The history of marketing specifically (Alderson, 1957), and of organizations generally (Chandler, 1962, 1977), is consistent with this perspective. Vertically integrated functional organisations (such as Ford at the time of the Model T) dominated the early years of the twentieth century, when relatively stable market environments characterised by low customer purchasing power and simple customer preferences, caused the focus to be on *production*. Following this, organisations became multi-divisional (e.g. General Motors in the Sloan years), in an attempt to be both *product- and market-oriented*. The environment of increased spending power and sophisticated tastes both permitted and necessitated this development. As power and sophistication intensified, however, multi-divisional organisations were supplanted by some form of matrix organisation, often attempting to align marketing more closely with science and engineering (Bartlett & Ghoshal, 1990). In the 1980s, matrices gave way to networks (Powell, 1990; Iacobucci, 1996), as it became apparent that many effective organisations, such as those in Japan and Korea, owed their success to factors outside the firm.

Duncan (1976) highlights a basic contradiction in organisational structures best suited to innovation versus efficient implementation. His proposal is that organisations should change shape in their transition from innovation to implementation. Analogously, in our model, changing from shaper mode to follower mode might mean becoming less organic and more mechanistic. Indeed, the interacting firm might require the most radical organisational form of all – one that is constantly changing shape, structure, processes, and even objectives. Hedberg, Nystrom & Starbuck (1976) describe, and Huber (1984) alludes to, the 'experimenting' organization, which is in a constant state of self-redesign, characterised by flexibility and adaptability. Others have referred to the effectiveness of adhocracies (Duncan, 1976). A recent article illustrates this phenomenon:

> To an unusual degree Silicon Valley's economy relies on what Joseph Schumpeter, an Austrian economist, called 'creative destruction' ... the basic idea is (that) old companies die, and new ones emerge, allowing capital, ideas and people to be re-allocated' (*Economist*, 1997: S-7).

It is tempting for managers to look at the strategic archetypes in Figure 4.2 and oversimplify by assuming there is one 'wrong' focus for an organisation (the isolate mode) and one ideal focus (the interact mode, which integrates customer and innovation orientations). While this might be appropriate in an ideal world, in reality there is no ideal or misplaced focus *per se*. Rather, it is more important that the mode in which the firm operates be pertinent to the environment in which it competes. As noted previously, a case can even be made for the isolation mode under certain circumstances, such as times of crisis in commodity markets or major corporate mergers. The greater risk to the organisation is a focus inappropriate to the circumstances, such as engaging customers in interaction when all the market requires is to be served, or attempting to serve and follow customers exclusively when the market is ripe for shaping. Decision makers might benefit more from understanding their current mode of focus and determining whether this is appropriate to the circumstances of the organisation, rather than merely attempting to attain a particular focus, regardless of the situation. We argue, therefore, that the issue is not one of insufficient customer focus or inadequate attention to innovation, but rather of an inappropriate focus on environmental circumstances. Measures of customer and innovation orientation may offer managers an accurate picture of their firm's strategic mode of operation, but without considering environmental circumstances, they will be unable to judge whether the current mode is suitable.

To summarise, it is not and was not our intent to present an apostasy of the customer orientation philosophy. Rather, we intended to demonstrate that there was more than one mode of achieving business success. Customer or market orientation has generally evolved to focus on the serving or keeping of customers (as a perusal of the items in the various instruments proposed to measure it confirm (Deshpande & Farley, 1998)). To fully embody the concept of a business as espoused by Drucker and others in the 1950s, there is a need to *create* customers. Innovation, with a focus on technology, is central to meeting this need.

In this chapter we have attempted to clarify and reconcile two of the most widely promoted theses in management: the need for customer orientation and the requirement of improved innovation management. Both are key to understanding Drucker's original concept of the business enterprise, but each has at times been advocated to the exclusion of the other. We believe that any philosophy of management that appears to suggest there is a 'magic bullet' does a disservice to both theory and practice. When considering customer and innovation orientations, managers must realise that they are not necessarily looking at an either/or decision, but rather they must ask which strategic posture will best help fulfil their companies' future goals and objectives.

References

Aaker, D. 1991. *Managing Brand Equity*, New York, NY: Free Press.

Alderson, W. 1957. *Marketing Behavior and Executive Action*, Homewood, IL: Richard D Irwin.

Band, J. 1991. *Creating Value for Customers,* New York, NY: John Wiley.

Bartlett, CA & Ghoshal, S. 1990. Matrix management: not a structure, a frame of mind. *Harvard Business Review*, July–August.

Beeby, W. 1983. Manufacturing information flow. *US Leadership in Manufacturing*, Washington, DC: National Academy of Engineering: 86.

Blattberg, RC & Deighton, J. 1991. Interactive marketing: exploiting the age of addressability. *Sloan Management Review*, Fall: 5–14.

Bloom, PN & Greyser, SA. 1981. The maturity of consumerism. *Harvard Business Review*, November–December: 130–139.

Brown, M. 1994. *Richard Branson: The Inside Story*, London, UK: Headline.

Bulgin, R. 1997. Enter the Puma, *The Daily Telegraph*, 21 June: C3.

Burns, T & Stalker, GM. 1977. *The Management of Innovation.* 2nd ed. London: Tavistock.

Capon, N, Farley, JU & Hulbert, JM. 1988. *Corporate Strategic Planning*, New York, NY: Columbia University Press.

Capon, N, Farley, JU, Lehmann, DR & Hulbert, JM. 1992. Profiles of product innovators among large US manufacturers. *Management Science*, 38 (February): 157–169.

Car. 1997a. No two rollers will be the same again. February: 10.

Car. 1997b. Building a class leading platform. April: 10.

Carpenter, GS & Nakamoto, K. 1989. Consumer preference formation and pioneering advantage. *Journal of Marketing Research*, 26 (August): 285–298.

Carpenter, GS, Glazer, R & Nakamoto, K. 1994. Meaningful brands from meaningless differentiation: the dependence on irrelevant attributes. *Journal of Marketing Research*, 31 (August): 339–350.

Carpenter, GS, Glazer, R & Nakamoto, K. 1997. *Readings on Market-Driving Strategies: Towards a New Theory of Competitive Advantage.* Addison-Wesley.

Chandler, AD. 1962. *Strategy and Structure.* Cambridge, MA: MIT Press.

Chandler, AD. 1977. *The Visible Hand: The Managerial Revolution in American Business,* Cambridge, MA: Harvard University Press.

Christensen, C. 1997. *The Innovator's Dilemma: When New Technologies Cause Great Firms to Fail,* Boston, MA: Harvard Business School Press.

Christensen, C & Bower, J. 1996. Customer power, strategic investment, and the failure of leading firms. *Strategic Management Journal*, 17(3): 197–218.

Clark, KB & Fujimoto, T. 1991. *Product Development Performance,* Boston, MA: Harvard Business School Press.

D'Aveni, R. 1994. *Hypercompetition,* New York, NY: Free Press.

Day, GS. 1990. *Market Driven Strategy: Processes for Creating Value,* New York, NY: Free Press.

Day, GS. 1994. Capabilities of market-driven organizations. *Journal of Marketing*, 58 (October): 37–52.

Deming WE. 1986. *Out of Crisis: Quality, Productivity and Competitive Position.* Cambridge: Cambridge University Press.

Deschamps, J-P. 1994. Managing the marketing/R&D interface. *Prism*, 4: 5–19.

Deshpande, R & Farley, JU. 1998. Measuring market orientation: generalization and synthesis. *Journal of Market Focused Management*, 2: 213–232.

Deshpande, R, Farley, JU & Webster, FE. 1993. Corporate culture, customer

◄ 84

orientation, and innovativeness in Japanese firms: a quadrad analysis. *Journal of Marketing,* 57 (January): 23–27.

Deshpande, R, Farley, JU & Webster, FE. 1997. *Factors affecting organizational performance: a five-country comparison.* Cambridge, MA: Marketing Science Institute Report No. 97–108.

Dickson, PR. 1992. Toward a general theory of competitive rationality. *Journal of Marketing,* 56 (January): 69–83.

Dickson, PR. 1993. *Marketing Management,* Fort Worth, TX: The Dryden Press.

Downes, L & Mui, C. 1998. *Unleashing the Killer App,* Boston, MA: Harvard Business School Publishing.

Drucker, PF. 1954. *The Practice of Management,* New York, NY: Harper and Row.

Drucker, PF. 1973. *Management: Tasks, Responsibilities, Practices,* New York, NY: Harper and Row.

Duncan, RB. 1976. The ambidextrous organization: designing dual structures for innovation in Kilman, RH, Pondy, LR & Slevin, DP. (eds). *The Management of Organizational Design,* Vol. 1. New York, NY: Elsevier

Economist. 1996. Freer than free. 17 August.

Economist. 1997. A survey of Silicon Valley. 29 March.

Economist. 1997. America Online. 1 February.

Fjellman, SM. 1992. *Vinyl leaves: Walt Disney and America,* Boulder, CO: Westview Press.

Flight International. 1993. Tailor made twinjet. 8 December.

Galbraith, JK. 1967. *The New Industrial State,* Boston, MA: Houghton Mifflin.

Gatignon, H & Xuereb, J-M. 1997. Strategic orientation of the firm and new product performance. *Journal of Marketing Research,* 34 (February): 77–90.

Glazer, R. 1991. Marketing in an information-intensive environment: strategic implications of knowledge as an asset. *Journal of Marketing,* 55 (October) 1–19.

Glazer, R. 1997. Strategy and structure in information-intensive markets: the relationship between marketing and IT. *Journal of Market-Focused Management,* (forthcoming).

Gouillart, F & Sturdivant, F. 1994. Spend a day in the life of your customers. *Harvard Business Review,* January–February.

Gupta, AK, Raj, SP & Wilemon, D. 1986. A model for studying R&D-marketing interface in the product innovation process. *Journal of Marketing,* April: 7–17.

Hall, W. 1980. Survival strategies in a hostile environment. *Harvard Business Review,* January–February: 75–83.

Hamel, G & Prahalad, CK. 1991. Corporate imagination and expeditionary marketing. *Harvard Business Review,* July–August: 81–92.

Hamel, G & Prahalad, CK. 1994. *Competing for the Future,* Harvard: Harvard Business School Press.

Hannan, MT & Freeman, J. 1977. The population ecology of organizations. *American Journal of Sociology,* 82: 929–963.

Hannan, MT & Freeman, J. 1984. Structural inertia and organizational change. *American Sociological Review,* 49 (April): 149–164.

Hedberg, B, Nystrom, PC & Starbuck, WH. 1976. Camping on seesaws: prescriptions for a self-designing organization. *Administrative Science Quarterly,* 21 (March): 41–65.

Heide, J & John, G. 1990. Alliances of industrial purchasing: the determinants of joint action in buyer-seller relationships. *Journal of Marketing Research,* XXVII (February): 24–36.

Hill, GWL & Jones, GR. 1998. *Strategic Management: An Integrated Approach,* Boston, MA: Houghton-Mifflin.

Hofer, C & Davoust, M. 1977. *Successful Strategic Management,* Chicago, IL: AT Kearney.

Huber, GP. 1984. The nature and design of post-industrial organizations. *Management Science,* 30 August: 928–951.

Hulbert, JM & Pitt, LF. 1996. Exit left center stage? The future of functional marketing. *European Management Journal,* 14(1): 47–60.

Iacobucci, D. (ed) 1996. *Networks in Marketing,* Thousand Oaks, CA: Sage.

Jaworski, BJ & Kohli, AJ. 1993. Market orientation: antecedents and consequences. *Journal of Marketing,* 57 (July): 53–70.

Johanson, J & Nonaka, I. 1987. Market research the Japanese way. *Harvard Business Review,* May–June: 29–32.

Keith, RJ. 1960. The marketing revolution. *Journal of Marketing,* 24 (January): 35–38.

Kodama, F. 1995. *Emerging Patterns of Innovation: Sources of Japan's Technological Edge,* Boston, MA: Harvard Business School Press.

Kohli, AK & Jaworski, BJ. 1990. Market orientation: the construct, research propositions and managerial implications. *Journal of Marketing,* 54 (April): 1–18.

Kohli, AK, Jaworski, BJ & Kumar, A. 1993. MARKOR: A measure of market orientation. *Journal of Market Research,* (November): 467–477.

Li, T. & Calantone, RJ. 1998. The impact of market knowledge competence on new product advantage: conceptualization and empirical examination. *Journal of Marketing,* 62 (October): 13, 29.

Macdonald, S. 1995. Too close for comfort: the strategic implications of getting close to the customer. *California Management Review,* 38 (3): 8–27.

Mander, J. 1991. *In the Absence of the Sacred: The Failure of Technology and the Survival of the Indian Nations,* San Francisco, CA: Sierra Club.

Martin, J. 1995. Ignore your customer. *Fortune,* May: 121–126.

McGarvey, J. 1995. Interactive kiosks make a fashion statement, *Inter@ctive Week,* 11 September: 24.

McKelvey, B & Aldrich, H. 1983. Populations, natural selection and organizational science. *Administrative Science Quarterly,* 281: 101–128.

McKitterick, JAB. 1957. What is the marketing concept? in Bass, FM (ed). *The Frontiers of Marketing Thought and Science,* Chicago, IL: The American Marketing Association: 71-82.

Miller, D & Friesen, PH. 1983. Strategy-making and environment: the third link. *Strategic Management Journal*, Summer: 221–235.

Morgan, RM & Hunt, SD. 1994. The commitment-trust theory of relationship marketing. *Journal of Marketing*, 58 (July): 20–38.

Morris, MH, Davis, DL & Allen, JA. 1991. Perceived environmental turbulence and its effect on selected entrepreneurship, marketing and organizational characteristics. *Journal of the Academy of Marketing Science*, 19 (Winter): 43–51.

Narver, JC & Slater, SF. 1990. The effect of a market orientation on business profitability. *Journal of Marketing*, 54 (October): 20–35.

Narver, JC, Park, SY & Slater, SF. 1990. Relative emphasis in a market orientation and its effect on business profitability. *AMA Summer Educators Conference Proceedings*, Chicago: American Marketing Association.

Naumann, E. 1995. *Creating Customer Value*, Cincinnati, OH: Thompson Executive Press.

Nonaka & Yamanouchi. 1989. Managing innovations: a self-renewing process. *Journal of Business Venturing*, 4: 299–315.

Packard, V. 1957. *The Hidden Persuaders,* New York, NY, Pocket Books.

Peppers, D & Rogers, M. 1993. *The One-to-One Future: Building Relationships One Customer at a Time*, New York, NY: Currency Doubleday.

Peppers, D & Rogers, M. 1998. Levi's buttons up a new customer in *INSIDE 1 to 1* Newsletter, 3 December:

Pilzer, PZ. 1990. *Unlimited Wealth: The Theory and Practice of Economic Alchemy*, New York, NY: Crown Publishers.

Pine, BJ II 1993. Making mass customization work. *Harvard Business Review*, September–October: 108–111.

Pine, BJ II, Peppers, D & Rogers, M. 1995. Do you want to keep your customers forever? *Harvard Business Review*, March-April: 103–114.

Powell, WW. 1990. Neither market nor hierarchy: network forms of organization in Cummings, LL & Staw, BM. *Research in Organizational Behavior,* Greenwich, CT: JAI, 295–336.

Quinn, JB. 1986. Managing innovation: controlled chaos. *Harvard Business Review*, May–June: 73–84.

Quinn, JB. 1992. *Intelligent Enterprise,* New York, NY: Free Press.

Romanelli, E & Tushman, ML. 1986. Inertia, environments and strategic choice: a quasi-experimental design for comparative-longitudinal research. *Management Science*, 32: 608–621.

Saxe, R & Weitz, BA. 1982. The SOCO Scale: A measure of the customer orientation of salespeople. *Journal of Marketing Research*, 19 (August): 343–351.

Schotter, A. 1981. *The Economic Theory of Social Institutions*, New York, NY: Cambridge University Press.

Schumpeter, J.1934. *The Theory of Economic Development: An Inquiry into Profits, Capital and the Business Cycle,* MA: Harvard University Press.

Schumpeter, JA. 1939. *Business Cycles*, New York, NY: McGraw-Hill.

Selnes, F, Jaworski, BJ & Kohli, AJ. 1997. *Report No 97–107*. Cambridge, MA: Marketing Science Institute.

Shanklin, WL & Ryans, JK Jr. 1984. Organizing for high-tech marketing. *Harvard Business Review*, November–December: 164–171.

Sinkula, JM. 1994. Market information processing and organizational learning. *Journal of Marketing*, 58 (January): 35–45.

Slater, SF & Narver, JC. 1991. Becoming more market oriented: an exploratory study of the programmatic and market-back approaches. *Report No 91–128*, Cambridge, MA: Marketing Science Institute.

Slater, SF & Narver, JC. 1995. Market orientation and the learning organization. *Journal of Marketing*, Vol 59 (July): 63–74.

Smith, L. 1980. A miracle in search of a market. *Fortune*, December (1): 92–98.

Souder, WE. 1987. *Managing New Product Innovations*, Lexington, Mass: Heath.

Spekman, RE & Salmond, D. 1992. A working consensus to collaborate: a field study of manufacturer-supplier dyads. *MSI Working Paper, Report No 92–134* Cambridge, MA: Marketing Science Institute, December.

The Times. 1997. Bentley goes back to the future, 19 July.

Tichy, NM & Devanna, MA. 1986. *The Transformational Leader,* New York, NY: Knopf.

Tushman, M & O'Reilly, C. 1996. Ambidextrous organizations: managing evolutionary and revolutionary change. *California Management Review*, 38(4): 8–30.

Urban, GL & Hauser, JR. 1980. *Design and Marketing of New Products,* Englewood Cliffs: NJ: Prentice-Hall.

Urban, GL, Carter, T, Gaskin, S & Mucha, Z. 1986. Market share rewards of pioneering brands: an exploratory analysis and strategic implications. *Management Science*, 32 (June): 645–659.

Utterback, J, Allen, TJ, Holloman, JH & Sirbu, MA Jr. 1976. The process of innovation in five industries in Europe and Japan. *IEEE Transactions on Engineering Management*, 23(1): 3–9.

Virany, B, Tushman, M & Romanelli, E. 1992. Executive succession and organizational outcomes in turbulent environments: an organizational learning approach. *Organization Science*, Vol 31: 72–92.

Von Hippel, E. 1977. Has a customer already developed your next product? *Sloan Management Review*, 182: 63–75.

Von Hippel, E. 1978. Successful industrial products from consumers' ideas. *Journal of Marketing*, 421: 9–49.

Webster, FE Jr. 1988. The rediscovery of the marketing concept. *Business Horizons*, 32(3) May–June.

Webster, FE Jr. 1994. *Market Driven Management: Using the New Marketing Concept to Create a Customer-Driven Company*, New York, NY: John Wiley and Sons.

Wiener, N. 1954. *The Human Use of Human Beings: Cybernetics and Society*, New York, NY: Doubleday.

Wind, J, Green, PE, Shifflet, D & Scarborough, M. 1989. Courtyard by Marriott:

Designing a hotel facility with consumer-based marketing models (copyright: The Institute of Management Sciences) in Lovelock, CH. 1992. *Managing Services: Marketing, Operations and Human Resources*, Englewood Cliffs, NJ: Prentice-Hall International: 119–137.

Woodruff, RT. 1997. Customer value: the next source for competitive advantage. *Journal of the Academy of Marketing Science*, 25(3): 139–153.

Zaltman, G, Duncan, R & Holbek, J. 1973. *Innovations and Organizations,* New York, NY: Wiley.

Appendix

Take the TOCO Test

If you want to gain a quick insight into how you think your organisation shapes up, take the TOCO test below. Then see what your results say.

The TOCO checklist

Instructions: Think about the organisation you work for – how it views its customers, its competitors, how it thinks about technology in the form of products and services, its perceptions of the business environment in which it operates, its employees, and of course, itself. Then complete the short questionnaire below. Read each of the four descriptions of an organisation, A, B, C and D, and then mark a '1' next to the description that you think *best fits* your organisation, a '2' next to the description that fits it next best, and so on, until you place a '4' next to the description that least describes your organisation. In many cases, you may find the descriptions quite similar, so read them carefully. In addition, there may be instances where you want to say, 'It all depends...' Don't worry too much about this – there are no right or wrong answers, so simply record your first impression.

Let's use an example to illustrate:
Suppose a statement read as follows, with four descriptions of an organisation:

Our organisation feels as follows about 'casual dress' or 'dressing down':
A. It is totally unacceptable _____
B. It is left to the discretion and good sense of the individual _____
C. It is acceptable on Fridays _____
D. It is encouraged at all times _____

Obviously there is overlap between some of the descriptions in the example, but let's assume you know or at least think that there is a 'casual on Fridays' arrangement in the organisation, and that while it wasn't necessarily encouraged at all times, it was at least left up to the good sense and discretion of individuals. You might also be certain that at least there wasn't a rule that casual dressing was unacceptable. You would place a '1' next to description C, and then perhaps a '2' next to description B, and a '3' next to description D. You would also place a '4' next to description A, since that was most like your organisation.

Complete the following:

1. Our organisation views customers as:

A. Necessary sources of revenue for the firm _____
B. The primary reason for the firm's existence _____
C. People who will respond positively to innovative products and services _____
D. Co-partners in the development of customised products and services _____

2. Our organisation views innovative products and services as:

A. A means to extract revenue from customers _____
B. A means of responding to the needs and wants of customers _____
C. The primary reason for the firm's existence _____
D. As something which is co-developed with customers _____

3. Our organisation views the business environment (factors such as the political and legal situation, the economy, and socio-cultural change) as:

A. Of primary importance, because of its impact on the firm _____
B. Of primary importance, because of its impact on customers _____
C. Of primary importance, because of its impact on innovative products and services _____
D. Of primary importance, because of its impact on the interaction between customers and innovative products and services _____

4. Our organisation views competitors as:

A. Rivals who attempt to take away our firm's market share and financial rewards _____
B. Rivals who attempt to satisfy customers needs and wants better than we do _____
C. Rivals who attempt to develop innovative products and services, and shape wants better than we do _____

D. Rivals who attempt to engage customers in
interaction with innovative products and services
better than we do   _____

5. *Our organisation views itself as:*

A. A vehicle for the creation of shareholder and
employee wealth   _____
B. A vehicle for the creation of satisfied customers _____
C. A vehicle for the creation of innovative products
and services   _____
D. A vehicle for the creation of interactions between
customers and innovative products and services   _____

6. *Our organisation views employees as:*

A. Dedicated to the service of the firm   _____
B. Dedicated to the service of the customer   _____
C. Dedicated to the development of innovative
products and services   _____
D. Dedicated to the establishment of interaction between
customers and innovative products and services   _____

Scoring

Once you have completed your impressions of the situations, add up
your scores for 'A' descriptions, and place them in the box under 'Type
A' firms below. Then do the same for all the 'B' descriptions, then the 'C'
ones, and so on.

Type 'A' firm	Type 'B' firm	Type 'C' firm	Type 'D' firm

Once you have filled in the four boxes, the figures should add up to 60.

Interpreting your scores

According to your impressions, you believe your organisation is most
like the firm type for which you have the lowest number, and least
like the type that has the highest number. For example, if you had a
lowest score of 9 in the type 'B' firm, your impression is that your
organisation is most like a type 'B' firm, and least, perhaps, like a type

'C' firm, where your highest score may have been 23. Alternatively, you may find that your two lowest scores are quite close together and possibly identical in some instances. This would mean that, in your opinion, while your firm is mostly type 'B', with a score of 10, it is often like type 'D', with a score of 12.

This enables us to identify four archetypal configurations:

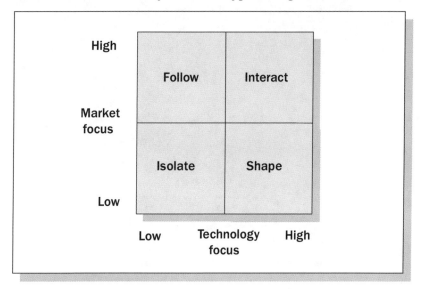

If your lowest score is for a type 'A' firm, you operate in what **isolate** mode, where there is little or no communication between technology and the market. If you scored lowest for a type 'B' firm, you operate in the **follow** mode. The firm relies heavily on market research – formal or structured (using surveys) and informal or unstructured ('walking in the customer's shoes') – to establish the parameters of products and services, and to drive their development. If you scored lowest for a type 'C' firm, technology is the focus rather than the market, and you follow a **shape** strategy; technology shapes the market. The market may not have even been aware that it needed or wanted the benefits derived from a particular technology until it became available. The product becomes quintessential in shaping or defining a given market. Finally, if your lowest score occurred for a type 'D' firm, it operates in the **interact** mode. Here, dialogue is established between the market and technology.

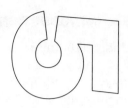

Introduction

Porter's 'Five Forces' model

Generic competitive strategies

A process model of competitive advantage

Competition and competitive strategies

5.1 INTRODUCTION

Understanding who its competitors are is one of the key factors that helps a firm define the business it is in. All organisations have competitors. While economists may define monopolies as organisations or firms that face no competition, in most situations today there is either direct competition or competitors may be just over the horizon in some shape or form. Very often, it is when firms are riding the crest of the wave of success, seemingly impervious to competition, that competitors emerge in another guise. Just when it seemed that a wonder drug like Glaxo's Zantac would take the firm profitably into the next century, it was found that stomach ulcers responded to simple generic antibiotics. Organisations such as Sun Micro Systems are beginning to speculate that the days of the PC are dead – just as Microsoft is riding the crest of the wave with Windows. The market that has made it successful may begin to erode before the firm's eyes. In order to understand marketing strategy from a competitive perspective, it is worthwhile considering some of the classic analyses of competitive strategy and competition in markets. Much of this work springs from the research and writings of Harvard Business School Professor, Michael Porter (Porter, 1980). While Porter is more of an economist and strategist than a marketing professor, marketers have much to learn from his views on competitive strategy. While not all of his work is accepted without argument, it provides a useful tool and platform for understanding competition.

5.2 PORTER'S 'FIVE FORCES' MODEL

Porter begins his analysis of industries and what makes them profitable with the question: Why are some industries more profitable than others? At the heart of the explanation lies the rivalry between competitors. This is illustrated in Figure 5.1.

If firms compete fiercely against one another, they need to spend considerable financial and other resources in their competitive efforts, which means that costs are driven upwards. At the same time, extreme competition places a heavy downward pressure on prices, as competitors attempt to attract customers with promises of better value through lower price. A simple analysis of industries globally would tend to demonstrate this point. Some are very profitable because the firms within them do not compete directly and aggressively. Other industries tend to be far less so, as they compete in various ways aggressively one against the other.

Figure 5.1: Porter's 'Five Forces' model

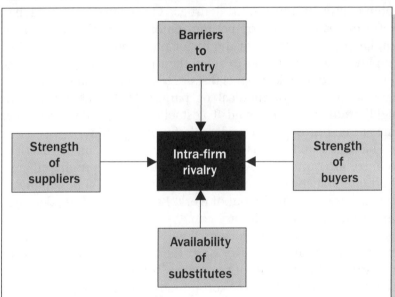

Four factors determine the extent of rivalry between firms. Firstly, as can be seen in Figure 5.1, rivalry is determined by the barriers to entry within an industry. Some industries are easy to enter. For example, it is not difficult for an individual with limited capital to enter some kind of food service business. However, for a single individual or a firm of limited resources to enter the motor manufacturing industry would be an awesome challenge. The capital and technology required, not to mention the technical, financial, procurement and marketing skills, would be beyond the reach of most individuals and organisations. The model in Figure 5.1 can be applied to two industries today: the pharmaceutical and airline industries. The pharmaceutical industry is a difficult business to enter for a number of reasons. Ethical drugs require considerable resources to be devoted to research and development. Companies may work for many years on a particular project without necessarily enjoying the benefits of a successful product pay-off. Furthermore, patents protect most ethical drugs. Only once the drug has come off patent can competitors enter the market and make similar products. Many of the major pharmaceutical companies employ large sales forces to detail their products to general practitioners and medical specialists. These individuals generally have some kind of medical or paramedical background, are highly trained and well paid. To establish a large pharmaceutical sales force represents considerable financial outlay.

The airline industry is relatively easy to enter, as the barriers to entry are quite low. Aircraft can be leased or purchased, and there are skilled flight and cabin crew who would be willing to transfer or may even be out of work. Labour, therefore, does not represent a considerable problem.

The second force in Porter's 'Five Forces' model that determines the extent of rivalry and, therefore, profitability in an industry, is the strength of the buyers confronting that industry. To what extent can buyers exert pressure on suppliers within the industry? Facing the pharmaceutical industry in most countries are large numbers of individuals as patients and users of ethical drugs. Individually, these patients cannot exert considerable pressure on any one company. Furthermore, the medical practitioner (as prescriber) generally makes the purchasing decision; he or she does not pay for the product and therefore is not that sensitive to its price. When a purchase concerns our own health or that of our family, we are not price sensitive, providing we can afford it. In many countries, government-run national health schemes pay for the purchase; neither the user nor the prescriber pay for the product.

When it comes to the airline industry, however, the buyer is faced with a range of choices. Between major destinations around the globe, travellers have a number of airlines from which to choose. Most travellers will not postpone vacations or business trips in order to remain loyal to a particular airline. Airlines are therefore unable to exert much pressure on buyers when there is choice available.

The third force in Porter's model concerns the availability of substitutes. To what extent are reasonable substitutes available for the particular product manufactured by firms within a particular industry? In some cases, there are many substitutes available for a particular product. A good, simple example of this is the number of substitutes for a product such as butter. The consumer can purchase margarine, low-fat spreads, spreads made from vegetable and olive oils, or do without.

Within the pharmaceutical industry, there are few substitutes for ethical drugs. When a medical practitioner prescribes a particular drug, the patient usually takes that particular drug and no substitution is allowed or permitted. Similarly, patent protection prohibits competitors from manufacturing identical products. Customers of the airline industry usually have a number of substitutes for air travel or transport. Besides other airlines, they can usually choose to travel by rail, road, boat or bus.

The fourth force in Porter's model is that of the strength of suppliers facing an industry. To what extent, can suppliers hold an industry or the firms within it 'to ransom'? In the case of the pharmaceutical industry, the answer is: 'to very little extent'. To make ethical drugs, pharmaceutical companies need to acquire very basic chemical compounds. These are available from various sources, most of which compete with one another on price. No supplier is able to exert any significant pressure on the pharmaceutical industry.

The suppliers confronting the airline industry tend to be somewhat stronger. There are only a handful of jet aircraft manufacturers. While these firms compete quite aggressively with one another, there are nevertheless delays in the supply of aircraft and pricing can play a significant role.

Our conclusion, therefore, is that the extensive rivalry among airlines makes this generally a low profit industry. Only a handful of airlines have earned significant profits since 1990. By contrast, pharmaceutical companies tend to be among the most profitable. The model explains this by alluding to the fact that these firms do not compete very aggressively; they rather compete alongside one another. There are some niggling questions, however. Why do some firms within theoretically profitable industries not perform well? Why do some firms within theoretically low-profit industries perform very profitably? What is the role of government in the model? Do industries change and what factors cause them to change?

Readers who have followed the discussion up to this point will question the overall validity of the model. They might comment that even within a notoriously low-profit industry, such as the airline industry, there have been firms that have made considerable profits in recent years (such as British Airways, Cathay Pacific, Singapore Airlines, and South West Airlines). Similarly, there have been competitors within the pharmaceutical industry who have not fared well. Many have been taken over, while others have simply closed down. The point is that management and strategy can have a profound effect on the performance of firms, regardless of the industry in which they compete. Effective management will be able to overcome and perhaps even exploit the deficiencies of a notoriously unprofitable industry. Even in the most potentially profitable industries, there will be few mitigating factors for ineffective management.

What is the role of government? When viewing Porter's model, many observers of the practical business scene would suggest that government should probably be represented as a sixth force. In most countries, government actions have shaped competition in significant ways. In some cases, the government itself has competed against private firms in various sectors. Michael Porter would argue that government is not so much a sixth force in the model, as a force that affects each of the other forces in various ways. For example, government could affect the extent of rivalry among competitors by limiting access to the market, through trade practices and the stringency of monopolistic or anti-monopoly legislation. Similarly, government could affect the strength of buyers by allowing purchasers to band together, or by dictating and allowing manufacturers and other service providers to fix prices. Government could also influence supply. In many countries, the government has been a supplier of major raw materials or services to industries and is therefore able to exert considerable monopolistic power over rivals within a particular market sphere. Government can even affect the availability of substitutes, by encouraging or discouraging the production of various products, or by entering substitute businesses as a supplier of products or services. Government can raise or lower the barriers to entry via legislation. It could, for example, exact expensive licence fees in certain industries, or only allow the operation of a restricted number of businesses within an industry.

Finally, there is the issue of whether industries change and what causes them to change? Industries do change. In many countries, for example, buyer strength is increasing in the pharmaceutical industry as the high cost of medical care forces both governments and private medical schemes to resist overly expensive products. Many medical schemes are agreeing only to pay a certain amount towards a prescription. Consequently, the user or patient is forced to pay the balance and resists high prices to a greater extent than he or she has in the past. On the other hand, frequent flyer schemes in the airline industry may be seen as tools that cause buyers to become less strong'. Buyers are less willing to shop around and, instead, want to enjoy the benefits of frequent flyer miles. In the pharmaceutical industry, the availability of generic substitutes and their aggressive marketing has seen a greater availability of substitutes for prescriptions. A factor that has considerably raised the barriers to entry in the airline industry is the availability of gates at airports. At many major airports, such as London's Heathrow, the value of a gate (a place where the aircraft can park and passengers can embark and disembark easily) has made individual airlines far more valuable. In some cases, airlines have been purchased by their competitors, not for any management skills, resources, or aircraft, but simply because they have gate access. Thus, industries are always in a state of flux. The five forces in the model are constantly changing, and this places incessant demands on the creative skills of managers – particularly marketing managers.

5.3 GENERIC COMPETITIVE STRATEGIES

It is a useful exercise for marketers and strategists to analyse the industries in which they operate according to Porter's model. Porter asserts that firms have only two fundamental or generic options when it comes to strategy. Firstly, a firm can compete on the basis of low cost. A firm that chooses to compete on cost is one that attempts to be the low cost producer of a product or a service. It is important to note that this is not a low price strategy. Rather, the firm concentrates on being able to manufacture a product or deliver a service at a cost that is significantly lower than that of its competitors. What are the benefits of a low-cost strategy? From an economic perspective, the benefits should be obvious. For example, if firm A is able to product a product for R1, while the average cost of all the other producers within the industry is R2, this firm enjoys a considerable advantage. This can be exploited in one or two ways. The firm can sell the product at the same price as its competitors (let us assume R3) and enjoy a far greater margin than its rivals. Alternatively, if the going price' in the market is R3, the firm can choose to sell at R2 and make the same margins as its competitors, while drawing a considerable proportion of customers to its product because it is less expensive. There are other alternatives within this range.

If a firm cannot be the lowest cost producer of the product or service in the market in which it competes, the alternative is for it to differentiate. In simple terms, differentiation means that the product or service must be made different to those of other producers, in a way the customer values and is prepared to pay for. Products may be made bigger or smaller, faster or slower, with more features, in a greater range of colours, in a different style, of greater quality or perceived quality, or in any other way that is important to customers within the market. Differentiation may not even be something that is done physically to the product or service; it may be something the organisation does to the customer's mind'. A firm may embark on a strategy that positions the product in the customer's mind, such that it leads him or her to believe or perceive that the product is different. Ole, a margarine brand, at one stage differentiated itself by claiming that it contained zero percent cholesterol. In fact, no margarine contains cholesterol.

There is also the dimension of focus that needs to be brought into generic strategies. Focus has to do with the extent to which the firm attempts to serve a market or a very narrow segment within a market. When the dimensions of differentiation and low cost are dichotomised, and the extent of focus is dichotomised, we can develop a simple but effective model of competitive strategy, as illustrated in Figure 5.2.

Figure 5.2: Generic competitive strategies

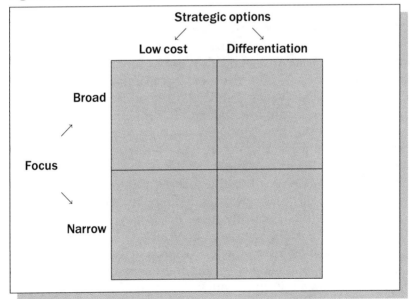

According to the figure, a firm can pursue four generic strategies. It can be broadly focused and low cost, broadly focused and differentiated, narrowly focused and low cost, or narrowly focused and differentiated. Each strategy has its advantages and requires not only a very different approach to managing the organisation, but also to marketing. Michael Porter would argue that any competitor within an industry should choose one of these strategies and pursue it exclusively. He would predict that being stuck in the middle' would be dangerous and non-productive. Being stuck in the middle would mean that the firm is neither low cost nor particularly well differentiated, neither narrowly focused nor broadly focused. He would even contend that a competitor couldn't be both low cost and differentiated. Nowadays many commentators on strategy and marketing might disagree with him. However, let's consider examples of firms pursuing one of the four generic strategies.

The broadly focused low-cost firm is one that strives to achieve the lowest cost for the product or service while serving a broad market. A good example of this strategy is Ivory soap, a highly successful product marketed by Proctor & Gamble. Ivory soap is not targeted at anyone in particular – it is a soap for whoever wishes to purchase an inexpensive but adequate soap. The product is always one of the cheapest brands and often competes directly against in-house brands. This does not mean that the product is low quality – indeed, the product is very high quality. The company continually attempts to drive the costs of production and marketing down, while simultaneously reaching as broad a market as possible.

A good example of a broadly focused differentiated strategy would be that of British Airways. Being The World's Favourite Airline' means that it can fly more customers to more destinations around the globe than any other airline. Its target markets consist of just about everyone who wishes to fly: holidaymakers, business travellers, people visiting friends and family. The airline differentiates itself through its meticulous attention to service. It is widely regarded as an airline that provides super-lative service – even though the cost of delivery means that it is not necessarily a low-cost operator. Thus, if one wished to emphasise price only in the purchase of an airline ticket, British Airways would not necessarily be the preferred choice. However, if one wished to travel to the widest range of destinations and enjoy good service on the way, the airline would be the preferred choice.

A good example of a narrowly focused low-cost strategy is that of the French hotel chain Formule 1. Formule 1s are intended for budget travellers or business travellers on the kind of budget where the individual gets to keep whatever he or she saves on accommodation. Formule 1 has attempted to eliminate everything that adds cost. It has no reservation service, it has no reservation or reception desk, there is no portering, and there is no restaurant. There is no reception desk, because travellers may wish to check in late at night and this would require staff at reception at all times. Rather, the guest does some of the work by using a credit card to automatically check in. There is no portering facility because not all guests need a porter (guests who do not need a porter would be subsidising those who do and this would increase the cost of operation). There is no restaurant in a Formule 1, because not every guest wishes to eat in the restaurant. The restaurant would have to remain open even if it was not full, again driving costs up. In most cases, independent restaurants and fast food chains have opened a branch very close to a Formule 1 for the convenience of its guests and for other diners.

There are few good examples of a focused differentiated strategy. It is a risky strategy, and many companies who have followed it have gone out of business. The strategy requires resisting the temptation to become broad-based simply because there appear to be opportunities, and cutting costs simply because it looks like good accounting. My favourite example of a focused differentiated strategy is that of TVR, a small but successful manufacturer of sports cars in the United Kingdom. These are thoroughbred sports cars that handle and perform in ways only a real enthusiast will appreciate. The company has long waiting lists for cars, does not compromise on quality, and has resisted increasing production. It has also resisted the temptation to expand into other markets – such as less expensive, lower specification products.

5.4 A PROCESS MODEL OF COMPETITIVE ADVANTAGE

For many years, marketers and strategists have debated and discussed the issue of competitive advantage. Sometimes this may have occurred without first attempting to understand what competitive advantage really is. Competitive advantage is best conceived of as a process. While some commentators have referred to 'sustainable competitive advantages', realists would probably agree that long-term sustainable competitive advantage is only achieved by organisations that give continuous attention to a process. Many firms recognise that competitive advantage is a process (Day & Wensley, 1988), and that it needs to be managed as such. This is the only way in which organisations will be able to keep up with the relentless cycle of competitive rationality. One of the most significant changes occurring in management thinking is that the outcome of the competitive advantage process is customer equity.

References

Porter, M. 1980. *Competitive Strategy*, New York, NY: The Free Press.
Day, GS & Wensley, R. 1988. Assessing advantage: a framework for diagnosing competitive superiority. *Journal of Marketing*, 52 (April): 1–20.

Market segmentation

Target marketing

Positioning strategy

Understanding customer behaviour

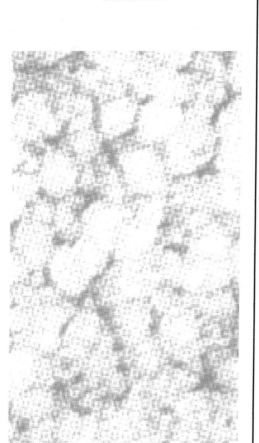

6 Market segmentation, target marketing and positioning

6.1 MARKET SEGMENTATION

We have briefly discussed why it is necessary for firms to segment markets, identify suitable target markets and develop a marketing mix for these target markets. In this chapter we focus on ways in which markets can be segmented, the requirements for effective target markets, and we look in more detail at the concept of positioning. As has been mentioned, there are very few products or services for which the entire world population, or even the population of a particular country, is a market. There are hardly any products or services that everyone uses. It is the task of the marketer to identify some meaningful and effective way of breaking heterogeneous populations into more specific homogeneous segments on which to focus.

Market segmentation is not a mechanical task; there are no 'easy to follow' formulas for segmenting markets. Market segmentation is really a very creative task, and some of the most effective recent marketing strategies have been successful not because of the development of creative marketing mixes, but because the market segmented in an imaginative and creative fashion. Traditionally, marketers have segmented markets in four ways: geographic, demographic, lifestyle (or psychographic) and benefit segmentation. We discuss each of these briefly in turn.

6.1.1 Geographic market segmentation

For many firms the segmentation of markets on a geographic basis is almost a self defined requirement. Particularly for small businesses, the focus is on a local market. Thus for retail outlets, restaurants and hotels the market is very often geographically defined. For retail stores the market will be the local population, or part thereof. That is to say, the majority of customers will be those people for whom the store is conveniently located. Of course, geography does play a role in the segmentation strategies for other products and services. Thus the market for items such as clothing, sporting goods and travel is frequently circumscribed by geography. Skiing equipment generally sells better around ski resorts, and surf boards and wind surfers are likely to be bought near the sea. Clothing is typically purchased on the basis of the climatic conditions that the wearer expects to experience where the item is purchased. However, for most products and services geographic segmentation on its own is not a very useful way to segment markets.

6.1.2 Demographic market segmentation

The demographics of a population are statistics which describe that population in broad terms. A particular population may be described in terms of such variables as gender, age distribution occupation, religion, race and, of course, income. Many of these variables influence consumption. For example, certain health-care products are consumed by women only, while other products are mainly used by men. However, in recent years some products have crossed traditional gender boundaries. Women have begun to buy male cosmetics in significant numbers, while razor manufacturers and the marketers of shavers have finally admitted that it is not only males who use their products. Similarly, age is a major determinant of consumption. Children consume items such as toys and games, while older consumers tend to be greater users of health-care products and retirement services.

Even demographic variables such as religion can determine consumption: the consumption of certain products is encouraged by some religious groups and forbidden by others. Race may also influence consumption: products such as sun-care lotion are used predominantly by people with lighter skins. When Gillette launched its convenience disposable razors in Japan in the late 1970s, many Japanese males bore the signs of use of the product! The company had not realised that the beards of Japanese males tend to be somewhat different from those of the groups at which the product had previously been targeted. Finally, income is a major factor in demographic market segmentation. Income permits or precludes the consumption of many products.

Indeed, without income one cannot speak of a market. However, very few markets can be segmented purely on a demographic basis.

6.1.3 *Psychographic market segmentation*

During the 1970s marketers and marketing research companies recognised the limitations of geographic and demographic market segmentation strategies. A famous article appeared entitled 'Are Grace Slick and Patricia Nixon Cox the same person?'. This article made the point that, in terms of demographics, Grace Slick (lead singer of the psychedelic rock band Jefferson Airplane) and Patricia Nixon Cox (daughter of president Richard Nixon) were identical: they were both female, of the same race, in the same age group, and indeed of similar income groups. However, the two women differed quite radically in terms of their lifestyles. That is to say, their attitudes, activities, interests and opinions differed significantly. The way in which they occupied their time, the things that they were interested in, and their opinions on a wide variety of subjects, differed widely. Marketers began to look at segmenting markets based on lifestyles, since they argued that consumers would consume products which fitted well with their lifestyles, rather than those which did not. In order to identify these segments, advanced marketing research tools were used to survey large samples of the population. The aim was to identify clusters of people who pursued similar activities and had similar interests and opinions. These studies of **activities**, **interests** and **opinions** became known as AIO analyses.

Lifestyle segmentation was popular among marketers, for it gave them the opportunity to have a more intimate knowledge of the customers who might purchase their products and services. It was also widely supported within the advertising industry, since advertising copywriters found it much easier to write creative copy when they knew what those comprising their markets spent most of their time doing, what they were interested in, and what they thought of various aspects of everyday life. It was much easier to write a catchy advertisement for a person who spent time in the outdoors, was interested in wildlife and the environment, and tended to be politically liberal and oppose big business, than it was to write something which might appeal to a 26-year-old male in the upper income group who lived in a particular geographic area. However, lifestyle segmentation was also not without its drawbacks. The main problem with lifestyle segments was that they tended to be unstable over time. A segment or lifestyle cluster which existed one day might not be there in five years. Furthermore, lifestyle segmentation required large sample studies and the use of sophisticated marketing research techniques. This was quite beyond the capabilities of most firms, and even beyond the capabilities of all but the very largest of the research companies.

6.1.4 Benefit segmentation

A further possibility is segmenting markets in terms of the benefits that the potential customer seeks. As consumers, we do not all look for the same benefits in the same kind of product. Thus, if one were able to identify the prime benefits that a particular customer sought in a product, one would be able to target the product specifically in such a way that it would appeal to that particular benefit segment.

This is perhaps best illustrated by means of a simple example: if one considers toothpaste, it is apparent that different groups of consumers might see different benefits from a toothpaste. For some consumers the major consideration might be the medical benefits of using the toothpaste: decreased plaque, fewer cavities, and generally better health care of the teeth and gums. For another target market the benefits sought might be mainly cosmetic: for example, the product's ability to make teeth bright and white and to promote fresh breath. A third benefit segment might be the consumer who sought toothpaste that was pleasant tasting, and which might also have visual appeal: brightly coloured, striped, and so on. There might even be a fourth benefit segment: the consumer for whom the major benefit to be sought in a toothpaste is value in terms of low price.

This segment might believe that all toothpastes effectively do the same thing, and simply purchase, therefore, whichever brand is cheapest.

With benefit segmentation it is also possible to couple the benefit sought to other market segmentation approaches. For example, consumers who seek mainly medical benefits in a toothpaste might be parents (particularly mothers in demographic terms), and in terms of behavioural or lifestyle characteristics they might also be very concerned about the care of their childrens teeth! Consumers who seek cosmetic benefits in toothpaste might be predominantly smokers, or perhaps young consumers wishing to look good! Likewise consumers who seek mainly what may be termed hedonistic benefits (pleasant taste) would probably be children, who would also be amused if the toothpaste were able to sparkle! The consumers who sought low price as the major benefit in toothpaste might be bargain seekers or people on a restricted budget. It is not too difficult to envision which brands would be most appealing to each of these benefit segments some brands emphasise the medical benefits, others the cosmetic benefits and yet others the taste or appearance of the product. Those consumers who seek only price as a major benefit would probably be the least brand loyal; they would inevitably purchase whichever brand happened to be on special in the supermarket, or even housebrands in supermarkets, should these be the cheapest product available.

If one considers benefit segmentation as a possible market segmentation strategy, it is worth looking at all the aspects of the marketing mix. Let us take for example home pregnancy tests. Simple demographic segmentation of the home pregnancy test market would reveal nothing of any real value or interest. The consumer of this product would obviously be a female in a particular age group. This offers no real insights. Even lifestyle segmentation might not give any clearer guidelines to a marketing strategy. However, when one considers benefit segmentation, useful implications arise. For some consumers a positive result may be greeted with great delight. For others a similar result might spell huge dismay. The marketing strategy for the first group might be to use attractive packaging, a suitable name and to display the product prominently in retail outlets. One can conjure up all kinds of appealing brand names for a product such as this, and one can also imagine that the price could be quite high, since this market would probably be relatively insensitive to the price. If the result is positive, whatever the price had been, this consumer would see it as a bargain! On the other hand, for the market for whom a positive result would be most unwelcome, the ideal marketing strategy would be very different. Here the product might be packaged more solemnly, be displayed less prominently in retail outlets, might be suitably named in terms of reassuring benefits and accuracy, and might be priced at a lower level, for here, whatever the result, the product would probably not be viewed as a bargain! Promotion could feature contact numbers for help and advisory services.

6.2 TARGET MARKETING

The purpose of market segmentation is to identify target markets upon which the marketer can focus a marketing mix. The market segment(s) which the marketer chooses is/are termed the target market: that market for which a marketing mix is developed. For a target market to be meaningful to a marketer, it should comply with certain basic requirements. Firstly, it should be large enough to be served effectively. That is to say, small target markets, although effectively defined, might not be large enough to warrant the development of a marketing strategy. Secondly, the target market should be defined in such a way that it can be reached effectively with existing media and through existing distribution channels. While the market might exist, if one cannot reach it effectively through existing media and through existing distribution channels, the pursuance of a marketing strategy might be not be feasible.

6.3 POSITIONING STRATEGY

The term positioning is one of the most common terms used in marketing strategy and management. It was born in work done by two advertising executives called Al Pies and Jack Trout, who wrote a very successful book in the early 1980s called *Positioning: The Battle for your Mind* (Pies & Trout, 1982). Pies and Trout had noted the spectacular failures of many organisations which had tried to compete with the opposition using a direct approach. They pointed to the sensational flops of companies such as General Electric and RCA in the 1960s in their attempts to enter the mainframe computer market in direct opposition to an entrenched company such as IBM. Pies and Trout explained the failure of these strategies by saying that it was very difficult to disenthrone an entrenched competitor from a market because that competitor was firmly positioned in the minds of prospects. Thus for one to say that one's firm was also a successful large manufacturer of mainframe computers was simply an imitation strategy, since the customer knew who the real big name was – in this case, IBM.

It would be far more effective, said Pies and Trout, to position products by looking for gaps in the perceptual maps in the minds of customers. Thus for Avis it made more sense to reinforce what the consumer already knew (that Hertz was the largest car rental company) and to position itself against Hertz, not as an equally large competitor, but as number two. Consumers could accept this; they knew that Avis was indeed the second largest competitor in the market. This position against the entrenched competitor enabled Avis to say that because it was number two it would have to try harder. The 'We Try Harder' campaign became one of the most successful advertising and positioning strategies of all time.

Positioning is not something that one does to a product. Rather, it is something that one does to the minds of customers. Marketers, psychologists and marketing researchers have made extensive use of the perceptual maps referred to previously to illustrate what the minds of those comprising their target markets might be summarised to look like. An example of a perceptual map is provided in Figure 6.1.

What might marketers use a perceptual map such as that displayed in Figure 6.1 for? Firstly, it enables marketers to see

Figure 6.1: A simple positioning map of some hotels in the Cape Town area

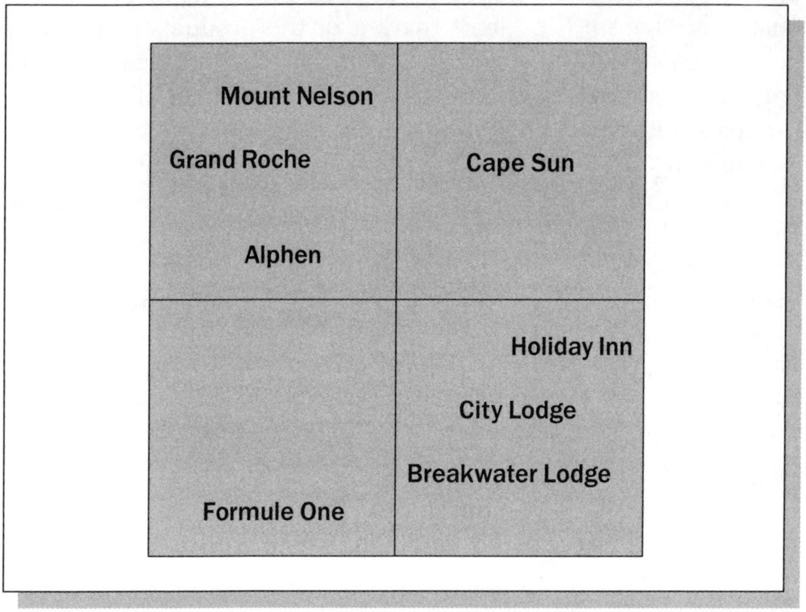

Mount Nelson **Grand Roche** **Alphen**	**Cape Sun**
   Formule One	**Holiday Inn** **City Lodge** **Breakwater Lodge**

where their products or brands (a hotel in this case) are positioned compared to others in the market place. Thus marketers can see where their brands are relative to a brand leader. Marketer scan also use such a map to determine the effectiveness or otherwise of marketing strategy, particularly marketing communication strategy. The map might also be useful to marketers who wish to identify a gap in the market. There may be a market for brands for which there is currently no position or closely associated position. However, just as one asks the question 'Is there a gap in the market?' one should also always ask the question 'Is there a market in the gap?' Indeed, there may be gaps in a particular market because there are no customers there. Naturally, maps such as the one in Figure 6.1 can be used to track the perceptions of a market over time. However, it should also be obvious that marketers must be sure that in doing the research for the map, researchers have spoken to and interviewed the target customers. While this may seem self evident, the reliability of maps such as these is heavily dependent on the knowledge of customers within the target market of the products or services concerned. Customers within the product or service category concerned should have at least a basic knowledge of the major brands studied, or they are not target customers.

This bring us to brand perception and brand recall. It is most useful to think of this at a series of levels. At the highest level, the most sought-after characteristic that marketers could wish for their brands is what is called top-of-mind awareness. Top-of-mind awareness refers to the fact that when a consumer is asked to name a brand of a product within a particular category, the marketer's brand will appear at the top of the list named. In many countries, for example, if one were to ask consumers to name a brand of coffee, the brand name Nescafé would be one of the first mentioned. This does not necessarily mean that the consumer concerned is a regular purchaser and user of Nescafé, but it does mean that Nescafé is one of the brands immediately thought of when coffee comes to mind. Psychologists refer to the phenomenon of top-of-mind awareness as the evoked set. The evoked set is simply the set of brands that the consumer will think of when thinking of the particular product category. Psychologist George Miller (1956) wrote a fascinating article in the 1950s called 'The magic number seven, plus or minus two'. What Miller was referring to was the individual's inability to remember not many more or less than seven items in any particular set – in this case, brands. Thus most consumers will probably not be able to remember more than seven brands of coffee; indeed most at any given time will not be able to remember more than four or five. While there are probably many brands of coffee on the shelves of major supermarkets, this means that many of them are not part of the evoked set of consumers. There is obviously a high correlation between membership of an evoked set, top-of-mind awareness and market share for most brands.

The next level of brand perception is brand awareness. This is when customers are aware of a particular brand, even though it may not be the first one mentioned in interviews. In the descending hierarchy of brand perception, the next level down is that of aided recall. Aided recall means that the consumer will be able to identify a brand if other cues are given. For example, while consumers may not be able to remember all the names of cigarette brands, if one were to suggest that a particular brand was linked to advertisements featuring a cowboy, this might aid some consumers to remember that the brand referred to was Marlboro. The lowest level in this hierarchy of brand familiarity is brand recognition. That is to say, when shown a picture of the product and the name of the brand, the respondent recognises both the product and the brand.

6.4 UNDERSTANDING CUSTOMER BEHAVIOUR AS A PREREQUISITE TO SEGMENTING, TARGETING AND POSITIONING

A complete discussion of consumer behaviour in industrial markets is beyond the scope of this book. However, a useful way of thinking about buyer behaviour is to consider the behaviour of customers as being influenced by two broad sets of variables: intrinsic (or internal) variables and extrinsic (or external) variables. Intrinsic variables are aspects of the individual's behaviour which are unique to that individual.

The major intrinsic variables which influence the behaviour of the individual are motivation and learning; attitudes; perception; and personality.

- Motivation has to do with the needs of individuals and how they behave in order to satisfy these needs. Obviously, marketers must study the needs and wants of individuals if they are to develop appropriate marketing strategies.

- Learning is an important aspect of customer behaviour which marketers must understand, because, from a consumer perspective, learning is the net effect of marketing strategy on the memory of customers.

- Attitudes are learned behaviours which predispose people to respond favourably or unfavourably to a specific person, object or idea. They are reasonably consistent; that is, they do not change in a dynamic fashion. However, attitudes do change, and attitude change is at the focus of many marketing strategies. A useful attitude model is presented in Figure 6.2.

Figure 6.2: The three components of attitude

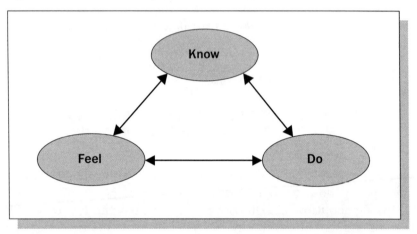

In this figure it can be seen that an attitude typically consists of three components: the cognitive (or knowing) component, the affective (feeling) component and the conative (doing) component of attitudes. Many marketers have been successful at changing attitudes by focusing on one of these components. Thus by changing the level of consumer knowing, for example, it may be possible to change the consumer's feelings toward the product, and indeed the consumer's behaviour toward (consumption or trying of) the product.

- It is also important that marketers understand perception. For most consumers, perception is reality. While marketers might believe their own reality of the product and be unable to comprehend why consumers do not perceive it in the same way, it is important for marketers to understand that the perception of the consumer is all that really matters.

Extrinsic variables which affect customer behaviour include culture, membership of peer groups, and family.

- Culture obviously has a tremendous impact on consumer behaviour. Cultures embody the values, attitudes and codes of living of large groups of people. Culture serves as a tool by which individuals judge their own behaviour. Thus cultures play a major role in encouraging or precluding the consumption of various products and services.
- Membership of peer groups also influences consumer behaviour: for example, adolescents may purchase certain products, use certain brands or wear certain clothes because these indicate membership of a group.
- The family has a significant effect on the behaviour of individuals. Many children grow up to purchase similar brands to those purchased by their parents. Additionally, in families there is the important issue of role-playing in the purchasing decision process, which is broadly paralleled in many organisational buying processes. We therefore frequently refer to roles such as that of:
  1. *user* (the person who uses the product)
  2. the *decision maker* (the person who makes the decision to purchase the product and the brand)
  3. the *influencer* (someone who influences the decision maker in the purchase)
  4. the *buyer* (the person who physically purchases the product or service)
  5. a *gatekeeper* (someone who controls the flow of information to and from the decision maker)

In the case of many purchases, these roles may be played by the same person. However, in numerous other purchasing situations, these roles are frequently played by different individuals. For example, the user of a baby food would probably be baby (who can only show his or her dislike of the product by not eating it); the decision maker might be the mother; a sibling, grandparent or physician may be an influencer; the buyer could be the father or another sibling; and gatekeepers may be involved, such as community nurses or childcare advisers. Obviously, similar roles can be found and identified in the organisational buying process, where marketers refer to the existence of buying centres. Buying centres are seen as a conglomerate of roles played in the purchasing process of large and small organisations in the pursuit of their activity.

6.5 CONCLUSION

This chapter has considered market segmentation, target marketing and positioning strategy. Various segmentation strategies were discussed, each with its own particular advantages and limitations. Target marketing tends to be a creative act, rather than something which can be applied in a piecemeal, fill in the right blocks fashion. Positioning is seen as something one does to the mind of a customer rather than to a product or service. Finally, we ended the chapter with a very brief discussion of some of the variables that impact on customer behaviour.

References

Miller, George A. 1956. The magical number seven, plus or minus two: Some limits on our capacity for processing information. *Psychological Review,* 63: 81, 97.

Ries, Al, & Trout, Jack. 1982. *Positioning: The Battle for Your Mind.* New York, NY: Warner Books.

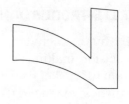

7

**Marketing research —
a manager's perspective**

Introduction

Ways of obtaining marketing
information

Steps in the marketing research
survey process

Relationships with
research suppliers

7.1 INTRODUCTION

If any one activity were to define managerial work it would be decision making. Managers make decisions. Obviously, all individuals make decisions; however, the one thing that distinguishes managerial work from other work is that managers make decisions about planning, organising, directing and controlling. Therefore, marketing managers make decisions about the planning, organising, directing and controlling of marketing activities. Now, while it is possible to make decisions, even good decisions, without having access to information, it is clear that informed decisions are more rational decisions. The object of this chapter is not to investigate management decision making in great detail. Nor is it to give a scholarly or academic perspective on marketing research. Rather, the objective of this chapter is to provide marketing managers with some guidelines so that they can be astute and critical users of marketing research. Nowadays, in most large organisations, marketing research tends not to be done in-house, but rather to be contracted out to specialist marketing research companies.

The marketing researcher usually requires no formal qualification. There are no formal bodies to mandate minimum levels of qualification or regulate the performance of marketing research practitioners and firms. Thus, almost anyone can enter the marketing research profession, whether that individual has received training or formal education in marketing research or not. Thus while there are many excellent and professional firms which practise marketing research at the highest level, the activity has also been known to attract some charlatans and opportunists who want to exploit a situation, make their fortunes, and disappear. Thus, the work of some firms could, if used in the management decision-making process, be downright dangerous. The purpose of this chapter is therefore to provide the marketing manager with a broad overview of the processes involved in marketing research. We also hope to provide a number of incisive questions to ask the providers of marketing information.

7.2 WAYS OF OBTAINING MARKETING INFORMATION

There are three ways of obtaining marketing information. These are by direct observation, by experiment, and by survey. While surveys are still the most common way of obtaining marketing information, marketers nowadays are turning increasingly to observation and experimentation as ways of achieving the same purpose. We therefore consider the first two briefly before moving on to the third in more detail.

7.2.1 Direct observation

Much information can be gained from observing the behaviour and actions of buyers, consumers and potential purchasers in the market place. When researchers select direct observation to gain information, they do not ask questions directly of potential respondents. Rather, by means of personal or mechanical observation they merely watch and record the actions in which they are interested. Mechanical observation means that the respondent is not observed by a human being but rather by means of some form of technology. Personal observation means that respondents are observed by a human observer and their actions are noted.

The simplest example of mechanical observation in marketing research would be the counting of cars by an electronic counter. This is a rubber cable across a road which notes the movement of a vehicle across it by recording the impact of the wheel. Nowadays, however, mechanical observation has become far more extensive and sophisticated. Retail stores use scanning technology to record the purchase of brands and allocate these purchases to the individual consumer.

Personal observation can be used to record a wide range of buyer activities. For example, observers stationed at the breakfast cereal section of a supermarket might observe the interaction between child and parent in the decision on a breakfast cereal purchase. Thus the observer can record whether children have any influence on the decision or not, what the nature of this influence is (is it on the type of cereal or on the brand?) and what negotiation strategies they use to exercise influence. Are these strategies rational, or do they often rely on some kind of threat (I'll stamp my feet, yell and throw a tantrum)?

The major advantage of observation as a marketing research technique is that it tends to be more objective. The researcher merely notes and records and does not bring any personal preference or bias into the picture. However, a drawback of observational techniques is that they can only record behaviour and actions and not infer the reasons for these. So, while the mechanical observation of cars can be used to record numbers and the direction of traffic flow, no inferences can be drawn on the reasons for this travel: why people were travelling and what they were going to do when they got to their destination. Such information can be gained only by direct questioning.

7.2.2 Experimentation in marketing research

In the physical sciences experimentation is a common technique used in research. Most experiments use an experimental design that involves the use of a control group as a benchmark on which the effects of an experimental variable are measured. While the use of experimentation in marketing research is growing, it is unlikely that this method will ever achieve the levels of usage as a research tool that it enjoys in the physical sciences. However, experiments have been used at a practical level by retailers for many years. A chain of stores may, for example, display a particular product at a certain price and in a certain way in ten stores, and at other prices and in other ways in ten others. The difference in store sales (a dependent variable) of that product can be compared and conclusions drawn as to the effect of the experimental variables such as price and means of display. The advantage of experiments is that the researcher can say with some degree of precision what did or did not cause changes in the outcome variable (in this case, sales). However, the problem with experimentation in marketing research in most cases is that it is difficult to isolate the effects of other variables. While the researcher in a laboratory studying the effects of various constituents in a rat's diet is able to rule out or exclude and therefore control most other variables, the marketing researcher does not have the same luxury. It is difficult, for example, to rule out the effects of competitive advertising and pricing strategies, and the interaction among respondents or the subjects of the study. Quite simply, consumers in shopping situations and other marketing environments do not behave like laboratory rats.

7.2.3 Survey research

Most marketing research today is still conducted by means of survey. That is, the researcher or individuals designated by the researcher ask questions of respondents, who are typically buyers or potential buyers of the product or service concerned. We therefore focus in the rest of this chapter on this most common tool of marketing research. We consider the steps conducted in a typical research survey and examine each of these in a little more detail to determine how they may be carried out more effectively.

7.3 STEPS IN THE MARKETING RESEARCH SURVEY PROCESS

What follows is a brief description of the steps which are typically carried out when a marketing research survey is conducted. Note that there is really no one right way approach to the steps in the research survey process. Rather, researchers have over the years identified some distinctive phases in a research project, which may be carried out in some more or less chronological order. Each of these steps is critical to the success of a survey. Mistakes made in any one of the steps in the process will introduce bias to the survey as a whole, which may make the results of such a survey questionable, and thus may hamper or jeopardise the decision-making process.

7.3.1 Defining the problem

The first step in the survey process is for the researcher to define the problem. While this sounds easy, in practice it requires a lot of common sense and hard thinking. The researcher must define the problem to be studied and hopefully solved very carefully, for this step determines all the others which follow, and the success or failure of each of these steps is therefore particularly dependent on this definition. Some researchers prefer to define the problem in terms of a hypothesis – in other words a tentative explanation and answer to a problem. Whichever is chosen, defining the problem is the critical first phase in the research process.

7.3.2 Defining the information required to solve the problem

Once the problem has been defined, the researcher can define what information will be needed to solve the problem. The researcher therefore makes a list of all the information which must be gathered in the survey and thinks carefully about where this information can be obtained. At this stage the researcher might also be thinking of two common types of information: secondary and primary data.

Secondary data is data that has already been collected by someone else at another time, typically for another purpose. The wise researcher turns to secondary data first in the effort to solve research problems. Indeed, there is much secondary data that the ordinary researcher would not be able to gather. Census data is a good example of this. Institutions such as a government and government departments, research facilities, universities, business schools and private individuals, as well as the media, may have collected data similar to that which the researcher requires. The benefits of accessing secondary data include a saving in time and a saving of money. However, researchers should question secondary data very carefully. They should ask why such data was gathered, by whom and how. Researchers will also examine whether the data is in a form that can be used for the project, and the age of the data. Data that is out of date is of no use at all.

If the secondary data is insufficient to answer the questions posed by the research problem, the researcher will need to gather primary data. Primary data can be defined as data that is gathered by the researcher for the first time. That is to say, no one else has gathered this kind of data before. In the steps that follow we concern ourselves mainly with the gathering of primary data.

7.3.3 *Defining the sources of information*

The next step in the survey process is for researchers to determine where they will access the data required. This step requires the researcher to identify at an individual level those parties who would be best qualified for and suited to providing information. This is critical in that it requires the researcher to think carefully about the method of survey and the design of the sample.

7.3.4 *Survey methods*

When a researcher conducts a survey, one of the most critical decisions for him or her to make is the method to be used in gathering the data. Typically the researcher has three choices in this regard. The researcher needs to decide whether respondents are to be interviewed personally, by telephone, or by means of a mailed questionnaire. Each of these three methods of survey has its advantages and disadvantages. Typically, these all revolve around the time needed to conduct the survey, the cost of the survey and the bias which may be introduced as a result of the choice of that particular method. Personal interviews typically enjoy high response rates (people tend to be more willing to respond to an individual face to face), much data can be gathered with little bias if carried out effectively, and generally cost more than the other methods. Telephone surveys have reasonably high levels of response, good quality of response, and are quick. They are not as expensive as personal interviews, but typically tend to cost more than mail surveys. However, an important problem with telephone surveys is that not all the population of interest may have telephones. Mail surveys are characterised by the fact that respondents can complete questionnaires in their own time and may therefore be more willing to participate, also given the added benefits of anonymity. However, the disadvantage of mail surveys is that a longer time is needed for the work to be completed, and, most importantly, typically there are low response rates. While it is frequently argued that mail surveys are cheaper, one must bear in mind that if the response rate to a mail survey is low, then the cost of receiving an actual response may approach the costs of telephone and personal surveys.

7.3.5 Sample design

Most marketing research surveys do not sample whole populations. That is to say, most surveys do not sample every potential buyer or customer for a product, or all the members of the population of a country or city. Marketing researchers, like other researchers in the physical and social sciences, tend to rely on a sample to conduct their research. Samples are used for a number of reasons, including the fact that they save time and are less expensive than surveying entire populations. Without wishing to go into the technical details of sampling, suffice it here to say that the researcher has two fundamental options when considering a sample: a random or nonrandom sample.

Random samples consist of various sampling techniques by which the researcher is able to determine with some level of statistical certainty the likelihood of an individual forming part of the sample. The simplest kind of random sampling is called, not surprisingly, a simple random sample. In a simple random sample for a survey, each individual in the population has an equal and known chance of forming part of the individuals to be interviewed. More sophisticated forms of random sampling include quota sampling (filling a quota of individuals of particular characteristics) and stratified sampling, where the population is divided into strata, from which a number will be chosen as part of the sample.

Nonrandom sampling, on the other hand, means that the researcher uses some decision criterion as to whether individuals will form part of the sample or not. In other words, not all individuals have an equal chance of forming part of the sample, and the sampling is not left to chance but is a decision on the part of the researcher. The simplest form of nonrandom sampling is convenience sampling, where the researcher chooses members of the sample on the basis of convenience. For example, respondents may have been people who were easy to access, were close by or could be accessed at low cost. Other forms of nonrandom sampling include judgemental sampling, where managers and researchers include or exclude members of the population based on some means of expert judgement.

Many people believe that random sampling is by definition better than nonrandom sampling. This is not strictly true. While it is right to say that statistical data analysis can be conducted effectively in most cases only on random samples, there are times when a judgement sample will be a better sample than some form of random sampling. For example, if in industrial research the sampling frame or population consisted of about fifty firms, six of which dominated the industry, a judgement sample may be more effective. If it were important that these six firms be interviewed in order to make decisions, then there searcher would use his or her judgement and ensure that these firms were included. A random sample of twenty firms could conceivably exclude the six most important, and the quality of the information and the resultant decisions made could suffer as a result.

7.3.6 *The use of questionnaires*

The next step in the survey process is for the researcher to design the questionnaire, referred to as the **instrument**, which will be used to gather the information. There are many excellent texts devoted exclusively to the subject of questionnaire design. Our purpose here is simply to alert both researchers and managers to the many pitfalls that may emerge in the design of questionnaires. First and foremost, it should be remembered that the survey process is essentially one of measurement. When we survey people and ask them questions, we are attempting to measure one or more things. If we regard the survey process as one of measurement then there are two very important issues for the manager to consider: the **reliability** and the **validity** of the measurement.

Human beings measure things each and every day of their lives. We use our alarm clocks and watches to measure time; we use the speedometers in our cars to measure how fast we are travelling. Likewise, in marketing research we attempt to measure who people are, what they do, what they think, what they feel and so forth. Again, the fundamental properties of reliability and validity are critical in measurement. Let us briefly consider what they are.

The **reliability** of a measuring instrument is the ability of that instrument to produce similar results under similar circumstances. The simplest example of reliability or a lack thereof can be illustrated by a bathroom scale. When an individual stands on a bathroom scale one evening and sees that he or she weighs 80 kg, the individual may either be delighted, horrified, or simply not surprised. However, if that same individual were to stand on that same bathroom scale the following evening and see that the scale now registers 70 kg, he or she could reach one of three conclusions. The first conclusion could be, 'Gee, my diet is working!', the second could be, 'Wow, I am really not well', and the third, which would probably be the most logical, would be 'There is something wrong with this bathroom scale'. Common sense leads the individual to realise that losing 10 kg overnight is very unlikely and that therefore there is something defective in the measuring instrument. It is simply not reliable. Likewise, if a researcher were to design a questionnaire and use it on a sample of respondents to obtain a measurement, the same researcher would be doubtful of the reliability of the questionnaire if he or she used it six months later and got very different results. Unless something had happened to make respondents answer very differently, it is unlikely that they would respond so differently. If one reads scholarly journals such as the *Journal of Marketing Research* and the *Journal of Consumer Research,* one will note the use of an indication of reliability called the **coefficient alpha** or, more commonly, **Cronbach's alpha**, to denote the reliability or lack thereof in the questionnaire(s) used. It is a manager's job to ask about the reliability of the questionnaires used by marketing researchers. A good question is simply, How do I know that your instrument was reliable?

Validity, broadly speaking, concerns the ability of the questionnaire to measure what it sets out to measure. Validity, at its most fundamental level, has to do with the truth: does this measure give me a true indication of what I sought to measure in the first place? Again, a simple example serves to explain the issue more effectively. For many years viewership of television has been based on things called ratings. Good ratings mean that the programme is successful and poor ones that it is not. Advertisers prefer to have their products or services advertised on or around programmes which have high ratings, and to avoid those programmes where the ratings are low. How are the ratings measured? Ratings are typically assessed by means of small electronic devices placed in television sets in the homes of large samples of the population. The problem is not one of sampling, but rather one of validity. The little instrument faithfully records when the television set is switched on and off and the channel to which it was tuned while it was on. It is then assumed that when a television set is switched on and tuned to a particular channel, someone will be watching. The problem with this reasoning is that it is not always true. The device may faithfully record that at 17:30 on Tuesday afternoon the television set in a particular home was switched on. However, this is not a valid measurement of television viewership, since no one may have been watching! The problem of validity is clear. Again, the astute manager will ask the research supplier to give good indications of validity: Can I really believe this research? How do I know that it is a true reflection of what we set out to measure? These are issues which the wise manager will want to think about carefully when evaluating the services of the research supplier.

7.3.7 Measurement

Another issue the researcher will consider in designing a questionnaire is that of levels of measurement. Measurement occurs at many levels, using different kinds of scales to measure the object of interest. The manager should also note that the type of scale itself is important. The type of scales used to measure also dictate what calculations you can do with the data. There are four basic levels of measurement which marketing researchers may use.

The first of these is the *nominal scale*. The nominal scale (nominal from the Latin word *nomen,* or name) is a scale which uses numbers simply to classify or name the variables in the study. Good examples of a nominal scale would be male or female in the case of gender, or types of store (supermarket, convenience or discount store). Note that when numbers are assigned to these categories they do not indicate more or less of a characteristic. So it is not possible to say that because we numbered a discount store 3 on our scale it possesses more or less of a property than a convenience store which was numbered 1. The numbers are used simply to categorise. It follows that the arithmetic functions which can be performed on the data are extremely limited. For example, if we had used 0 to indicate male and 1 to indicate female on our nominal scale, we cannot calculate an average! There is no such thing as average gender, and while computers may faithfully calculate such an average and indicate that the average person was a ,46, this will simply not be true!

The next level of measurement is the *ordinal scale.* The ordinal scale is able to indicate direction; that is, it can be used to indicate more or less of something. Typical ordinal scales, sometimes referred to as ranking scales, are frequently used in marketing research: for instance, they may employ words that permit the respondent to indicate strength of feeling. The respondent may therefore strongly agree or strongly disagree with a statement, using a seven-point scale. This kind of measurement has limitations. A figure of 6 indicating strong agreement does not necessarily mean exactly twice as much agreement as 3 on the same scale. It will also be noted that different people interpret points on these scales in different ways. For example, to one individual a 5 might mean 'really good', while to another it might convey a feeling of 'pretty good, at least not bad'. Finally, ordinal scales are also quite limited as far as the application of statistical techniques is concerned; one cannot do many meaningful arithmetic calculations. A lot of marketing data is collected using ordinal scales and then interval properties are assumed: attitudes, opinions likes and dislikes. This might be because the ordinal data is the only tool the researcher has. However, it is important to note that we cannot really say that $6 - 4 = 3 - 1$ on an ordinal scale! While marketing researchers happily apply the calculations of average or mean scores to ordinal data, real statisticians are horrified by this, realising the problems that this causes for interpretation. In order to do these types of calculations properly we need a higher level of measurement.

A level up from the ordinal scale we find the *interval scale*. interval scales are distinguished from ordinal scales by having an arbitrary zero. Therefore, on this type of scale we can actually say that $6 - 4 = 3 - 1$. The best example of an arbitrary zero on scale is on a thermometer. If we are using a centigrade thermometer to measure temperature, then zero is arbitrary: it doesn't mean the complete absence of what we are measuring, in this case temperature. Neither does it equate to zero on the Fahrenheit scale (where zero is a lot colder). It is arbitrary because the scientists who developed the metric measurement system chose the point at which water freezes to be zero, the point at which it boils to be 100, and scaled in other temperatures in between. They could have chosen whisky, but they just happen to have chosen water. The interval on the scale are equally spaced, however, and so we can do many more types of calculation on interval data, including the calculation of a mean. For example, we can say that the average maximum summer temperature for

Johannesburg is 28 °C. What we cannot do is to assume that $\frac{40}{20} = \frac{20}{10}$; in other words, the ratios of points on the scale are not equal. The highest level of measurement (meaning that virtually any kind of arithmetic calculation can be conducted on the data gathered) is a *ratio scale*. A ratio scale has a true zero. Zero on the scale really does mean a complete absence of whatever it is we are trying to measure. Zero on my car's speedometer means a complete absence of velocity: my car should be standing still. Zero money in my pocket means just that. Someone earning R200 000 per year can indeed be said to be earning twice as much as someone earning R100 000. Thus, on a ratio scale, not only is $6 - 4 = 3 - 1$, but $\frac{40}{20}$ is also equal to $\frac{20}{10}$. In theory, it would be ideal for marketers to be able to measure as many things as possible on ratio scales, but in reality many of the phenomena they are interested in can never be expressed as ratios, for instance attitudes, feelings or likelihood of purchase.

The purpose of this brief discussion on measurement has not been to make you an expert in scaling techniques, but rather to give you a basic understanding of what can or cannot be done with scales. If you want to be a critical user of marketing research rather than a research expert, then this knowledge is useful. I have seen many marketing researchers who still do not understand measurement and what kind of analysis the data from various scales can or cannot be subjected to. I have seen nominal scales averaged and definite conclusions reached from small samples using ordinal scales. If you come across this, be aware that the results of the research should be treated with caution as the information is not reliable!

7.3.8 A simple look at questionnaire design

The questionnaire is the researcher's measuring instrument. If it is well designed, using appropriate scales, it can do a reliable and valid job which will yield valuable managerial insights. If it is not, then the data that is gathered can be worthless, even dangerous. Unfortunately, there are no golden rules of questionnaire design; much of what we know about the topic is common sense, flavoured with generous helpings of the experience we gain over the years. Frequently one learns as much by doing things wrong as by doing them right. In order to illustrate some of the pitfalls of questionnaire design, we will use the simple questionnaire in Table 7.1 as a small case study.

Assume a brewery asked consumers the questions, on the questionnaire in Table 7.1. How do you feel about each question? What do you think is wrong with it? How would you fix it?

Table 7.1: The Laga Breweries customer questionnaire

Hello, I'm from Laga Breweries and I want you to answer some important questions.

1. What is your income to the nearest R100? _____
2. Do you drink beer often or seldom?   Often _____   Seldom _____
3. Do you like Laga Beer?   Yes _____   No _____
4. How many advertisements for beer have you seen on television this year? _____
   How many last year? _____
5. In your opinion, which attributes of a beer are the most salient and determinant? List seven: _____
   _____
   _____
6. How often do you get drunk? _____
7. Do you think it right that the government impose an excise tax on beer, thereby causing such severe problems for the brewing industry that several thousand people might lose their jobs?
   Yes _____   No _____
8. Choose the point on the scale below which best describes your feelings about the price of Laga Beer:

   Too cheap ☐   Cheap ☐   OK ☐   Too expensive ☐   Far too expensive ☐

The first problem is the introduction. It does not tell respondents why they should cooperate, let alone what the research is about, why it is important and who it is important to. It does not even include the word please. Question 1 is a sensitive item, dealing with a topic that many people feel is private. If you need to ask questions like this, avoid placing them right at the front; rather place them nearer the end. Also, we are asking the respondent something many people might not know: their income to the nearest R100. In addition, do we mean income per month or per year, and is it gross or net income? A question such as this would be better asked at the end of the questionnaire, more specifically, and perhaps using a multiple-choice format rather than an open-ended response.

Question 2 is confusing. What is often and what is seldom? To some people often might mean once a week, while to otters it might mean every day, and the same applies for seldom. A respondent could also tick both alternatives: he or she might drink beer often in summer and seldom in winter.

Question 3 is very vague: what does the word like mean to the respondent? What if the respondent had never heard of let alone tasted, Laga Beer? Question 4 taxes the respondent's memory: who counts advertisements for beer on television? Who cares? Most people might at least remember watching television last night, so at the very most you might ask whether they can remember any beer commercials from the previous evenings viewing.

Question 5 has words that might sound impressive in an academic marketing research journal, but which will simply confuse the ordinary respondent. Why not something like, in your own words, what are the most important things about a good beer? And who can think of seven characteristics of a beer, apart from a qualified brewer? Question 6 uses the word often, which might mean very different things to different people. Some people might find the question offensive, or at least too personal. Just what does drunk mean to the respondent? To some it might mean, I smile and giggle a little more than I normally do. To others it might mean, I fall down, pass out and have to be carried home.

Question 7 is a loaded, double-barrelled question, and the ordinary individual can only answer, no, to it. He or she might feel that it is acceptable to impose an excise tax on beer, but not if it is going to cost jobs. Of courser we could phrase the question in another way that would guarantee a yes: Do you think it is right that the government imposes an excise tax on beer and use the money to purchase school books for underprivileged children?

This is why we often hear that marketing research can give you whatever results you want. It can if a questionnaire is badly designed. The point is that the question is loaded, in that it attempts to get a specific answer. It is also double-barrelled: there are two issues here, not one. Make two questions of it, at the very least.

Finally, question 8 uses a scale for the respondent to answer on. However, for a start, the scale is unbalanced. Far too at the one end of the scale is more extreme than 'Too' at the other, so the scale is weighted to the right. OK is not the middle point on the scale, and what does 'OK' mean? 'Cheap' is also not the opposite of 'expensive': the opposite of 'expensive' is 'inexpensive'. Improperly balanced scales cause more problems in survey research than just about anything else. A more appropriate format for the scale would be something like:

Very inexpensive ... Inexpensive ... Neither expensive nor inexpensive ...
Expensive ... Very expensive ...

The scale is now balanced with appropriate antonyms, and an indifferent midpoint. Some might say this is being pedantic, and won't make much difference. But marketing research is imprecise at best, so why make it even worse by sloppy scaling?

We have learned a few tips on questionnaire design from the mistakes made in Table 7.1. Note that these mistakes were drawn from real questionnaires. The problem with poor questionnaires is that most respondents will not simply ignore them or say, 'This is an improperly designed questionnaire that does not deserve to be answered'. Most respondents are kind souls who will give answers, even to the most stupid of questions: they will guess, interpret in their own way, or even just lie. The researcher will then use the data gathered, subject it to sophisticated data analysis and present it to the decision maker, who may very well use it to make important marketing decisions.

Some other important aspects of questionnaire design is question sequence, layout and design. Layout and design are important to interviewers in personal or telephone interviews, where it should be easy for the interviewer to record the responses quickly and accurately. In the case of mail surveys, a well-designed, aesthetically appealing questionnaire with a well-written introductory letter is the best way of ensuring a good response rate.

7.3.9 Fieldwork

Once the questionnaire has been designed and tested, it is sent out into the field. This means that it is administered by interviewers in the case of telephone or personal surveys, or sent out by mail in mail surveys. The better marketing research firms spend a great deal of time and effort recruiting, training, motivating and controlling interviewers, for they know that the best designed and conceptualised research studies can go wrong at this stage. Cheating can be a problem, with interviewers who do not stick to sampling schedules, simply call friends or other convenient respondents, or, worse still, complete questionnaires themselves.

7.3.10 Data analysis

Once questionnaires have been returned, they should be edited for completeness and correctness and entered into some kind of computer program which will allow the further manipulation of the data to test the hypothesis/hypotheses formulated in the first stage of the research process. Again, there is ample opportunity here to flaw the study by improper editing, error-laden data entry and the application of inappropriate statistical techniques.

However, this is not intended to be a text on statistics. One cannot do much with statistics in marketing research. In fact, we can do only three things. Firstly, we can describe data. We can summarise a particular set of questionnaires and responses using tables and graphs, and some measure of central tendency. That is, we can use statistics to describe where most of the values lie, and in some cases to indicate what the average is and also to what extent the data is spread about the average, or the central measure. In simple terms, rather than say what each individual respondent spent on product category in supermarkets last month, one could say that the average respondent spent R34.50 and say what the extremes of expenditure were to either side of this average, that is, how this spending was spread.

Secondly, we can use statistics to look at differences. Is the spending of men on our product different from that of women? Do older consumers use more of the product than younger consumers? There are various statistical tests which can be used to determine these differences, and their use depends on the levels of measurement (nominal, ordinal, interval, ratio) which we discussed earlier.

At this point we need to introduce the concept of significance. Statisticians and good marketing researchers are interested in the significance of a difference, and the astute manager should be as well. So, for example, if the results seem to indicate that women in our survey on average spend more on product A than do men, we want to know whether this is significant. Many researchers present findings something like this: Women spent R56.00 per month on the product, and men only R53.25; therefore we can say that females spent more than males. This is nonsense. A good researcher would do a test of difference and report the probability of this occurring by chance alone. When researchers do this, they usually report the level of significance of the test in terms of a probability, such as 'the probability of this occurring merely by chance is less than 5%'. In other words, the difference looks statistically significant. As a manager, therefore, you know that it is probable that you will be about 95% right! If your marketing research supplier consistently fails to report significance levels in observations of difference, you might like to ask why.

Thirdly, one can use statistics to explain associations. In other words, one can use statistics to determine whether there is a relationship between two or more variables, how strong this relationship is, and whether it is significant. In some instances we may simply want to see whether two variables are related (this is called correlation); for instance, the manager might be interested to know whether sales of soft drinks are related to the average daily temperature. In other cases we may wish to determine whether changes in one actually led to changes in the other (regression). The manager might, for instance, want to know whether increases in average income cause increases in sales of a product.

7.3.11 Writing the report

The final step in the research process is a writing up of the project in the form of a report. In this report, the researcher outlines all the steps taken in the project, reports the results, and draws conclusions. If required, the researcher may even make certain recommendations. The manager or client uses the report as a basis for marketing decisions. Even at this late stage, a badly conceptualised and poorly written report can lead to misunderstandings and incorrect interpretations.

7.4 RELATIONSHIPS WITH RESEARCH SUPPLIERS

This chapter has not attempted to make a marketing research expert out of you. Rather, it has sought to give an overview of the research process, pointing out that at every step of the way errors can creep into the research process. The intelligent manager uses marketing research in the way a sober person uses a lamp-post: for illumination. Ineffective managers tend to utilise marketing research in much the same way that a drunk uses a lamp-post: for support for ill-conceived decisions that may already have been made. So how should one manage a relationship with a research supplier, bearing in mind that there are a host of marketing research firms out there competing for business? Some of these firms show tremendous insight, skills and innovation. Others, however, may be less qualified than almost anyone in your own firm to conduct an assignment.

So choose the research firm carefully. Find out who they have worked for in the past, and check the big names out by calling them. Ask researcher's clients whether they thought the research was well conducted, and whether they acted upon the results. Look at the company's research records, and ask for qualifications and experience of key researchers. Search for a mix of quantitative and qualitative skills, as well as a knowledge of the real world of marketing. Take things such as publications seriously: people who do things well are not shy about their successes. They write about them in managerial and academic journals, and present interesting findings at conferences. This is not sham academia; these are people who are confident enough in what they have done to want to share it with a critical audience of their peers.

Ask in-depth questions about measurement and questionnaire design. Ask how reliability and validity will be determined, and if you have access to a good psychologist, sociologist or statistician get such specialists to check the answers for you. Ask for more statistics than mere summary tables, and if the request cannot be met, the supplier should be treated with particular circum-spection. Ask about significance, even if you don't understand it perfectly (and this text will not have given you those skills if you did not already have them). However, if you are shrewd you will probably be able to tell just from the look on the researchers face whether the firm has even considered this aspect or not.

7.5 CONCLUSION

This chapter provided a brief overview of the marketing research process to enable the manager to evaluate potential suppliers. Each step is crucial in determining the value of the information gained. If the manager thinks seriously about marketing research and uses it well, it can illuminate a lot of his or her decision-making.

In most situations researchers test a sample of the population. How would you feel if your doctor said, I have to test your blood. All of it. We are generally quite happy to accept the results of blood tests conducted on small samples!

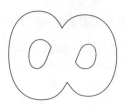

Introduction

Conventional product strategy

The product life cycle

What are the real decisions when it comes to product and branding?

Managing the product

8.1 INTRODUCTION

Most standard marketing texts include several chapters on product management. We will do things somewhat differently and discuss all of these issues in one chapter. There are two reasons for this. First, in many marketing texts, much of what is discussed about product management is either so obvious or so irrelevant that it justifies little managerial attention. Second, many of the worthwhile issues regarding new products are specialised and technical, that they fall beyond the borders of a general marketing text.

8.2 CONVENTIONAL PRODUCT STRATEGY

What topics concerning product strategy do conventional marketing texts cover? Perhaps the best way to deal with the conventional topics of product strategy quickly and easily is to refer to Ted Levitt's (1980) seminal article on product differentiation. Levitt sees a product as existing at three levels, as illustrated in Figure 8.1:

Figure 8.1: Three levels of product (Levitt)

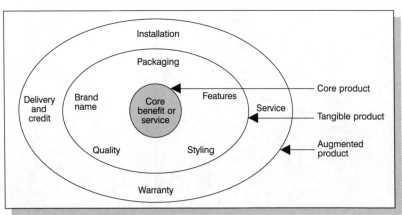

The manager needs to make decisions in each of the three circles or 'levels of product'. The *core product* is the basic benefit or service the customer receives from what he or she has purchased. The frequently used example is a drill; the customer supposedly doesn't buy a drill, but holes in a piece of wood, or metal, or in a wall.

The *tangible product* consists of those visible properties of the product that can make it different from those of competitors. Here, the manager will need to make certain decisions:

- How will the product be packaged? The basic purpose of packaging is to contain the product, protect it and prolong its life. However, for many products, the packaging is a 'silent salesperson'. Packaging communicates to customers that they should purchase this particular product rather than one of the available alternatives. In the example of the drill, packaging will contain and protect it, but can also be used to sell it. The packaging might consist of a case in which not only the drill can be stored and carried, but also additional chucks, bits, extension leads and even small tools.

- What features will the product have? What abilities will the product have that make it different from alternatives? In the case of the drill, features might include dual speeds, emergency power cut-offs and switch locks.

- What styling will be applied to the product? Will it look modern, conventional, or old-fashioned? What range of colours will be available?

- What 'quality' will the product possess? This is not as easy a question as it first appears. While it might be quite simple to say 'as high as possible', the manager must decide whether the market he or she intends to serve really wants the highest quality and is prepared to pay for it. A professional who uses a drill every day in order to make a living, might want and be prepared to pay for a product that will last a long time and offer high performance. On the other hand, a home user who uses a drill once or twice a year to hang a picture may not be prepared to pay for this or need it. Another good example of this dilemma is razor blades. It is technically possible to manufacture a razor blade that would last forever. However, most shavers would probably not be prepared to pay the price that this would require for the firm to be profitable, and most manufacturers would not want to make a product that sold infrequently. The quality has to be 'right' and not necessarily the best at any cost.

- What name will be given to the product? A clever, creative brand name will have a very positive effect on the success of a product. Should the company name be prominent? Should family branding be used, where an established brand is extended to new products? Should the manufacturer simply allow someone else, such as a retailer, to name the product? Later in this chapter, we look at a more extensive discussion of the role of brands, which should shed further light on these critical issues.

The *augmented product* consists of aspects that, while important, are not palpable and probably not even visible. These are attributes of the product the customer has to 'take on faith' and believe they are there. Nevertheless, the manager has to make some fundamental decisions, for as Levitt points out, they can turn mere commodities into specialised offerings; they can differentiate an offering from many other 'me-too's'.

- *Installation:* How will the customer get the purchase to work? This is particularly important in the case of industrial purchases, such as large machines and computer networks. However, it should not be overlooked in consumer purchases. Marketers who make it easy for the customer to 'install' the product will enjoy considerable advantage.

- *Delivery and credit*: How easy is it for the customer to pay for the product and how easy is it to obtain? Many companies have differentiated themselves from competitors by offering credit terms to the customer that no one else can match. For example, in the case of small cars, where product parity is becoming a norm, some manufacturers have differentiated themselves by providing interest-free repayments. The customer's thinking may well be along these lines: 'Most small cars are similar, with no single product being much better or worse than others. All things being equal, I'll choose the product that offers the best credit terms.' And let's not forget delivery. Domino's Pizza has become successful not only for the taste of its products, but for the speed and reliability of delivery.

- *Warranty*: The customer has to believe that the manufacturer will honour a warranty if one accompanies the product. The manager has to decide exactly what the terms of this guarantee will be. For the customer, the one hope is that the warranty will never have to be tested; in fact, the only opportunity the customer will have to do so is when the product breaks down!

- *Service:* Very few products are sold without any service component. What the manager needs to decide is how much service will be added to the product. If this is done successfully, service can provide the supreme differentiation.

8.3 THE PRODUCT LIFE CYCLE

Apart from the 4 Ps of the marketing mix, one thing that everyone wants to take away with them from a conventional marketing course is the story of the product life cycle. The product life cycle is a simple theory that says that all products (or services) go through a life cycle, during which they are born, grow, mature, decline and eventually die. If we plot the history of a product's sales over time, this will give an indication of its life cycle, often referred to as the PLC. Most PLCs in marketing texts are portrayed as a normal distribution curve and marked with the distinguishing phases shown in Figure 8.2.

The PLC is an entirely appealing concept. Teachers like it because it is easy to teach and can be made quite interesting; students like it because it is simple to remember and a perfect 'shoe in' as an exam question. Generally, managers like it because it has what I call intuitive appeal: 'I like it because I understand it.' While it does seem to make so much sense, think about these questions:

Figure 8.2: The product life cycle

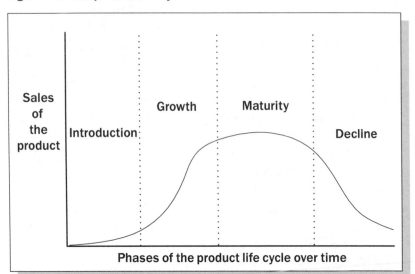

1. Has anyone ever seen a product life cycle and did it look like the curve in Figure 8.2?
2. What about products that seem to go on forever, like Coca-Cola?
3. Are we talking about the PLC for the industry, the product, or the brand?
4. Do you know anyone who has every used the PLC to do strategic market planning?
5. Do you know what the product life cycle looked like in the past? Are you certain that the past is going to be a good predictor of the future?
6. Would you feel safe dropping a product, even if you were certain it was at the end of its PLC?

These might appear to be simple questions, but the answers are difficult. I sometimes feel that the PLC is such a simple concept that it is not very useful at all. In fact, I think it is probably a better way of explaining past behaviour and events than a tool for future planning. Perhaps managers shouldn't like it quite as much?

My *answers* to the questions posed above are:

1. Most PLCs that I have seen do not look remotely like the one in Figure 8.2. Some are like spikes; some seem to be never-ending, like Coca-Cola; some come to a very abrupt end in the middle of the so-called growth phase. And the ones that do? In *South African Marketing Cases* (Pitt, Bromfield & Nel, 1995), the case of the Volkswagen CITIGolf, a product long past its first PLC, is reviewed. According to the PLC enthusiast, the sales curve seems to be 'maturing' until 1991. Was it time to start managing for decline? In the years after the case was written, CITIGolf sales really took off! If Volkswagen SA managers had taken the PLC seriously, the CITIGolf would never have been the phenomenal success story it is!

2. Coca-Cola seems to go on forever. Or is it just a particularly long maturity phase? If it is, how useful is the PLC?

3. It really does make a difference! Some industries seem to go on forever. Some product categories thrive (VHS video format), while others die (Betamax video format). Some products have extraordinarily long life cycles (house paint), while others don't (Rubik cubes). Some brands last longer than any human beings (Marmite), while countless millions are forgotten each year. I don't believe this makes thinking about PLCs simpler, as many would claim; rather, it makes it more confusing.

4. While many managers espouse the PLC, and most know it, only a minority claim to use it. Mike Morris and I did some research on managers in the USA and in South Africa and found that most didn't use it in strategic marketing planning (Morris & Pitt, 1993). Surely the value lies in the use?

5. The past is not always a good predictor of the future. There is a lot to be said for some methods of time series forecasting, but most statisticians will tell you that good times series tend

to be longer, with lots of reliable data. Many products and brands have shorter lives than a time series forecaster would find comfortable.

6. You might. I wouldn't. Some people might be old enough to remember the Bristol Myers toothpaste brand, Ipana (the one with the big red dot on the I). The story goes that Bristol Myers did some PLC analysis and decided the brand was well into decline, and that they should get rid of it. They sold the brand, manufacturing and marketing rights to engineers, who then made a fortune reviving the brand, manufacturing toothpaste on old machines that they had set up in one of their garages. Perhaps Bristol Myers didn't need the money?

8.4 WHAT ARE THE REAL DECISIONS WHEN IT COMES TO PRODUCT AND BRANDING?[1]

From the foregoing discussion, it should be apparent that, while there are certain basic issues to be considered, and perhaps even a certain minimum amount of knowledge needed to understand products and brands, real success comes from how they are managed. Some fundamental questions need to be considered:

- What do brands do for customers and firms? Can other entities fulfil the same functions?

- The product or brand manager system has been broadly and successfully followed in the past. Is it appropriate for the future?

- How should an organisation be structured to maximise its abilities to manage product innovation and interact with customers?

- Is there a best way to organise marketing?

- What scenarios might emerge for product management in the future?

---

[1] Based on Berthon, PR, Hulbert, J & Pitt, LF. 1999. Brand management prognostications. *Sloan Management Review*, 40, 2 (Winter): 53–65

8.4.1 What do brands do?

The quintessential function of branding is to create differences between entities with potential for need satisfaction. From this primary distinction, a series of utilities or benefits are enabled for both buyers and sellers. The benefits branding provides for both buyers and sellers are illustrated in Figure 8.3. For buyers, brands effectively perform a function of *reduction*: Brands help buyers by identifying specific products, thereby *reducing search costs*. Brands also provide an assurance of quality to buyers that can be extended to new products, thereby *reducing the buyer's perceived risk*. The buyer receives certain psychological rewards by purchasing brands that symbolise status and prestige, thereby *reducing the social and psychological risks* associated with owning and using the 'wrong' product.

Figure 8.3: Brand functions for buyers and sellers

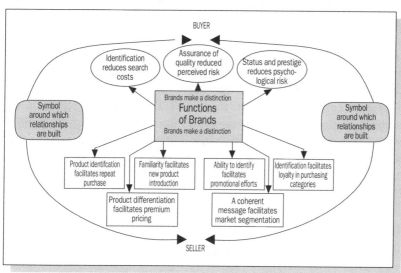

For sellers, brands perform a *facilitation* function – they make certain tasks that the seller has to perform easier. Because brands enable customers to identify and re-identify products, this *facilitates repeat purchases* on which the seller relies to enhance corporate financial performance. Brands *facilitate the introduction of new products*. If existing products carry familiar brands, customers will generally be more willing to try a new product if it carries the same familiar brand. They *facilitate promotional efforts* by giving the firm something to identify, and a name on which to focus. Brands *facilitate premium pricing* by creating a basic level of differentiation that should preclude the product from becoming a commodity. They also *facilitate market segmentation* by enabling the marketer to communicate a coherent message to a target customer group, effectively telling them for whom the brand is intended and, just as importantly, for whom it is not intended. Finally (and we would argue that this is a facilitative function distinct from that of identification), brands *facilitate brand loyalty*, which is particularly important in product categories where loyal purchasing is a feature of buying behaviour. It is interesting to note that brands appear to fulfil more functions for sellers than they do for buyers. However, this is simple counting and does not reflect the value of the functions to each party. Since relationships must ultimately reflect some ongoing equity, in certain contexts this disparity may explain why consumers appear more equivocal towards brands than the managers and companies who 'own' and manage them.

Overall, brands have performed a fundamental function of bringing buyers and sellers together: For buyers and sellers alike, brands accomplish the unifying role of acting as symbols around which both parties can establish a relationship, thereby creating a focus of identity. Despite venerable historical status, however, the pressures on both branding and the brand management system are increasing.

8.4.2 The brand manager system

Many firms' strategies have rested almost entirely on building brands. The brand manager, as brand custodian, has reigned supreme, particularly in the most admired consumer goods companies of the world. Other types of firms have observed these 'world champions of marketing' and attempted to emulate their successes by instituting similar brand or product manager systems. Organisations as diverse as car manufacturers and insurance companies, banks and industrial chemical producers, have structured themselves along brand and product lines, and have made individuals responsible for the success of single brands or product categories. Nonetheless, the wisdom of the brand management approach, and the very value of brands themselves, have been questioned of late. Articles with provocative titles such as 'The death of the brand manager' (*The Economist*, 1994) have appeared in the business press. The questions and concerns include:

- What is the point of marketing without brands?
- If brand managers no longer assume responsibility for brands, who will?
- Is the brand manager dead or merely ailing?
- Will brand management rise again, phoenix-like, in a modified format?

8.4.3 How might marketing be organised in the future?

8.4.3.1 Alternative modes of organising

Other approaches to organising marketing (other than brand or product management) have long contended for managerial attention. These have included, first, a functional approach, whereby marketing is split into specialised functions, including research, sales and advertising, and individuals with particular skills in these areas charged with responsibility for them. Second, a geographic segment approach, whereby marketing is organised by regions of a country or even the world, recognises that different regions require different marketing acumen. Third, a market or market segment approach, whereby marketing is organised by different target markets, and managers made responsible for each of these. Business-to-business marketers particularly favour industry or end-use organisations. Thus, a computer company may divide its market into various applications, such as banking and financial services, manufacturing, transport services, and retailing, and managers might be made responsible for these.

Various pressures for change in the business environment will undoubtedly have a dramatic impact on both brands and brand management, especially on the functions that brands perform for buyers and sellers engaged in a marketing relationship. A majority of these impacts might be negative, which will not bring great joy to brands' proponents. For example, for the buyer, a brand's function of reducing search costs can be replaced by technology; for the seller, the changing values of customers will mean that they may seek value to a greater extent than status, to the detriment of brand loyalty. However, the picture is not exclusively one of doom and gloom, for there are some positive implications of the environmental forces on brands – again, with reference to the functions that they perform for buyers and sellers. For example, for the buyer, technology has the ability to facilitate one-to-one communication that can enhance the risk reduction ability of the brand; for the seller, the customer's changing values can facilitate new product introduction because sophisticated customers will be more receptive to new products that genuinely add value.

8.4.3.2 Some future alternatives for brand management

As discussed above, a brand or product manager system is one of many ways to organise marketing. It could be argued that much of marketing does not need to be organised as a specialist function, for if it is seen as a general management function, it is the job of everyone within the organisation (Hulbert & Pitt, 1996). Despite the fact that each way of organising has its advantages and limitations, brand management has shown unusual resilience. Yet there is a substantial difference between the idea of a brand manager and managing brands. Three possible scenarios for brand management *per se* labelled the evolutionary, the intermediate and the revolutionary, are summarised in Table 8.1.

Table 8.1: *Scenarios for the evolution of brand management*

Approach	Organisational structure	Strategy	Systems	Management of human resources
Evolutionary	• Rationalise brands and product lines • Separate management of brand/product combinations (e.g. Nestlé) • Increased use of cross-functional teams	• Brand/product emphasis weakens • Corporate/umbrella brand strengthens	• Augment traditional financial/market measures with brand equity health checks • Activity-based product costing	• Fewer, better educated brand managers • Movement toward more seniority of remaining brand managers as minor brands are dropped
Inter-mediate	• Shift to corporate/umbrella structures with great simplification	• Proximal customers emphasised; co-operative strategy development	• Customer satisfaction measurement and incentives implemented • 'Hot line' listening system in place	• Hire from customers • Customer involvement sought in recruitment, training and development
Revolutionary	• Customer- and market-based structures • Not product or brand based	• Focus on increasing long-term value of customers • 'Partnership' contracts at all levels	• IT used to emphasise 'segment of one' and even 'one-to-one' • Vision of customer proactive communication	• Empathetic: total immersion with customers • Regular interaction (use groups/clinics) • Two-way emphasised • Look for similarity

An *evolutionary scenario* will see a continuation of current trends. As markets become more competitive and trade customers more assertive, the tail of brands will shorten. Convenience store retailing, with its growth linked to affluence and two-worker households will, because of its restricted shelf space, accentuate the pressure on many other-than-leading brands. Supermarkets seeking growth by adding new categories will likewise place increased pressure on manufacturers' brands with less-than-leading positions in traditional categories. As companies sort out their brand systems and ranges, one might expect to see less emphasis on product-level branding and more on corporate- and family-level umbrella branding, and issues of brand architecture to become more prominent. Indeed, service firms have long recognised the cardinal position of the corporate brand (Berry, Lefkowith & Clark, 1988), and after years of learning marketing lessons from consumer goods marketers, perhaps in the future the roles will be reversed.

These changes alone will tend to thin the ranks of brand managers, leaving a residual of undoubtedly greater seniority. Those who remain, however, will increasingly work in cross-functional teams, organised around categories and/or processes – a distinct change from the traditional model of brand management. One might expect more companies to follow the lead of firms like Nestlé in consciously elevating the hierarchical level of responsibility for brand equity guardianship. Traditional financial and market measures of performance will be augmented by brand equity-based measures, and these will be given real teeth in the evaluation process. As retailers pursue direct product profitability (DPP) and category management to more sophisticated levels, so will manufacturers seek ever-better product costing, using tools like activity-based costing. Shareholder value philosophy will penetrate further into the organisation, with increasing numbers of brands and decisions being reviewed for economic rather than accounting profit.[2] Dealing with these changes will demand a better and more roundly educated cadre of brand managers than is currently employed by many firms. Indeed, if the prognosis of some marketing scholars is correct, future brand and marketing managers will

---

[2] Economic profit is typically defined as operating profit less a charge for capital utilised, based on the company's cost of capital. Assuming an accurate cost accounting system (often a big assumption), economic profit contributes to increased shareholder value.

need both the skills of the analyst and the financial aptitude of an investment banker (Sheth, 1995), not to mention the interpersonal sensitivity of a skilled diplomat.

The *intermediate scenario* is at least partially in place in some companies. Simplified brand and organisation structures will become strongly focused on trade customers: retail chains in the developed world, but emerging large wholesalers in some less developed markets. Manufacturers will increasingly develop joint strategies with these proximal trade customers, although approaches will vary in different parts of the globe. In the USA, more retailers may follow K-Mart-like examples of subcontracting category management, or even jointly developing store-based micro-marketing strategies as advocated by Kraft General Foods. In Europe, relationships tend to be more difficult, and the large French retailers, in particular, tend to resist this level of co-operation. How South African marketers will respond to this is critical. Focusing on proximal customers in the distribution system, however, will lead to considerable advances in efficient consumer response (ECR) initiatives, improvements in delivery and assortment performance, and more sophisticated attempts to measure customer satisfaction.

As part of the attempt to become more customer-focused, one might expect significant changes in human resource management. Manufacturers will follow the example of service providers such as Southwest Airlines in co-opting customers (frequent flyers) to assist them in recruiting, screening and selection procedures. More companies will involve customers directly in training and development activities, not only as speakers but also as co-participants. Hiring from customers will be seen as another means to instil customer thinking into the organisation, even though the impact will dissipate over time. Some companies are experimenting with job swapping – on a temporary basis – between supplier and customer. Certainly, multi-level multi-functional contact with the customer is likely to become the norm.

Unfortunately, in the enthusiasm to embrace the proximal customer, there is the danger that the consumer or ultimate customer plays second fiddle. Direct feedback from consumer or end-user to company is a valuable input in many marketing decisions, and recent novel approaches to marketing research are a formal acknowledgment of this. Such insight is also invaluable in helping to offset emergent intermediary power and should be part of the marketer's inventory of tools. A similar example is afforded by the 1-800 'Freephone' numbers that are almost universal on US packaged goods. These have long been treasured as a consumer resource by Japanese companies like Kao, but are still quite rare in Europe and other parts of the world. Again, one is only left to wonder with what success they will be used in countries such as South Africa.

The *revolutionary scenario* is in many ways the most exciting, for it requires a radical rethinking of the role of both brands and customers in the management equation. As discussed earlier, brands play an important role in buying behaviour through the *functions* they perform for the customer. Customers process an enormous amount of information in the course of their daily activities and need to develop efficient ways of dealing with it. Their heuristics or decision-rules include the use of selective attention, memory shortcuts and rules of thumb. Brands can serve as devices that signify larger chunks of information, simplifying information handling and processing. At a minimum, brands should assure quality, to simplify choice and reduce risk. Whether or not product-level branding is the best way of serving these functions is, however, questionable.

Information technology is the lever that could enable a complete rethinking of brand management. Technology enables firms to identify customers individually, with the economics of doing so becoming ever more favourable. Major airlines, direct marketers such as LL Bean and Land's End, and leading retailers like Tesco in the UK, are already heavily committed, but this capability now exists irrespective of the size of the firm, the nature of industry or the product/service. In South Africa, retailers such as Click's use a loyalty card to track customer purchases, while the Wine of the Month Club has a large database of enthusiastic wine consumers whom they can track as indivi-

duals. A small Stellenbosch-based travel agent, African Alternatives, operates its business entirely via a home page on the World
Wide Web, enabling it do business with customers worldwide on
a very personal basis. The revolutionary scenario involves organising and managing on a customer basis rather than a product
basis. As Schultz (1995) noted in an article criticising brand management, 'Most organisations need a structure that can evolve
from brand management into a more practical and forward looking format.'

Very few organisations are built on the basis of 'once-only'
clientele, yet only recently have firms started to realise that
they have much to gain by thinking about their customers in
relational rather than transactional terms. A longer time frame
on how the organisation's actions either add to, or subtract from,
the development and maintenance of relationships with customers seems both sensible and economically desirable. The
nature of service firms has typically led them to think of building
longer term relationships with their customers, for better service
was seen as a way to retain customers and ward off competition.
This is particularly true in firms within industries that require
high customer acquisition spending and a cost structure with
disproportionate fixed costs. For example, in the cellular telephone business, acquisition costs are very high because companies 'give' telephones away at prices so low they are almost 'free'.
Low usage rate subscribers have to be on the books for many
years before they eventually repay the costs of their acquisition
– and if they leave before then, the company loses money. However, it is just as prudent for manufacturers of goods to think of
the value of consumers over longer periods. A consumer loyally
using a brand typically represents substantial cash flow over time
to the firm marketing the brand. If, however, we focus on the
consumer – rather than the brand – as the 'unit of analysis',
we should concomitantly begin to consider the consumer
holistically, across brands and products. This perspective will
change the seller's perception of the economics of the relationship for any multi-product company, since the discounted cash
flows of the bundles of purchases should be significantly greater.

Just as importantly, the holistic view affords the possibility of a significant increase in customer insight on the part of the seller.

Unfortunately, neither brand managers nor firms typically think of consumers in this way (holistically or empathetically). Historically, companies have not selected brand managers for these traits, and do not include these capabilities in development and training, or in evaluation and reward systems. An enormous paradigm shift is required if we are to consider moving to managing consumers rather than, or at least as well as, brands and products.

Beginning with the customer, rather than products, brands or geography will change the firm's entire marketing structure. This would require a clear line of authority for every customer, although managers would normally be responsible for a group of customers of a determined size and determinable value. A 'portfolio' of customers is perhaps the most appropriate term. Given that customers have some lifetime value, it captures the spirit of viewing them as an investment.[3]

The role of the brand or product manager will not be one of selling the brand to as many customers as possible, but a more supportive one of being a product or brand expert, supporting the firm's customer portfolio managers in developing and providing the products and brands they need to increase their customers' lifetime values. It may also mean realising that there will be customer portfolios to whom a particular brand or product *will not be sold*, based on a computation of the impact on the net present value of the customer portfolio. Customer portfolio managers will have the responsibility of managing the firm's relationships with individual customers in a portfolio, rather than having merely brand and product managers to superintend a brand name. Brand managers will no longer research markets to

---

[3] Our thinking has been influenced to a considerable extent by the terminology of Peppers & Rogers (1993), and Blattberg & Deighton (1996). Managing marketing by the customer equity test, *Harvard Business Review*, July–August: 136–144.

identify what a reasonably large segment of 'average' customers will want. Neither will they price, promote and distribute products to best reach this target market in as large numbers as possible.

For this to happen, the changes in organisational structure will be quite profound. They imply quantum shifts in thinking and conceptualisation for many branded goods companies. Rather than turning the organisation on its head, perhaps the current marketing structure should lie on its side. The thinking process is illustrated in Figure 8.4, moving from a brand structure, in which the brand is paramount, to a customer-based structure, in which the brand manager almost becomes a staff function.

Figure 8.4: Turning the organisation on its side

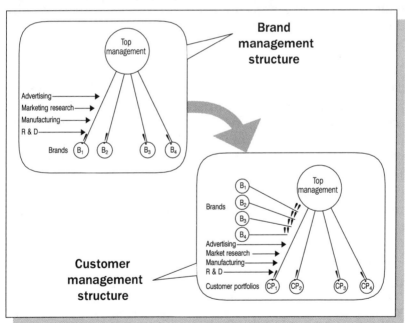

In Figure 8.4, the two organisational possibilities of brand management and customer management structures are shown.

In the case of the former, brands (B1...B4...Bn) are the pillars of the firm, with all other functional activities serving if not subservient to them. In the case of the latter, customer portfolios (CP1...CP4...CPn) are the pillars with other functions *and* brands serving them. From the perspective of the *brand(s)* the organisation has effectively been turned on its side.

For this Peppers and Rogers-like vision to become a reality, very significant changes would be required. The possibilities for true consumer insight, however, would multiply. In this scenario, empathetic managers could literally 'immerse' with their consumers or buyers. Interaction would be continuous; product and brand blinders would diminish. Personal, multi-faceted dialogue has the potential to result in both managers and consumers becoming more proactive in the exchange process. Cohort matching would now become even more important, for contact with 'your' manager becomes an experience to be carefully engineered.

8.5 CONCLUSION

This chapter has considered product strategy and the management of products. It offered a brief overview of some of the more conventional aspects of product management. It then described and questioned the value of the product life cycle. A major focus of the chapter was brands and what they do for customers and firms alike. The very pervasive brand management structure was discussed and questioned, and some alternatives presented, ending with what is perhaps the most revolutionary structure of all – a customer portfolio structure.

References

Berry, LL, Lefkowith, EF & Clark, T. 1988. In services, what's in a name? *Harvard Business Review*, September-October: 28–30.

Blattberg, RC & Deighton, J. 1996. Managing marketing by the customer equity test. *Harvard Business Review*, July–August: 136–144.

Death of the brand manager. 1994 *The Economist*, 9 April: 67–68.

Hulbert, JR & Pitt, L. 1996. Exit left centre stage? The future of functional marketing. *European Management Journal*, 14, 1 (February): 47–60.

Levitt, T. 1980. Marketing success through differentiation – of anything. *Harvard Business Review*, January-February: 83–91.

Peppers, D & Rogers, M. 1993. *The One-to-One Future: Building Relationships One Customer at a Time*, New York, NY: Century Doubleday.

Pitt, LF, Bromfield, D & Nel, D. 1992. *South African Marketing: Cases for Decision Makers*, Kenwyn, South Africa: Juta & Co Ltd.

Pitt, LF & Morris, MH. 1994. Implementing marketing strategies in the US and South Africa. *Long Range Planning*, 27, 1: 56–71.

Schultz, D. 1995. A better way to organize. *Marketing News*, 27 March, 12: 15.

Sheth, JN & Sisodia, RJ. 1995. Feeling the heat. *Marketing Management*, 4(2): 8–23.

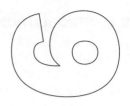

Introduction

What factors should managers consider when setting a price?

Pricing is too important to be left to accountants

9.1 INTRODUCTION

Of all the elements of the marketing mix, decisions on the price the ultimate customer is to pay for the product or service are the ones least likely to be taken by marketing people. In many cases the pricing decision is seen as a financial decision at best, or, at worst, as a mechanical accounting decision. This is very unfortunate, because in these days of product and service parity, super-efficient distribution and elegant marketing communication, pricing offers the final frontier for real marketing creativity.

The following cases in miniature illustrate this point:

When the international pharmaceutical giant Glaxo launched its anti-ulcer drug Zantac in the early 1980s, company chairman Sir Paul Ghirolami surprised not only the industry but most of the members of his management team by insisting that the product be sold at a premium price. Conventional wisdom would have dictated that Zantac be sold at a discount to the leading brand, SmithKlines Tagamet. After all, Tagamet had been the first of the new H2 blockers; in fact, its developer won a Nobel prize in medicine for his work. The drug had also established a huge share of the anti-ulcer market for itself. Zantac was seen by many as being a similar product to Tagamet, with few really significant advantages over it. Surely, to have any chance of success, it should be priced as a less expensive, equally good alternative to the market leader? Ghirolami stuck to his guns, however, and priced Zantac significantly higher than Tagamet. Glaxo also concentrated its salesforce massively, and struck strategic alliances with former competitors in many countries. Zantac was sold to the same doctor on multiple occasions by different sales representatives, often detailing different benefits. Within a short time Zantac had become the number one anti-ulcer drug in most world markets, including the USA, despite the fact that the FDA had reinforced the fact that it offered no significant new advantages. Tagamet was being dealt severe blows on all fronts. Zantac's success and the margins enjoyed through premium pricing saw Glaxo leap from being just another player in the international ethical drug industry to the worlds largest pharmaceutical firm and most profitable company in 1993. Zantac alone accounted for 2 billion pounds sterling in revenue.

In 1994 the president of Taco Bell, John Martin, announced that the fast food chain would hold all prices until the year 2000; this despite the fact that the

Mexican-style restaurants, a subsidiary of PepsiCo with more than 1 500 outlets, had earlier been committed by Martin to *increasing the food* cost proportion of sales by constantly seeking higher quality and therefore more expensive raw materials. As he put it, 'If I were a consumer paying a dollar for fast food, and I found out it had cost the restaurant 27 cents, I'd feel ripped off. We want to get to the stage where, when consumers buy a dollar's worth of food from us, they get a dollar's worth of food.' Taco Bell's focus on value for the customer in terms of good food served at the right temperature in clean surroundings, and fast, efficient service, delivered at *the lowest price,* had become Martin's obsession. The strategy seemed to be paying off: surveys had shown that consumers perceived Taco Bell to be delivering far better value for money than burger giant McDonalds. Taco Bell's financial performance had seen a constant rise in sales and return on investment (through better utilisation of assets and huge increases in the span of management) since 1989, whereas most fast food chains had been hard-hit by fierce competition in a stagnant market.

Marc Andreessen was a twenty-two-year-old student at the National Center for Supercomputing at the University of Illinois towards the end of 1993 when he developed first Mosaic, and then Netscape, two pieces of browser software. These software packages are used to browse or surf the World Wide Web, the multimedia platform on the Internet. The Internet is an inter-connection of tens of thousands of public and private networks worldwide, providing more than 30 million users with access to information from around the globe. Mosaic and Netscape were distributed free of charge, despite the fact that the software had very obvious value. Millions of individuals and organisations availed themselves of the free offer, and quickly learned to use and love the software as the vehicle to access all manner of information and entertainment. When Andreessen (as vice president of technology) floated a company with Jim Clark (former chairman of Silicon Graphics) as president in August 1995, it was one of the hottest new listings in financial history. Netscape Communications Corporation shares opened for trading at multiples of the offer price, despite the fact that the company had until that time not really sold a single product. Marc Andreessen's personal wealth on the day of the listing was estimated to be in excess of $58 million.

Pricing at premium, pricing at minimum, and pricing at zero – all different strategies, but all arguably key elements in eventual organisational success. Pricing represents one of the more visible decision variables confronting a firm's managers, and is the only marketing mix variable which is directly related to revenue. The prices charged for products and services send clear messages regarding customer value and company objectives. In most firms, however, pricing is one of the least emphasised of strategic issues, and an issue desperately lacking in creativity, which managers have often appeared hesitant to discuss.

Many managers have tended to take price for granted, assuming that its principal function was to cover costs and to generate a reasonable rate of return. Others assumed that most firms were charging about the same amount of money, or that legal and regulatory constraints limited their ability to use price as a strategic weapon. However, a more fundamental explanation for price avoidance on the part of managers has been the fact that many did not really understand how to price, and were insecure about the adequacy of the pricing approach they employed. As a result, they relied on overly simplistic rules of thumb, and placed an exaggerated amount of emphasis on cost-based formulas.

Nevertheless, this state of affairs may be changing. Firms are beginning to adopt more sophisticated approaches to price management, and are coming to appreciate the strategic importance of the price variable. A number of notable examples exist of companies and industries where prices are managed in a fairly proactive and value-based manner. Some firms, such as banks and financial institutions, are developing more complex price structures in their efforts to build relationships with, and cater to the individual needs of, large corporate clients. Others such as hotels and car rental firms are initiating more frequent price changes, not only to overcome the perishability problems of being in this kind of service business, but also constantly to communicate innovative messages and strategies to their markets. Still other firms, as diverse as telecommunications companies, airlines and printers, are customising their prices to individual market segments, and even taking this down to the level of the individual customer. Anyone who doubts this should inquire of his or her fellow passengers what they paid for their airline tickets next time they fly – the odds today are very much in favour of everyone having paid a different fare! See the workshop at the end of this chapter on pricing.

These changes do not represent isolated events or random occurrences. Rather, firms in general are being forced to change their approaches to pricing, and these changes are environmentally driven. In many industries in many countries, ranging from utilities such as power and water to the professions, legislation has opened up markets and forced firms to compete against one another without being able to fix prices. A lowered rate of inflation in many countries has meant that customers will no longer accept annual escalation clauses in contracts, and are insisting on annual price decreases instead. A major sociocultural shift has seen customers actively seeking value to the extent that brands are under threat. In supermarket after supermarket and in category after category, many brands are being decimated by in-house brands offering similar value at lower prices. Even Coca Cola and Pepsi Cola have suffered badly at the hands of supermarket cola products. Information technology in the form of scanner systems and large databases enables marketers to obtain instant feedback on price sensitivity at the retail level, thereby conducting on-going real-time experiments to test, measure and react to buyer responses to price. Increasing levels of turbulence in the external environments of firms are therefore forcing managers to become more strategic in their pricing behaviour in order for their firms simply to survive, let alone prosper.

9.2 WHAT FACTORS SHOULD MANAGERS CONSIDER WHEN SETTING A PRICE?

Apart from external forces such as legislation, which may to a large extent dictate prices in certain industries in certain countries, there are three fundamental factors which managers should consider when setting the price for a product or service: **costs, competition and customer demand**. While these may seem obvious, in the past there has probably been a far greater concentration on the first two factors, costs and competition, perhaps because they are more visible and easier to understand. In the future, marketers will move toward an integration of the three, particularly as the techniques available to estimate and understand customer demand more effectively become better known. Let us consider the three fundamental pricing factors in a little more detail.

9.2.1 But costs must be covered . . . mustn't they?

There is a simple rule in business: firms that consistently price under cost will not survive. A firm needs to price its products or services in the long term in such a way that the costs directly associated with production (such as raw materials) are covered by the price, and that there is sufficient margin (commonly referred to as 'gross margin') left to cover the fixed costs, or overheads, associated with running the business. Additional margin over this begins to contribute to the profitability of the firm. This type of thinking is frequently used as a pricing rule-of-thumb and is known as break-even analysis.

How does a simple firm manufacturing and marketing one small product break even (that is, show neither a profit nor a loss)? It needs to sell enough products at a particular gross margin so that the number of products sold, multiplied by the gross margin per product, equals the total fixed costs. The following example illustrates the point:

Assume Company XYZ has total fixed costs of R1 000.

Assume the selling price for its de luxe Widget product is R10, and that the total variable costs involved in manufacturing it (materials, direct labour, etc) amount to R5. The gross margin on a single product is therefore R10 – R5 = R5.

XYZ therefore needs to sell 200 de luxe Widgets to break even: R1 000/R5.

If XYZ sold 201 products, it would make a net profit of R5.

Break-even analysis is a very powerful tool, enabling managers to consider the impacts of different price levels to gauge the effects of changes in variable costs and the burden of overheads, and to budget for profit. Managers can therefore quite easily set prices based on cost, because they can see what the effects of this will be on financial performance. Many firms still use so-called cost-plus pricing to determine the selling price the customer will pay for the product or service, where all prices are set by means of a standard mark-up on cost, for example, 50% mark-up on cost.

However, this kind of cost-focused reasoning ignores what competitors might be charging for similar products or services. It also does not consider whether customers might actually be willing to pay the price for the product or service, and frequently misses the fact that they might even be willing to pay more! Cost-based pricing tends to be arbitrary. While some managers might try to convince us that there is a very good reason for a 50% mark-up, the fact remains that 50% is often an arbitrary figure.

9.2.2 Watching the competition

Many firms set prices by watching competitors carefully and pricing products or services at very similar levels. The thinking behind this is that as long the price is the same as or even a little less than the competitor's, then all other things being equal, the firm should get its fair share of business. No firm wants to be seriously 'out' on its prices. Of course, it is important to observe and study competitor prices carefully, but there are two problems in this. Firstly, who is to say that competitors aren't watching you? In fact, there is every possibility of a recursive situation developing in this way, with every competitor watching the other. Secondly, and perhaps more importantly, competitive pricing suggests that the product or service has reached the level of a commodity, in which case price becomes the only thing that really matters. Better products, premium service, clever positioning through creative marketing, communication, superior distribution – all count for nothing. When competitors in a market have succeeded in convincing the buyer that all that matters is price, marketing is irrelevant.

9.2.3 Understanding demand: what the product or service is worth to the buyer

Despite the above, however, buyers do not really care what the product or service cost the seller to produce or provide. They care about what it is worth to them in terms of its abilities to satisfy their needs and wants. Unless they perceive the product or service as a commodity, they are not so much concerned about how many different competitors supply the product or service as they are about which particular competitor in the market place is best able to give them what they really want. Calculating what the product or service may really be worth to the customer is in actual fact the missing link in pricing strategy.

Consider the following little game related to pricing which I like to play with students, and which I call 'Selling the service'. It involves two individuals in role-play, with one, the seller, a computer programmer, who has been requested by the buyer to write some software. Very little additional information is available to him, except that he knows that he can do the work very easily, and also what his charge-out rate is to his employer (i.e. how much his department charges for his work per hour to other departments). He has no idea what his work will be worth to the buyer. The buyer, on the other hand, owns a medium-sized chain of fashion boutiques for which she needs some software produced. She knows very little about computers or software. All she knows is what other people have quoted her for the work, and how big the savings from investing in the software will be. She does not know what effort is involved, or how long it will take, and has no idea about the seller's internal charge-out rate. These individuals must then agree on a price for the work. On completion of the role-play, I ask each party whether they are happy with the deal they've just done. Inevitably, both are. I then ask the buyer what the MOST was she would have paid for the work, and the seller what the LEAST was that he would have accepted. Now you will find that one of the two parties is not nearly as happy as he or she was at first. Usually it turns out that the buyer would have paid much more than the seller received, although this is not always the case. This may be regarded as a clever little game in negotiating and sales skills, which to some extent it is, but it is really much more than that. The valuable lesson here is a pricing one. In those cases where the seller has got the worst part of the bargain, selling far too low because the buyer would have paid more (and this turns out in around nine out of ten times), what could the seller do in future to make sure this doesn't happen again? Obviously the answer is: ask the buyer lots of questions. In that way he will begin to discover what the service is really worth to the buyer. Ask questions like, 'How does your business work, and what will this work do to make it more effective? Have you looked at other potential sources of supply? What were they charging? Have you estimated what this work might save you, and how much is that worth to you?' An expert marketer will ask lots of questions, get the buyer talking, and find out exactly what the service is worth to her and what she might be willing to spend. He will then receive about as much as she is willing to pay.

We should all do a lot more questioning in pricing, and attempt to find out what the product or service is worth to the buyer. Those who do not will be likely to suffer what behavioural psychologists call the 'winner's curse': They may get the business, but they will always be plagued by the nagging thought that they could have got just that little bit more.

So how can we make more effective pricing decisions? In an insightful article in the *Harvard Business Review,* Dolan lists eight steps which should ensure a better price. Let us study some of Dolan's (1995) pointers and consider the process of pricing as a whole.

1. Do we know *what value* our customers place on our product or service? We might know the value that *we* place on the product, based primarily on its cost, but do we have a really good idea of the value it has to the customer? In the case of Glaxo's ZANTAC against SmithKlines Tagamet, the decision makers understood that by pricing the new product at a higher price than the market incumbent, they would be implying it was of

higher quality. In any event, the prescriber was not the person who actually paid for the product. So long as the prescriber was convinced of the products effectiveness and quality, it would be prescribed, regardless of its higher price.

2. Is there *variation* in the way in which customers value the product? For example, in the case of an airline ticket, some passengers place far more value on the particular ticket than do others. The business traveller who specifically wishes to fly on the Friday afternoon flight leaving at 17:30 in order to get home on time will not be nearly as susceptible to a bargain as the vacationer. Airlines today understand this very well, and are able to incorporate many of these insights into their pricing strategies. Other issues to consider are:

- *Do customers vary in their intensity of use?* For example, some cellular phone subscribers use their cellphones for business while others use theirs for emergencies only. Cellphone companies have catered for both of these markets by varying the prices of both subscriptions and call rates. The regular user pays a reasonably high subscription rate but a low per call price, whereas the emergency user pays a low subscription rate with a high per call charge.

- *Do customers use the product differently?* For example, a five kilowatt motor used by a refinery in emergency power shut-downs only will differ in value to the refinery than would a similar motor in constant use at a food factory.

- *Does product or service performance matter more to some customers than to others?* For example, a customer who wished to guarantee an express courier delivery by 10:30 tomorrow would be willing to pay more than the customer who merely wanted the package to be there sometime this week.

3. Assess the customer's price sensitivity: that is, how sensitive to the price will the customer be in overall terms? Ask questions such as:

- *Will the customer pay for the product personally?* Most people are less price sensitive when spending someone else's money.
- *Is the price a considerable portion of the buyer's total expenditure?* All things being equal, the average buyer will be more sensitive to the price of meat, which could represent a higher proportion of the grocery bill, than to the price of a tube of toothpaste, which would not.
- *Does price signal quality?* In many cases there seems to be a connection in the buyer's mind between price and quality: higher price = higher quality. There is a danger that by pricing too low, you signal low quality to the buyer. While this might not be true, the buyer perceives it as such.
- *Is it costly for the buyer to shop around?* In some cases the buyer might have to spend a lot of money and considerable time shopping around, and might therefore be willing to accept a less than optimal price in order to avoid this.
- *Are switching costs high?* Frequently a buyer might be able to get a lower price for a product or service, but will not purchase it because of the presence of high switching costs. A truck fleet which has predominantly vehicle type A in it will probably not easily switch to buying vehicle type B because it would have to retrain drivers and service technicians, and reinvest in parts. You might not want to change all your financial affairs from bank X to bank Y for a small reduction in overdraft rate, merely because of the inconvenience that this involves.
- *Is the buyer the end-user?* Buyers who are not end-users tend to be more price sensitive. An office manager might purchase a less expensive chair for a typist because he or she does not personally have to experience the discomfort of it.

4. Attempt to identify an optimal pricing structure by seeing the overall pricing picture. So, for example:
   - *Should we price individual components or some package?* Both Club Med and Disney take a lot of the inconvenience out of pricing for their customers by offering all-inclusive

packages, rather than pricing individual room rates, meals, drinks and sporting facilities, or individual theme park rides. Customers see themselves as receiving a tremendous bargain, and do not have to keep purchasing tickets for individual services. At the same time this generally makes the firms own administration of pricing much simpler.

- *Should we offer quantity (bulk) discounts?* One of the oldest questions in pricing is whether customers who purchase more products or services, or those who pay cash, should receive some kind of incentive.

5. Consider competitors' reactions: What might competitors do? Most firms consider what competitors might do *only in terms of price retaliation*. While this is important, it is not the only reaction competitors could have to a price change. Often, in fact, a 'nonprice' reaction can be far more serious: changes may be made in promotional strategies, in the product or service itself, or in the distribution strategy. A good manager should try to anticipate competitor's reactions.

6. Monitor prices realised at the transaction level. Ask this question: What will the difference between list price and the final transaction price be? In many cases, envisaged pricing strategy differs from realised pricing strategy. If salespeople have considerable freedom in being able to offer discounts, for example, what the customer actually pays for the product or service maybe very different from the list price. If the pricing strategy behind the list price was to establish the product as a premium luxury brand, then the reality in the market place might be that the product is now being positioned as a cheap brand which is inevitably discounted.

7. What will the customer's emotional response be? Pricing is not just about being rational. For the buyer, especially, emotions maybe involved. Attempt to assess these and the effects your

price will have on them. What might the price say about your product or service?

8. Are the returns worth the cost to serve? Many pricing policies might be great in theory, but in reality they might cost more to administer than the benefits they deliver. For example, some non-profit organisations have complex pricing schemes which originally had good intentions, but now, in reality, cause administrative nightmares to managers and appear frustratingly complex to customers. A particular metropolitan museum charged different prices for different days of the week and different months of the year, probably under the assumption that visits to a museum are seasonal. Furthermore, it offered special rates to the elderly, schoolchildren, registered students and members of certain charitable organisations who reserved before visiting. When a new director was appointed, she made some rapid changes. The four people who had been collecting the pittances charged for admissions were now changed into 'welcomers': individuals who would welcome visitors personally, and offer to give them help and advice on particular exhibits. And from now on admission was to be free, with visitors asked to donate an amount which suited their pockets and matched their enjoyment on leaving the museum. She quickly quashed the resistance of her board by pointing out that the annual salaries of the four individuals who had been collecting admissions was only exceeded by admission fees by around 10%. Within a year she was also able to demonstrate in real terms to her board that the amount raised by the voluntary donations of visitors exceeded the previous year's admission fees by around 16%.

Overall, says Dolan, managers need to consider the extent to which the pricing process complements the overall marketing strategy. Consider the Korean automaker Daewoo's entry into the British market. It wanted to offer motorists an overall trouble- free motoring package, rather than an advanced sporty car or a huge range of options. It researched the market carefully and found that most car buyers hated haggling over price or horse-trading with a pushy salesperson. So it announced a fixed price strategy: what was advertised would be the price you paid, so that buyers would have no nagging fears that they might have squeezed the salesperson for a little more discount.

In addition, according to Dolan, marketers need to consider the extent to which their pricing strategy is coordinated and holistic. Here you might want to consider the following questions:

- *What are other perspectives, e.g. accounting sales, operations?*
- *What are our pricing objectives?*
- *Does everyone understand these objectives?*

9.2.4 Workshop

9.2.4.1 Differential pricing – Customers are different, so why should they all pay the same price?

Next time you fly somewhere, ask the passenger sitting on the left of you what he or she paid for his or her ticket. Then ask the passenger on your right. Don't be surprised if you all paid different prices. The airlines have become admirably good at yield management, that is, using capacity management systems to make sure they sell most of the seats on an aircraft. However, they have also understood that an air ticket is worth different amounts to different people. Why do they give passengers discounts if they are willing to stay away on a Saturday night? Because business travellers do not want to stay away over a weekend and would rather get home on Friday evening. So they charge business travellers premium prices for the same service. In the same way, telephone companies charge higher rates for calls in business hours and rental car companies charge lower rates on weekends. They have all learned about differential pricing: charging different customers different prices for the same product or service because in some way they are able to estimate the value that the product or service has to the customer. To see whether differential pricing will work in your situation, take the following simple test.

9.2.4.2 Differential pricing in services: A checklist

Will differential pricing – that is, charging different prices to different customer groups, or at different times – work in your organisation? Please indicate the extent of your agreement with the following statements by circling the appropriate point on the scale provided. If you disagree strongly, circle number 1. If you agree strongly, circle 7. If your feelings are less strong, circle one of the numbers in the middle. There are no right or wrong answers: all you need to do is circle a number that best reflects your opinions.

1. Different groups of customers have different responses to prices, i.e. they value the product or service differently.	1 2 3 4 5 6 7 I disagree strongly I agree strongly
2. Different market segments are easily identifiable, and mechanisms exist to price them differently.	1 2 3 4 5 6 7 I disagree strongly I agree strongly
3. There is no opportunity for individuals in one segment who have paid a low price to sell their tickets to other segments.	1 2 3 4 5 6 7 I disagree strongly I agree strongly
4. Segments are large enough to make the exercise worthwhile.	1 2 3 4 5 6 7 I disagree strongly I agree strongly
5. The costs of charging different prices will not exceed the incremental revenues obtained.	1 2 3 4 5 6 7 I disagree strongly I agree strongly
6. Customers will not become confused by the use of different prices.	1 2 3 4 5 6 7 I disagree strongly I agree strongly

Now add up your scores on the 6 items.

How to interpret the scores:

> 35   Great opportunities exist for differential pricing and you are probably using it already!

28–35   You can carefully explore opportunities for differential pricing.

21–27   Approach differential pricing with extreme caution.

< 21   Forget differential pricing.

9.3 CONCLUSION

Pricing presents the last frontier for marketing creativity. To achieve creative pricing, firms will have to move away from many of the traditional approaches to pricing, such as cost-based pricing or an obsessive focus on competition. There are real advantages to be had from a better understanding of customer perceptions of price, and of what value really means to the individual customer. A checklist is presented which will help marketers to make better pricing decisions. Finally, differential pricing is discussed, with a short test to determine whether differential pricing is appropriate in a given situation.

Introduction

Distribution channel structure

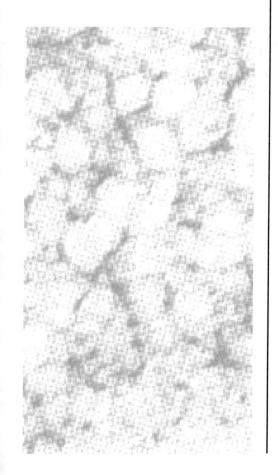

10

Distribution: understanding changes in channel structure

10.1 INTRODUCTION

Distribution, or 'place' as it is referred to in a simple discussion of the marketing mix, is a complicated issue, as it involves all the activities which must occur for the product to move from producer to customer. Not only must all the physical movements occur, but also the negotiations and administrative procedures to transfer ownership of the goods. We do not intend to cover every aspect of distribution here. Rather, our aim is to develop a simple but robust theory for explaining distribution channel structure.

10.2 DISTRIBUTION CHANNEL STRUCTURE

Why are distribution channels structured in the particular way they are? Why, for example, can one buy strawberries direct from a farmer; or from a convenience store, which purchased them from a distributor, who bought them from the farmer or indeed from a supermarket, which purchased them from an importer, who bought them from an exporter, who bought them from an agricultural cooperative, which bought them from, you guessed it, a farmer? Why does the distribution channel for capital equipment tend to be direct from buyer to seller, while in the case of medicines it tends to assume a classic manufacturer–wholesaler–retailer–consumer structure? Why do some retail types disappear, and new kinds of stores enter the market?

These are the questions we will attempt to answer, and our simple theory of channel structure will enable us to do this and more. It will enable us to explain why distribution channel structures have changed in the past, and why distribution channels in particular markets are currently shaped the way they are. It will also allow us to speculate on how particular channels might evolve and change in the future.

To begin the development of our theory we need to ask a simple question. What activities must occur if a product is to

◀ 182

move from producer to customer?[1] A farmer has produced potatoes, and some customers want to buy them. What must occur for the potatoes to move from farmer to customer?

10.2.1 *The basic functions of marketing*

There are six basic marketing functions necessary for a product to move from producer to consumer. These are:

- reassortment
- storage
- transportation
- financing
- carrying risk
- selling activities.

Let us examine each in a little more detail.

10.2.1.1 *Reassortment*

The term reassortment refers to all activities involved in grading, bulk breaking and packaging. The average potato farmer might produce ninety tons of potatoes. The average consumer wants to buy only a few kilos at a time. Someone has to 'break the bulk': divide the many tons of potatoes into more manageable quantities for the consumer. Sometimes the farmer produces a variety of sizes of potatoes. The average consumer probably only wants to buy one size at a time. So someone has to sort and grade the potatoes. The average customer wants the potatoes packaged, so that they are protected, contained, and easy to carry, and the farmer might want the potatoes packaged in an identifiable way. Someone will therefore also have to package the potatoes.

---

[1] We make a few simplifying assumptions at this stage: firstly, that the product has been produced, and is ready for the customer to purchase; secondly, we will limit the discussion to a simple agricultural product, rather than more complex goods. One should understand that for this to be a good theory, there should be, and are no exceptions (at least I hope not!), but it is easier in the beginning of our explanation to work with simple products. We will obviously extend the discussion to more complex products and services at a later stage.

The farmer could do all these things – bulk breaking, grading and sorting them, and packing them into bags. But it could also be someone else, including the customer, who does this! The farmer might say that consumers can visit the farm, dig up their own potatoes, pack the potatoes into their own bags, and pay for them, in the same way as strawberry farmers sometimes do. Or someone else might perform this activity: specialist graders and packaging companies, a wholesaler who buys in bulk from the farmer, or perhaps a retailer. The point is simply that the activities must happen if the product is to move from belonging to the producer to being owned by the customer.

10.2.1.2 Storage

At some point the product must be stored or held in inventory even if it is for a short period. The reason for this is that, with products, the time of production and the time of consumption are separated. There are many different reasons for this, the most important of which are as follows.

a. Seasonal production

The production of many products, particularly fresh produce, is seasonal. Consumers want to eat apples throughout the year, but the apple farmer produces only in winter. So in order to meet the demand for apples throughout the year, they are stored in sophisticated cold rooms.

b. Seasonal consumption

The consumption of many products is seasonal. This may be dependent on the season itself (soft drinks and beer are consumed more in summer, for example, and sporting equipment such as rugby and soccer kits are purchased more in winter), or on important occasions on the calendar, such as Christmas or Ramadan. A firm such as Coca Cola prefers to produce its soft drinks throughout the year, because the production efficiencies this permits the canning and bottling plants. However, consumption of Coca Cola is seasonal: while consumers do drink the product in the winter, they drink much larger quantities in summer. Coca Cola evens out demand and supply by storing stock. The company does not need to switch to a four-day week in the winter, because winter stock which is not consumed is stored for summer. Similarly, the company does not need to work overtime in summer, because it can rely to some extent on stocks made in winter and stored.

c. Certain products improve with storage

There are products which improve with time, and for this reason they are not consumed immediately after production. The best examples are fine red wines, brandies and whiskies, all of which might need many years of storage to mature to maximum quality.

As with reassortment, someone has to perform the task of storage. It might be the producer, but it may also be another party such as a wholesaler, a retailer, a firm which specialises in storage and warehousing, or even the customer. Wine lovers who buy young red wines from estates and then lay them down for five years perform the function of storage to improve the product for their own consumption.

10.2.1.3 Transportation

Transportation is necessary because the place of production and the place of consumption are separated by distance. It is therefore necessary for the product to be physically moved in order for it to be used. The producer might do this – the farmer may have a truck in which to take the potatoes to market – or it might be the consumer (who uses a car to visit the farm and takes the potatoes home). In some channels transport may be handled by the wholesaler or retailer, or by a specialised transport provider. In South Africa, for example, motor vehicle production tends to be geographically concentrated (around cities such as Port Elizabeth and Pretoria), while customers are everywhere. Neither manufacturers, customers nor dealers (retailers) provide most of the transport in this channel. A specialist operator, Motorvia, transports most new cars around the country.

10.2.1.4 Financing

Someone has to finance these various activities. Think of a wine estate, with hundreds of cases of fine red wine maturing in a cellar, or a whisky producer, with fine scotch maturing in vats. The producer expended considerable resources in getting the product to this stage, and it might be many years before the product is sold and cash is realised. And storage must still be financed. Similarly, in the case of a new car, most customers do not walk around with R70 000 in their pockets, enter a dealership, and say, 'I'll have that one there, now start counting the money'. Usually, someone other than the buyer finances the deal. The dealer or the manufacturer could provide a finance scheme (some years ago in the US General Motors was making more money out of financing its cars than manufacturing them), or separate institutions might enter the channel to specialise in this function.

10.2.1.5 Carrying risk

All the activities described so far carry risk. For example, all kinds of things could happen to stock stored in a warehouse, or being transported in a truck. The warehouse could burn down in a fire, the stock could be eaten by rats or the refrigeration equipment could break down and the stock could spoil. Alternatively, the stock could be stolen by dishonest employees, customers could shoplift it off the floor of a store, or the truck carrying the goods could be hijacked. A third possibility is that the goods just may not sell; customers might not want them after all. Those purple wet-look shirts which were such a hit a season or two ago, and which a clothing retailer decided to stock up on so as not to be caught short, might suddenly go out of fashion and could just as well be glued to the boutique floor.

◄ 186

We have just illustrated three kinds of risk. The first are what might be called natural risks, and fires, floods and other kinds of natural destruction occur somewhere or other in the world on an almost daily basis. Insurance companies call these 'acts of God' because they have no other way of explaining them. So they study the frequency of these occurrences to determine their probability, calculate the likely payout should such a disaster occur, and base the premiums they charge on these likelihoods. Obviously, it is possible to insure against such risk. By paying a premium to an insurer, the insured will be covered in the event of the catastrophe occurring. The second group of risks are what we might call 'human risks': the possibility that dishonest or careless humans could cause the damage described above. Again it is possible to insure against these risks by paying a premium to an insurer, who will pay out if the insured goods are stolen or lost through some form of human carelessness.

The third group of risks, which we might call 'market risks' are more complex, and are really what business and entrepreneurship are all about! Everyone in business takes the risk that the market might not buy the product at the price they had hoped to realise for it. Red wine in the style you make might go out of favour, and the purple wet-look shirts might not be snapped up if fish-net sweaters become all the fashion rage. In most cases it is not possible to insure against this type of risk, although there are exceptions. Anyone who can remember the wonderful Eddie Murphy and Dan Ackroyd movie, *Trading Places,* will recall that they were trading orange juice futures on the floor of the Chicago Board of Trade. This was not a figment of the producer's imagination, but a daily occurrence on the Chicago Futures Market, and indeed on the floors of futures and options exchanges all over the world. Briefly, it works in the following way. An orange farmer has all his assets tied up in this year's orange crop. If it is a bumper crop, he should do well, and if it is a dreadful crop, he might not. On the other hand, if everyone else also has a bumper crop, then the price of oranges will plunge and he still will not do well. He could take the chance that he will have a bumper crop and that most others will not, but decide that a good fair price, guaranteed, will be preferable to an uncertain great price. So he sells a contract to deliver the oranges on a specified date to, say, an orange juice canning firm at an agreed price. In this way the farmer is assured of a price for the crop, and indeed has the money in the bank. The juice business is assured of some raw material. However, the contract has some value in itself, regardless of physical items such as oranges. Someone else might believe that the price of oranges will be a lot higher in the season than the price paid by the juice firm and offer to buy the contract from them at a premium (so the juice firm makes a profit on the contract rather than the oranges). On the other hand, the juice firm may realise that the crop is going to be a lot better than it at first thought, and that it may have paid too much for the oranges. It decides to cut its losses and sell the contract now so that it can buy at a lower price later. Again, someone else might spot some differences in the price of contracts and decide to trade in the orange juice contracts market just for the profits to be made from trading, but without ever wanting to own the oranges and with no intention of actually having them delivered. Futures and options contracts in many commodities are traded on this type of market: wheat, maize, silver and gold, wool, pork bellies and orange juice. Irrespective of the item being traded, it seems to be a pretty exciting business. At least, it looked like fun in the movie.

However, as far as I am aware, there is no market (yet) for futures contracts in wet-look shirts. So our little retail boutique will just have to carry their own risk that the product might not sell. The point is that while we can shift the risk to an insurance company in some cases or to a market such as a futures market in others, or indeed carry it ourselves, someone ultimately has to carry the risk.

10.2.1.6 Selling activities

I am not in favour of the above term, but it seems the most appropriate. These activities are not marketing activities, because marketing is a lot more strategic and overall, but on the other hand these activities involve a lot more than just one-on-one selling. They include all the actions involved in resolving what economists call the problem of search: producers have to find customers, and customers have to find producers. So this set of activities includes all those involved in finding out who the buyer might be and might want. It involves displaying the product, merchandising it and advertising it. It involves selling to the customer in the sense of convincing a customer to buy, serving customers while they purchase and servicing them after the event. The best way to think of this activity is to conceive of it as including all those things which go with selling, in the sense of transferring the product to the customer for a return.

Again, someone has to perform these activities of seeking out the customer or the producer. When a strawberry farmer puts up a hand-written sign that says, 'Fresh strawberries, R5 a punnet', this is an act of search on the producer's behalf: the farmer is seeking customers. Similarly, when a family takes a drive into the countryside on a Sunday afternoon to look for fresh strawberries, they are engaged in search. When a buyer in a large industrial firm publishes an insert in a trade magazine seeking potential suppliers of new machinery, he or she is engaged in search.

Usually an intermediary enters the channel to specialise in search. A supermarket seeks suppliers, which simplifies the supplier's need to search for lots of small customers. Similarly, the supermarket simplifies the consumer's search by having many of the products the consumer will need under one roof. Rather than visit many small producers, consumers can find much of what they need in one place. A travel agent searches for many small customers for a multitude of travel service suppliers, such as airlines, tour operators and hotels, while performing a similar function for many small customers by searching for solutions to all their travel needs.

To repeat: someone must perform this search function and all the selling activities that it requires. It can be the producer, the customer, or any one of a number of intermediaries who enter the distribution channel in order to fulfil it. However, each of the steps in the distribution chain costs money!

Some people ask whether retailing or wholesaling are functions, for these are very visible parts of distribution channel structure. The answer is, quite simply, no, and the reason for this is clear: intermediaries only enter the channel when they can do so profitably, since each of these six functions costs money. Furthermore, no one really wants to perform these functions! Therefore, as long as someone else can perform the function efficiently and at lower cost, all parties are quite prepared to pay for this. Consumers are happy for supermarkets and other retailers to perform a lot of their search for them. Producers allow specialist transport firms and warehousing companies to perform transport and inventory functions. Many parties prefer to pay someone else (such as an insurance company) to carry their risk for them. Purchasers of expensive products and services are willing to pay someone else to finance their acquisitions, in the form of interest-bearing premiums.

Thus, intermediaries enter the channel to perform one or more marketing functions when they can do so at the lowest cost, and have to leave the channel when another party can perform the function at an even lower cost. It is this performance of functions, and the cost implications involved, that cause channel evolution to occur and the shape of distribution channel structures to change. We can now explain why channels change shape, why new intermediaries enter and whole new forms of distribution emerge, and also why long established intermediaries sometimes disappear. This also allows us to understand the current shape of distribution channel structure and to speculate on what changes might occur in the future. The story of the grocer and the supermarket will provide an example on which to test our theory.

10.2.2 *The grocer and the supermarket*

Some readers might remember the traditional grocery store where our parents or our grandparents purchased their groceries. They would have bought most of the family food there, as well as a large range of other household necessities. In some of these establishments the owner, the grocer, would have been actively busy in the running of the store, often even dressed for the part, in a striped apron and a straw hat. Most of the provisions would have been ordered from wholesalers, who in turn would have ordered them from producers, but some may have been ordered directly from manufacturers.

Let us now look at the six functions of marketing, and ask whether the old grocer performed them.

Function	Did the old grocer perform it?	Reasoning
Re-assortment	Yes	The old grocer bought in bulk and reassorted to a fine degree. Shoppers could have ham sliced thinly or thickly, and weighed to their specifications. They could buy flour which would be weighed on the spot, to their precise requirements, or rice, potatoes, and even a half loaf of bread. It would then be hand-wrapped (packaged) by the grocer or the grocer's assistant.
Storage	Yes	The grocer purchased stock in bulk, paid for it, and held it in inventory for customers.
Transport	Yes	The grocer not only fetched much of the stock from wholesalers and producers, but also provided a delivery service for customers. A boy on a bicycle would deliver the week's purchases to a customer at no extra charge.
Finance	Yes	The grocer would pay for many purchases beforehand, or within a very reasonable time. Many grocers would extend very generous credit to their customers – a customer could go 'on the book', and pay their account, or part thereof, at the end of the month (or, when times were tough, when they had the money!)
Carrying risk	Yes	The old grocer carried all of the three types of risk we identified, or paid for an insurance company to carry the first two. The grocer ran the risk of fire and flood, and that rats, mice or weevils would spoil the provisions. The grocer also ran the risk that the stocks he had purchased would not find favour among the customers and spend a long time on the shelves.

Function	Did the old grocer perform it?	Reasoning
Selling	Yes	The old grocer did spend a little money on local advertising. More importantly, this form of retailing provided substantial services to customers, who were all served personally, the regular ones greeted by name, and packages either carried to the car or delivered.

Now let us complete the same table for the supermarket of today. We are going to be very hard on supermarkets, because we want to test our theory quite rigorously.

Function	Does the supermarket perform it?	Reasoning
Re-assortment	No (not really)	In the case of the modern supermarket, much of the reassortment is performed by producers, who pre-package goods before they are placed on supermarket shelves. Consumers also do quite a bit of reassortment themselves, for example by weighing their own fruit and vegetables and placing them in a bag, or by serving themselves with pre-made salads.
Storage	Partially	Supermarkets do not really carry much inventory. In fact, this is one of the secrets of a well-run supermarket. Nowadays, so-called 'just-in-time' stock control systems ensure that just as the last package is about to move off the shelf the supplier's truck enters the offloading bay. Furthermore, many manufacturers would argue that supermarkets do not carry stock, for they are not paid until well after the goods have been sold. In a physical sense, however, the supermarket does store large quantities of products in the shop.
Transport	No	Suppliers deliver all merchandise to the supermarket. Consumers fetch it in their cars and carry it away. The supermarket does not really do any transportation.

Function	Does the supermarket perform it?	Reasoning
Finance	No	Suppliers all extend very generous credit terms to supermarkets, very often more than 90 days. If they did not, many of them would find it difficult to get their products placed on shelves. So they finance the supermarket. Customers of supermarkets all pay cash, or by credit card (which is the same as cash). By doing so, they finance the supermarket as well (or the credit card company does, indirectly).
Carrying risk	Partially	In general supermarkets do carry natural and human risks. There is always the danger of fire, flood and spoilage. Very serious losses can be occasioned by dishonest staff, or by the shoplifting activities of some customers. However, in many cases they don' t carry market risk. Many stores carry certain products on consignment. It works like this: the manufacturer asks the store to carry the product. The store will agree, on condition that the manufacturer pays for the shelf space up front. If it sells, they then agree to take a further mark-up and pay the manufacturer on credit, for instance, after 90 days. If the product does not sell, the manufacturer must come and remove the products. Supermarkets therefore do not bear much of the risk.
Selling	Partially	Supermarkets spend a huge amount of money on advertising. However, much of this is actually paid for by the manufacturers whose products are featured in the commercials. Supermarkets provide very little in terms of personal service to customers: no-one is served personally or greeted by name, and one usually has to pay if one wants one' s packages carried to the car.

Why has a form of retailing (the grocer) which provided so many services and fulfilled so many marketing functions, been replaced by a form of retailing which provides so few services and performs so few marketing functions?

The answer is, cost. Performing marketing functions costs money, and these costs have to be recovered. Supermarkets perform very few of these functions, and are able to pass this on to the consumer in the form of lower prices. As pleasant as they were, all those services the old grocer provided cost money, and unfortunately customers were just not prepared to pay for them. So, the supermarket performs a search facility and provides a place for producers and consumers to meet, but performs few marketing functions itself, for those would add to its costs. In this way it has managed to enter the distribution channel. By doing so, it has changed distribution channel structure.

There are many other examples of this. Think of how personal computers were sold ten years ago (specialised dealers), and how they are sold today (discount stores, appliance stores, mail order). There are countless other examples. In fact, many years ago, in the area of retailing specifically, a marketing professor called Malcolm McNair (1958) termed this process of evolution the 'wheel of retailing'. Let us look at this below.

10.2.3 The wheel of retailing

Very briefly, the wheel of retailing (Hollander, 1960) suggests that high service, high cost, high price retail establishments are gradually replaced by low service, low cost, low price retail establishments. But, as the wheel turns, these low price establishments begin to compete with one another on more than just price, and so start to add services. Of course, this increases their cost burden and makes them vulnerable to a new form of low service, low cost, low price retail establishment and so the wheel turns. We see evidence of this in many situations: department stores, which offered lots of service but suffered the burdens of high costs, were in many cases replaced by discount stores, which did not carry the range of products the department store did and provided very little in the way of service, but were able to offer substantially lower prices. Small toy stores with large specialised stocks for modelling enthusiasts and advice on educational playthings were replaced by megastores such as Toys Я Us. Small local pharmacies in many areas have been replaced by 'hyper-pharmacies' and chain drugstores.

Thus some readers may have noticed supermarkets beginning to assist in taking bags to the car, or opening a checkout whenever a line of more than two customers formed, or even having additional staff on the floor to assist customers find products or make choices. The outlets are doing what anyone who is hard pressed to compete on price would do: offering more service. This is what the wheel of retailing suggests. But it also adds that these institutions will add to their cost structure, since carrying staff, checkout cashiers and in-store advisers costs money. Supermarkets are therefore vulnerable to the next turn of the wheel, whatever that will be. Some supermarkets have addressed the issue by setting up hyperstores, or megasupermarkets. My own feeling is that change might come in the form of so- called club warehouses. Consider the example of CostCo below.

In December 1993 I was contacted by BBC Television, which was doing a business programme on a company called CostCo and wanted expert insights into how this business was run. What they needed was someone impartial to explain to viewers how CostCo worked, for, to the amazement of everyone, this huge megaretailer was not spending a single penny on advertising. CostCo was quite happy that television crews should visit the stores to film, but management declined to do any interviews. I armed myself with CostCo's year-end report for 1992 in the USA, and headed out to a British branch of the company.

CostCo is a store from hell. It is located in what can only be described as a giant aircraft hangar: a huge, charmless building which seems to be constructed only of scaffolding and steel sheeting. Things were no better inside: bare concrete floors, grey shelves and bright neon lighting, with products stacked to the root some still in boxes, other in cartons which had been slashed open with a Stanley knife. In some cases, hand-scribbled signs displayed prices. In addition, you have to pay to be a member and to shop at CostCo. You also have to apply for membership, which is why these institutions are known as club warehouses. The application forms, however, really only require one to be a member of the human race or to know someone who is!

The best way to describe operations at CostCo is to complete one more table in the same way we did for grocers and supermarkets, for we can then make a useful comparison.

Function	Does CostCo perform it?	Reasoning
Reassortment	Not at all	CostCo does not even unpack boxes which contain products. If suppliers are not prepared to merchandise products themselves, CostCo will simply stack cardboard cartons and the customer will have to purchase a carton, minimum. It was interesting to compare wine merchandising: Some suppliers had unpacked cases of wine and priced individual bottles so it was possible to purchase a single bottle of wine. Others were a little lazier and had not unpacked the box, but had at least ripped it open and stuck up a hand-written sign indicating price and that it was possible to purchase a single bottle. Others had not done anything and so the customer had to take a whole case.
Storage	Partially	In this function CostCo was still rather like a supermarket. It does not really carry much inventory, but applies the 'just-in-time' stock control systems. Also, a lot of the stock on the floor was on consignment.
Transport	No	Suppliers deliver all merchandise to CostCo. Because CostCo also sells white and brown goods such as washing machines and television sets, transport can be a problem for customers. An enterprising van rental company had set up business alongside, and this firm also rented or sold roof racks.
Finance	Surprisingly, a bit more than supermarkets.	CostCo offered no credit facilities to customers. However, I was able to ascertain that in some cases they would pay a supplier before delivery. What happened was that they would negotiate with a supplier (say a wine supplier, to keep the argument constant) by asking what the best deal would be, let us say, on 2 000 cases. The supplier might quote something like £18 a case on 90 days, a deal similar to that offered to a large supermarket chain. CostCo would then ask what the price would be if they paid up front, and the answer might be something like £16 a case. CostCo would then sell the case in store for something like £17.50, 50p lower than what a supermarket would be buying at. Needless to say, one could not help but be impressed by the extremely low prices on many of the products in the store.
Carrying risk	Partially	Just like supermarkets, CostCo does face natural and human risks, including fire, flood, spoilage and losses occasioned by dishonest staff and customers. Apart from inventory purchased before sale, however, many products were on consignment.

Function	Does CostCo perform it?	Reasoning
Selling	Absolutely not!	CostCo does not advertise at all, and there is absolutely no personal assistance of any kind within the store.

CostCo would not be my happy vision of an ideal shopping experience. However, if you wanted to purchase a reasonably large number of products at very low prices, it would be an eminently sensible place to visit. A look at the financial statements from the 1992 CostCo annual report in the USA revealed the following: The company had turned over approximately $10 000 000 000. It had made a net profit before tax of approximately $250 000 000. It had roughly 10 000 000 members. As the annual membership fee in the USA was $25, the picture is clear: CostCo runs a retail store to break even. The profits come from membership. Therefore, to make more profit the company needs more members (regardless of whether they buy or not!). The CostCo story allows us to complete our picture of how distribution channel structure evolves. Channels change because of an inexorable state of flux in the performance of distribution functions.

10.2.3.1 What about the exceptions?

Some will say that we have been too hard on the supermarkets and that there are supermarkets who actually do nice things for suppliers and customers (and now we know why). There are also those who will point out that not all the small grocers have disappeared, and that there are still department stores and tiny local pharmacies who have someone on a red scooter who delivers your medicine. Exactly; our theory generalises, but it does not preclude the fact that many structures in the older distribution channel still exist, albeit on a smaller scale. Our theory also allows us to explain why they exist! The fact that there are still small grocers or small pharmacies who manage to survive, despite their disadvantageous cost structures, means that they are able to pass these costs on to their customers in the form of increased prices. Just as importantly, it means that there is a small but significant group of customers who really want the added service and are prepared to pay for it! This is not new in marketing. We call it market segmentation!

To summarise, what does our simple theory of distribution channel structure allow us to do? It allows us to:

- explain why channels have changed in the past;
- look at existing channels and account for their current structure;
- look at a channel and try to understand what might happen to it in the future by predicting how shifts in the fulfilment of marketing functions will reshape it.

We will end this discussion by looking at the forces that shake distribution channel structure enough to change it.

10.2.4 What might cause shifts?

Most changes in marketing are caused by changes in the business environment. Changes in legislation, the economy, customer behaviour, technological developments and competitors are all forces which have affected existing distribution channel structures enough to change them. That was our premise in Chapter 2, when we discussed strategic marketing. We will discuss the following changes to make the point: changes in customer behaviour, changes in technology, changes in legislation, and changes in the channel itself

10.2.4.1 Changes in customer behaviour

Changes in customer behaviour can create changes in distribution channel structure. If we think of the distribution channel for personal computers we referred to earlier, we have an excellent example of this. When personal computers were first marketed in the early to mid-1980s, they were sold through specialised dealers. There was good reason for this: the average buyer was ignorant about the new product, and needed a lot of reassurance, which was provided by reasonably skilled sales staff within the store (selling activities). The store carried a full range of stock, provided finance, and would deliver and set the machine up. Nowadays this type of distribution for the product has all but disappeared, and most customers buy their computers through discount stores, computer hyperstores and, increasingly, through mail order outlets. Let us take the latter as an example and explain why this form of selling has become so prevalent.

Computer buyers today are a lot more informed than their counterparts of fourteen or fifteen years ago. The expert salesperson is not as necessary as in the past. If we look at the mail order computer outfit and test whether it does all those marketing functions, we find that the answer is no in most cases. Do they reassort? No: they ship in boxes which have been put together by manufacturers. Do they carry inventory? Again no. Most actually order from the manufacturer after they have received the customer's order. Do they provide transport? Of course not. The package is delivered by a specialist transport provider. Do they carry risk? Not much, since they don't hold much stock. Do they provide finance? No, this is generally provided by credit card companies or, on rare occasions, the customer will pay cash on delivery. Do they do any selling? A few advertisements in magazines and some well-constructed catalogues, yes. Do they provide knowledgeable service and sales advice over the telephone? Forget it! Just order the product by number from the catalogue. What has made this possible, and why has distribution channel structure changed? The customer has changed, has learnt a lot about the product, and this has made most of the previously important functions superfluous.

10.2.4.2 *Changes in technology*

Technological change can create major changes in channel structure. If we think of the basic function performed by agents and brokers of services, we quickly realise it is one of search. Travel agents seek holidays and travel arrangements for their customers, and seek customers for their suppliers, such as airlines, hotels and tour operators. Insurance brokers seek the best insurance deals for their clients, and seek customers for their suppliers, the insurance companies.

Now, what happens when search becomes easy for customers because they can do it themselves, through technology? Using the World Wide Web one can log into the British Airways site, look at their flight schedules, find the best fare, reserve a seat and pay for the ticket. One can then log into the Holiday Inn Web site, find a hotel in the city one is visiting, get room rates and availability and reserve a room. Similarly, one can search all the Web sites of insurance companies and get quotes for car insurance. Once one has the best deal at the best rate, one can insure one's vehicle over the Internet. Given that all this is possible, there are clearly problems looming for travel agents, insurance brokers and other service intermediaries.

10.2.4.3 Changes in legislation

A few years ago there was great consternation among South African pharmacists when the retail discount store group Clicks announced that it wanted to dispense medicines countrywide from its chain of shops. This would have required changes to existing legislation covering the dispensing of scheduled drugs, and for a time it looked as if the laws might change. They did not change at that time, but this illustrates the forces that cause changes in distribution channel structure. Clicks entering the channel would have resulted in a substantial reduction in the price of medicine (pharmacists actually fixed prices at the time, with government consent!), but probably also in a reduction of service to customers. For example, it is unlikely that Clicks would have employed someone to deliver the medicine. The consequences for pharmaceutical wholesalers might also have been dire, for the giant retail chain would undoubtedly have flexed its buying muscle and purchased directly from pharmaceutical manufacturers. Thus, in order to understand what changes might occur in distribution channel structure in any market, examine possible changes in legislation which might affect this market.

10.2.4.4 Changes in the channel itself

Sometimes changes within the channel itself are so radical that they alter distribution channel structure forever. This can be because of a change in the way any one of the six marketing functions is performed. Frequently this change is the result of technological change. For example, transport systems in many countries have improved so dramatically in the past twenty years that whole distribution channels have changed as a result. Companies such as Federal Express and United Parcel Service have introduced delivery and logistics systems so efficient and cheap that the new distribution systems and even entirely new businesses have been made possible. In the US today there is a firm called Calyx and Corolla, which sells fresh cut flowers by direct mail. This firm does not have a florist shop, only an office with some telephones, modems and computers. They take orders over the telephone and these are passed on to growers all over the country. The package delivery service Federal Express collects the arrangements from growers and delivers them to the recipients. The recipient is guaranteed of the freshest, longest lasting flowers available. Rapid, efficient, low-cost delivery systems are thus changing the traditionally long distribution channel (grower–distributor–wholesaler–retailer) for fresh flowers.

10.3 CONCLUSION

We have attempted in this chapter to develop a theory that will allow us to understand distribution channel structure, to explain how they have evolved, and to predict how they might continue to develop in the future. This theory is based on the fundamental marketing functions (reassortment, storage, transportation, finance, carrying risk and selling) which have to be performed for a product to move from producer to customer. The theory states that each of these functions has to be performed, which costs money, but that no one wants to perform them if someone else can do so more efficiently and at lower cost. Thus intermediaries will enter the channel when they are able either to perform one or more of the functions at lower cost, or if they are able to shift these functions on to someone else and pass this benefit on to the customer in the form of lower price. We have tested our theory to explain changes and evolution in a number of channel settings, and have also identified some of the forces that will initiate changes in distribution channel structure.

References

Hollander, Stanley C. 1960. The wheel of retailing. *Journal of Marketing,* July: 37–42.

McNair, Malcolm P. 1958. Significant trends and developments in the postwar period, in Smith, AB (ed). *Competitive Distribution in a Free, High-Level Economy and its Implications for the University.* Pittsburgh, PN: University of Pittsburgh Press, 1–25.

Juta & Co Ltd

Introduction

Some basics of
communication theory

What are we trying to achieve in
marketing communication?

Advertising: What is it? What can
it do and what can it not do?

Personal selling

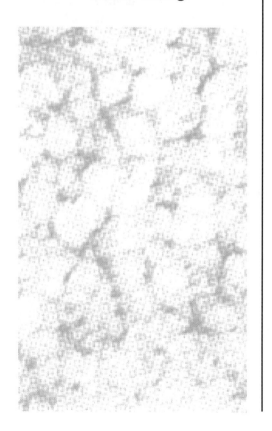

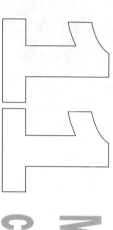

11
Marketing communication: conversations with the market

11.1 INTRODUCTION

Marketing communication involves the exchange of information between sellers and buyers. It is the most visible activity in marketing management decision-making, and to many people it tends to symbolise what marketing really is. It is a critical implement of marketing strategy, one of the four Ps we referred to in our introductory chapters.

11.2 SOME BASICS OF COMMUNICATION THEORY

Most simple models of the communication process involve a sender (the person who wants to communicate), a message (that which is to be communicated), a medium (something through which the message is transmitted or carried), and a receiver (a person who is the intended recipient of the sender's message). In one-way communication the process ends with the receiver taking in the message, whereas in two-way communication the receiver in turn communicates back to the sender, a process which closes the communication loop and which is called feedback.

One-way communication tends to be quicker and easier for the sender. Two-way communication takes more time, and is more difficult for the sender if he or she wishes to ensure that the receiver has comprehended the message. In marketing communication the most common forms of one-way communication are advertising and publicity, and the most obvious form of two-way communication is personal selling. Our focus in this chapter will be on advertising and personal selling.

11.3 WHAT ARE WE TRYING TO ACHIEVE IN MARKETING COMMUNICATION?

One way of developing a reasoned approach to marketing communication strategy is to use what consumer psychologists have called 'hierarchy of effects' models, and then to consider what the various forms of marketing communication can do to achieve maximum communication effectiveness. Hierarchy of effects models are attempts to describe the mental steps customers go through from the time they first begin to think about a particular need or want, until the time they satisfy this need or want through purchase, and even on to the time after purchase and consumption when they evaluate whether the purchase and consumption was really that great after all. The steps are essentially the same for consumers and industrial buyers, as is illustrated in the first two columns in Table 11.1 below.

Table 11.1 What do we want to achieve in marketing communication?

New customer/ prospect buying phase	Complex consumer buying process	Key seller communications objectives and tasks		Relative communication effectiveness
		Communications objectives	*Task*	Low High
1. Need recognition	1. Awareness of needs	Generate awareness	Prospecting	
2. Developing product specifications	2. Information processing	Feature comprehension	Opening relationship, qualifying prospect	
3. Search for and evaluation of suppliers	3. Evaluation processing	Lead-generation	Qualifying prospect	
4. Evaluation	4. Purchase decision	Performance comprehension	Presenting sales message	
5. Supplier selection	5. Purchase	Negotiation of terms/Offer customisation	Closing sale	
6. Purchase feedback	6. Post-purchase evaluation	Reassurance	Account service	Advertising Personal Selling

For both industrial buyers and consumers, the steps involved typically include recognising the need, seeking information and developing product specifications (what might satisfy the need?), evaluating the alternatives in terms of products and suppliers, making the purchase, and evaluating the purchase after the time. As can be seen from the third column in Table 11.1, the communication tasks facing the marketer differ down the hierarchy, or as the buyer moves through the various stages. In the beginning, the marketer's tasks tend to revolve around making customers aware of needs, or encouraging them to recognise needs. Customers then need to be given information, so that they can better understand the characteristics of the product that will best satisfy their need. This needs to be done on quite a large base in order for the marketer to have access to sufficient customers. Next, buyers' choices need to be narrowed down, and they can then be moved to actual purchase. And finally, once purchase has occurred, buyers need to be assured that they have made the right decision so that they can make a similar one in the future when the need arises again.

Obviously, not all customer purchases are made in this way. Firms do not go through the same process every time they need envelopes — they merely place a repeat order with an established stationery supplier. Similarly, consumers don't go through the process every time they buy milk, bread or dishwashing liquid. These purchasing patterns are usually so well-established as to be mechanical. However, the processes form a useful framework for marketers, because they show that to accomplish the objectives at each stage of the process, the marketer must accomplish defined tasks. This is shown from a personal selling perspective in column 4 in Table 11.1, A salesperson typically prospects (finds enough customers who might have a need for the product); qualifies (ranks prospects in terms of likelihood of purchase); presents information in the form of a sales message so that the prospect can be moved towards a decision; closes the sale by signing a deal or getting the prospect to purchase; and then follows up to offer reassurance that a good deal has indeed been done and to identify opportunities for future business.

As can be seen from the last two columns in Table 11.1, one-way and two-way communication (advertising and personal selling respectively) vary considerably in terms of their effectiveness in the phases of the decision hierarchy. Generally, advertising is at its most effective in the early stages of the decision-making process, and personal selling at its best towards

◂ 206

the end of the process. Advertising is very effective at making a lot of people aware of a need and at informing them of the existence of a product which might satisfy it. It is much less effective at actually getting the customer to buy the product ('doing the deal'), or at offering personal reassurance that the customer has made the right decision.

Personal selling is a clumsy way of attempting to make a lot of customers aware of a need in a short time) and at low cost. Particularly if the market is large, it would be prohibitively expensive to use a large salesforce merely to make customers aware of a need and the product that might satisfy it. However, personal selling is a very effective way of convincing individual customers that they should sign on the dotted line, and at visiting them after the purchase to determine whether everything is satisfactory. The final thing shown in Table 11.1 is that really effective marketing communication is integrated: the best marketing communication strategies will use tools such as advertising where they are most effective (for example, generating awareness), and personal selling where it works best (closing the sale). Of course, other media forms are emerging today, such as the World Wide Web, which allow for even more integration. We look at these in Chapter 11.

11.4 ADVERTISING: WHAT IS IT? WHAT CAN IT DO AND WHAT CAN IT NOT DO?

Advertising is one-way, paid-for communication through mass media by an identifiable sponsor, directed at making the target audience aware of something, persuading it of something or reminding it of something. A brief look at this simple definition is worthwhile. Advertising is one-way, which makes it different from personal selling (which is two-way). It is also paid for, which makes it different from publicity (which is, strictly speaking, free). It uses mass media, such as the press, radio, television and billboards. The sponsor of an advertising message is identifiable, which makes advertising different from propaganda, in which it can be more difficult or impossible to identify the sponsor. There is a target audience, and advertising can do three things to this audience:

- It can make potential customers *aware* of something of which they were previously unaware. It can therefore inform the customer of a new or improved product, a change in price or the opening of a new store, etc.
- Advertising can *persuade* customers to do something. For example, it can get customers to send off for further information, call for further details, sample a product or visit a new store.
- Advertising can also *remind* customers of a product or service and of past occasions on which it was used and enjoyed. Many people wonder why well-known, established brands are still advertised. The reason is that if customers are not reminded of the product or service they may actually forget about it. A brand such as Marmite, which is well known to most consumers in the UK and South Africa (being almost 100 years old), is still advertised today, just to ensure that consumers remember about it. Advertisers can also boost sales by reminding consumers of occasions, for instance, 'It's the weekend — don't forget the beer', 'Next Friday is St Valentine's day — don't forget to say it with flowers' or 'Only twenty-three more shopping days to Christmas'.

11.4.1 How powerful is broadcast advertising?

Just how influential is the advertising that permeates so much of our everyday life? Many people might answer that it is a strong force, as marketers would not appear to spend so much time and money on it. Others see advertising as a very powerful, almost sinister influence that can get gullible customers to buy things they don't want, don't need and can't afford. In reality, advertising is actually very weak, simply because for the individual company and brand in a single commercial, the communication effect is diluted to an extreme.

To explain: Assume that the annual amount spent on broadcast advertising (or what advertising agency executives like to call 'above the line'[1]) in South Africa is R10 billion. We know there are about 40 million people in the country, thus by division (10 000 000 000 ÷ 40 000 000) we can conclude that the average South African is exposed to R250 worth of advertising each year. Now let us consider a really big advertising budget, such as R100 million. Probably only one or two firms in the country spend this sort of money. We now divide the R100 000 000 by 40 000 000 consumers, and we end up with R2.50. In other words, even the largest advertisers are directing only R2.50's worth of advertising at a consumer who is getting a total of R250's worth.

On the other hand, advertising executives argue that their messages are much more focused than this, and are targeted not at the average customer but at the one who really mattered, which would mean that the net effect would be far greater on the individual. This point was worth noting.

A second point is that if your advertising money is so weak you must spend it wisely. Make sure the message is tested well, make sure you choose and manage your media carefully, and make sure that the effects of your advertising are not only measurable, but are measured.

---

[1] The phrases 'above the line' and 'below the line' are advertising jargon which mean the following: originally, advertisers distinguished between promotional material for which it was easy to budget and that which was not. 'Above the line' of course referred to the 'bottom line' so beloved of accountants, and 'below the line' referred to those expenditures for which it was less easy to budget. It was easy to budget for radio or television spots. You bought time, and multiplied this by the number of planned spots. Similarly, for newspapers and magazines you bought space and multiplied the space rate by the number of spots. So these activities were above the line (of net profit). However, it was less easy to budget for other promotional activities such as giveaways, including pens, calendars, discount promotions and so on, and so these became almost incidental and therefore 'below the line'.

11.4.2 So what are the most important advertising decisions a marketer needs to make?

Most advertising decisions fall into three sets of activities: advertising objectives; message and media; and advertising budget.

11.4.2.1 Advertising objectives

Before embarking on an advertising initiative, marketers need to consider what the objectives will be: what is the advertising meant to achieve? This helps to determine whether the advertising worked. If we were to ask most advertisers what the objectives of their advertising campaigns are, the answer would almost certainly be, 'To increase sales'.

However, most advertising does not have a direct effect on sales. This is because advertising is only one of a number of variables (good product, right price, availability and so on) which affect sales, and its effect on sales is usually so indirect as to be unmeasurable.

The things advertising can do are inform, persuade and remind. By thinking of advertising objectives in this sense, it is possible to define advertising objectives which are realistic, measurable and important. By informing, advertising achieves changes in awareness. These changes are realistic (if more people are not more aware of a product or service as a result of a campaign, the advertisement has probably not worked); important (customers have to be aware before they can move further down the purchasing hierarchy); and measurable (only 20% of customers were aware of the new product before the advertising campaign, and now 80% are). Similarly persuasion is important, realistic and measurable (how many people tried the free sample, visited the new store while the campaign was on, wrote off for the free brochure?), as is the ability of advertising to remind (What is the first brand of instant coffee that springs to mind? And the second?).

11.4.2.2 What to say and where to say it: A look at message and media

Most large firms employ the services of an advertising agency: a firm which specialises in broadcast communication. The agency is given the responsibility for crafting the creative message, selecting the media (print, radio, television etc) in which it will be conveyed, and timing the messages. This is generally an effective arrangement, for most firms are not large enough to employ the considerable talents and skills which a large advertising agency is able to bring to the table. In addition, most firms prefer to leave the marketing communication to specialists. The evidence also suggests that advertising works best when the firm selects a good agency and trusts them to design the best campaign for them, even when it appears to be risky. Perhaps the best example of this is that given by Bob Townsend in his book *Up the Organisation*. Townsend, as chief executive officer of Avis Car Rental, thought the slogan, 'We're number 2. We try harder', was risky, and could lead to Avis being perceived as inferior. However, he stuck with the agreement made with the agency that he would let them do the creative work, and let the campaign proceed. It is remembered as one of the most successful positioning campaigns in history.

This does not mean you should give the agency free rein to do as it pleases without some involvement from your side. The astute marketer will be critical, and have a reasonable understanding of what media are available, what they cost, and what the advantages and limitations of each are. However, the intelligent marketer will also not do the agency's work for them. If you like the ad, simply pay for it and let it run. If you don't like the campaign, tell the agency and suggest they start again. Don't agonise over small print, the angle of a photo shoot, or the smile on the face of a model: that's what you're paying them for!

11.4.2.3 The advertising budget: How much to spend?

One of the really difficult decisions that marketers face is how much to spend on advertising. Some even hope there may be some kind of magic formula out there that will tell them how much to invest, but each advertising campaign is different.

Two problems confuse the issue of how much to spend. Firstly, the utility of advertising is not linear, but S-shaped. In simple terms this means that spending below a certain amount is entirely wasted: it is so small it doesn't get noticed and therefore makes no difference. At the other extreme, one can also spend too much: beyond a certain point, additional advertising has no positive effect on awareness, persuasion or remembering, let alone sales. Secondly, advertising has what we call a residual effect, which is difficult to quantify in simple accounting terms. It is not the kind of expenditure which is spent in one year, with the benefits being reaped the same year. If the advertising works, the benefits may last for avery long time. For example, the slogan 'Things go better with Coca Cola' is still remembered more than twenty years after it was first created by Coca Cola's ad agency.

How, then, are advertising budgets determined? Usually it is set as an arbitrary percentage of sales, say five or 10%. Accountants approve of this method because it is simple, and with spreadsheets, one can do all kinds of 'what-if' calculations. The problem with it is that it has no logic attached to it. Firstly, the percentage chosen is arbitrary. Secondly, it can lead to gross overspending, or substantial underspending.

The best way to determine an advertising budget is neither easy nor precise, but it is certainly better than picking an arbitrary number. It involves a look once more at the objectives set for the advertising. We then carefully consider what we need to do to achieve those objectives. Next, we calculate the cost of this in terms of message creation and, of course, the media budget. And that will be the advertising budget. If that kind of money is not available, the overambitious objectives might have to be cut, or better ways of achieving them found.

11.4.3 Some problems with advertising agencies

No formal qualifications are required for advertising. Therefore, although many advertising executives are intelligent, creative and talented, there are also a good number of fly-by-nights. It is therefore advisable to be careful, and to consider a few things that may make working with your agency easier and more profitable.

Select your agency carefully. One of the best ways of doing this is to let your own judgement rule. If you see advertisements you like, find the agency who did them. Many firms like to ask a number of agencies to tender for business, and then select. Be careful of this: many of the better and larger firms don't tender for business unless it is a really large account, simply because they don't need to. So the ones who tender may need to! On smaller accounts particularly, agencies may calculate their chances of getting the business and not put their best tender forward, merely one that stands a chance of getting the business. It can also be informative to call clients of the agency and ask them what the agency is like to work with.

Agree on what the campaign should achieve, and also agree on ways in which this will be measured. If you don't do this beforehand, it will be difficult to call the agency to task if the objectives are not achieved. Insist on some kind of measurement afterwards and, if you have the budget, have this done independently.

If you are a small advertiser using an agency that manages some much larger accounts, beware of being used as their training guinea pig. Some large agencies will put junior staff on smaller accounts, reserving the stars for the really big accounts.

Beware of putting too much emphasis on advertising awards. Like most activities of creative endeavour, advertising is an industry that delights in mutual adulation. Clients should be aware that most of the awards are given for what matters to creative people (creativity), not for what matters to business people (product success, sales growth, market share, profitability, and customer satisfaction).

11.5 PERSONAL SELLING

While advertising has been defined as one-way communication between a firm and its target audience, personal selling is characterised by the fact that it is two-way communication between a salesperson and a customer, where the intention of the former is to persuade the latter to take some course of action. However, our focus is not on selling techniques or on how to be a good salesperson, so we will not go into these in any detail. Rather, we give attention to the fundamentals of the sales manager's job: what are the decisions a sales manager needs to take?

11.5.1 A sales manager is a people manager

While the primary responsibility of a sales manager might be sales, most of the activities involved have to do with people (salespeople), and so, just as with most other jobs which entail the management of human beings, the sales manager's job concerns recruiting, screening and selecting salespeople; training them; motivating and rewarding them; organising them; and controlling them. We will therefore look at each of these activities.

11.5.1.1 Recruiting, screening and selecting salespeople

A sales manager needs someone to manage! Salesforces are established and grow, and then salespeople leave, retire or die and need to be replaced. Thus, a considerable part of a professional sales manager's job is taken up by recruiting salespeople, screening them and selecting those who should become part of the sales team.

A frequently asked question is: what makes a good salesperson? If we were to elicit the characteristics of a good salesperson from a group of marketers, we would soon fill a blackboard with important traits: product knowledge, the 'gift of the gab', tenacity, a 'thick skin', good communication skills and so forth. The issue has been one which has received considerable attention in marketing and personnel research over many years, and while much of this research has offered valuable insights, we have yet to develop a definitive description of what one should ideally look for in a salesperson.

A study conducted by Mayer and Greenberg (1964) over forty years ago stated that the successful salesperson possesses just two important traits: empathy and ego drive. Empathy is the ability to 'feel with someone'; in other words, to understand the other person and that person's environment and problems. Ego drive (which they also refer to as 'ego strength' or the 'will to win') is the need to succeed just for the sake of it. It is understandable that this might be a desirable trait, given the vicissitudes of the selling job. What makes selling so daunting to many of us is what makes it exciting to the successful salesperson: it is so variable, and there is the guarantee of failure somewhere along the line. Most conventional jobs are fairly predictable and the person doing them does not go through the highs of success or depressing lows of failure that the salesperson experiences. Good salespeople thrive on this: sales failures spur them on rather than depress them. It is the ego drive which facilitates this.

So, what things should the sales manager take into account when recruiting? Some of them are:

- Use good psychometric tests as a tool, but do not emphasise them at the expense of good judgement.
- Look for personality more than industry experience. Some industry experience might be valuable, but it is more important to find people with the right personality.
- Build up some kind of quantitative performance database: keep good records on successful and unsuccessful salespeople, so that you can build up evidence of what seems to work in your market and what does not. Don't rely on your memory!

11.5.1.2 Sales training

The easiest way for a manager to think logically about sales training is to consider the following six fundamental questions: who? what? when? where? how? and why? There are no right or wrong answers to these questions; rather, they need to be considered in order to develop a logical framework for sales training strategy.

Who?

'Who' refers not only to who will be trained, but who will train. Who will be trained: will it be new recruits, the existing sales-force, or both? Will the trainer come from inside the firm, bringing valuable experience and knowledge, but with the possibility of insularity; or will the firm use specialist trainers, with access to a broad skills base and the latest techniques, but who may be unable to appreciate the firm's unique business situation?

What?

The 'what' question broadly covers the content of sales training: what does the effective salesperson need to know and be able to do? The best way to simplify this might be to distinguish between knowledge and skills. Knowledge has to do with certain basic minimum levels of understanding that a salesperson needs to be able to do the job. It will cover issues such as knowing the company itself, the product, knowing the customers and their business, and knowing the alternatives the customers have (competitors). It is unlikely that this knowledge can be imparted by external training, and so this sort of training is probably best done internally.

Skills are what the salesperson needs to do the job well. By learning them, and then continually practising them, the sales-person becomes ever more proficient at the selling job. Skills are imparted when a salesperson is given the ability to perform selling tasks (such as those outlined in column 4 in Table 11.1) in a creative and original way. They are what will distinguish the great salesperson from the average. This type of training is often best sourced externally, using a sales skills trainer.

When?

The sales manager needs to decide on time for training. This encompasses not only a seasonal aspect of time, but also such issues as training regularity, and company political aspects of time. A major problem with training is that it takes the salesforce out of selling, and the real costs and opportunity costs of this are high. Issues to look at include time of year, time of month, and even time of week and time of day. Also, should training be in an intense burst, ongoing or both? Finally, there are what we might term the polltical aspects of training time: in whose time should the training take place? Should the company use its own time only, or should it expect trainees to give up some of their time as well, for example over a weekend?

Where?

The sales manager needs to decide where training will take place. The obvious benefits of in-house training at the firm's location are that it is convenient, easy and inexpensive, particularly if the company has a good training infrastructure. However, problems are caused by the fact that training feels no different from the usual day at the office, and that training can easily be disrupted by urgent meetings, telephone calls, customer problems and the like. Training away from the office has certain advantages. It may show that the firm is serious about training, and prepared to spend money on it. Certain locations might be motivated, and facilitate the kind of intense work the firm expects trainees to go through in their training. Also, distractions can be minimised. However, it also has its own problems, not the least of which is cost. Additionally, if not managed carefully, 'away training' can be seen by some trainees as a holiday at the company's expense, and might not be taken seriously.

How?

The sales manager needs to decide on the best methods for imparting skills, knowledge and abilities to the salesforce. Lectures with notes, videos and good sales texts are a good way to impart knowledge, but might be seen by some trainees as being too theoretical. On the other hand, techniques such as case studies, role-plays and simulations are excellent ways of showing what might work and what might not, and give the trainee an opportunity to practise tools and techniques in more realistic situations. However, some people believe that simulated experience is no substitute for the real thing. So some firms use 'on-the-job' training, where a more senior colleague accompanies the trainee on a call, and then comments afterwards on what was done well, what was done poorly, and what lessons can be learned. The advantages of this approach are that it is entirely realistic and, if done well and managed by a skilled trainer, can bring huge benefits of good experience. It does have drawbacks, however: it can be threatening to both salesperson and customer. If criticism and praise are not skillfully balanced, the value of the learning might be affected. And what could be done if something goes so badly wrong that a major customer is lost? Unlike role plays, simulations and case studies, in the real world there are rarely opportunities to go back, re-run the script and fix the mistakes.

Why?

The 'why' question seems so obvious that it hardly appears worth discussing. Surely we train salespeople in order that they should sell more effectively, so that the firm does more business, and is more profitable? However, there are other less direct yet fundamentally solid reasons for training salespeople. Training is an investment in human skills, and particularly in skills which can be used in a wider activity than sales alone. Training is also a great motivator. It shows the salespeople that they are valuable enough for the firm to invest in them.

11.5.1.3 *Organising the sales force*

The sales manager must decide:
- how to organise the salesforce as a whole
- how to divide potential sales territories equitably among the salesforce
- how to assign salespeople to territories in a way that will provide for the best fit between the individuals and the customers they will serve.

There are a number of ways in which the salesforce as a whole can be organised, each of which has its advantages and its limitations. The simplest and most common way of organising the salesforce is on a geographic basis, so that each salesperson has a defined geographic territory to cover. Alternatively, the salesforce can be organised by product, so that each individual sells only certain of the firm's products or services. This allows the individual to develop product expertise, but also means that the salesperson may have a large geographic territory to cover, and that some customers may be called upon by more than one representative of the firm. Some firms organise the salesforce by customer, so that a salesperson may only call on a particular type of client or, indeed, only one client (this, or variations on the arrangement, is sometimes referred to as key account selling). In this way a salesperson can build up expertise in a particular kind of custo-mer's business, such as banking, manufacturing, research or whatever.

It is also important for the sales manager to organise the sales-force in such a way that

- everyone does his or her fair share
- all customers are visited in relation to their importance and need
- by hard work the individual salesperson is able to maximise his or her rewards.

The sales manager therefore has to find a way of dividing the total potential workload in such a way that

- all salespeople are given a reasonably similar loading
- customers get the service they require in relation to the po-tential business the firm can get them from them
- any one particular salesperson is not able to earn more simply because he or she has a much easier or much more valuable territory.

At the micro-level, the sales manager should try to ensure that each individual salesperson best matches his or her territory. This is best illustrated by a simple example. The sales manager of a veterinary pharmaceutical company might wish to ensure that she sends a salesperson to call on cattle farmers who not only has knowledge of the products and cattle, but can 'speak' the cattle farmer's language. It might help to build relationships with the farmer if the salesperson is not afraid of a cow pat or two, getting those new shoes a little dirty, and spending some time out in the open.

11.5.1.4 Motivating the sales force

The most important thing about motivating salespeople is deciding not only how much, but how to, pay them. The acronym 'SELF' indicates the elements of a balanced remuneration scheme:

- SIMPLICITY (easy for company and salesperson alike to understand, and easy to administer)
- EFFECTIVENESS (leads to maximum effort from the salesperson, and inevitably to the highest desirable levels of sales)
- LOW COST (should not cost the firm more than it needs to)
- FAIRNESS (does not penalise salespeople for things beyond their control)

At their simplest, most monetary decisions on salesperson remuneration revolve around whether the salesperson will receive a salary only, a commission only, or a combination of the two. The extremes are typically found a lot less than some kind of combination, although each of the three solutions have their merits and problems.

According to Maslow's well-known hierarchy of needs model, promotion is a great motivator. However, not all great sales people make good sales managers, and many would rather be selling than managing. Thus, although promotion may work as a motivator, it can also cause problems.

11.5.1.5 Controlling the sales force

Like all managers, sales managers need to set objectives for the salesforce, compare reality to objectives and take corrective action where reality falls short. This is the managerial task of control. While it does not differ fundamentally in sales management from most other situations, there are a few issues worth noting.

Firstly, unlike many other control situations, where the subjects of control are on the same site, here the subjects of control are selling in their sales territories. The sales manager is therefore controlling people he or she doesn't see most of the time.

Secondly, many of the mechanisms used to control salespeople have to be taken on faith. For example, most salespeople are required to complete call reports — which customer they saw, when, and what the result of the call was. When this is approached insensitively by a sales manager, it can at best become a bureaucratic process for the salesperson; at worst, it can lead to blatant dishonesty. 'Called on Purchasing Manager R Jones' can mean, 'I called on him, he was busy, I stuck my head through the office door and waved. He waved back'. Call accomplished, and duly logged. No real dishonesty in the strictest sense, but not a real call either. Or it can mean 'I didn't call on Jones, but I booked the call anyway, because I doubt whether you or your control system will check'.

Thirdly, the only variable that really matters to salespeople and sales managers is sales. However, sales tend to be an outcome variable. The problem is that if the factors that lead to sales are not controlled, including prospecting, sales techniques, call ratios, selling to the right price and so forth, then by the time we get to trying to control sales it may well be too late. Which leads us to the final point.

In sales what gets rewarded gets done. Reward salespeople for volume and they will give you volume. Reward for new accounts opened and a good salesperson will open scores. Reward for selling to the right price and the smart salesperson will not move much product, but will give no discount away either. This is a particular problem for the sales manager who often wants to control a number of variables, yet also give reward where it is due and where it matters most. How does a sales manager achieve this, especially when despite his or her best efforts, sales territories might not be perfectly balanced, and certain salespeople should be able to achieve relatively better results merely by virtue of where they operate?

One approach to this problem has been the development of simple weighted quota evaluations, with reward systems based on these. An example of this method is shown in very simple form in Figure 11.1

As can be seen from Figure 11.1, the fictitious firm uses a weighted quota system to control its salesforce. For each salesperson quotas (shown in the second column) are set on say four activities of performance (shown in the first column). The activity quotas in this case are VOLUME (some kind of sales volume), NEW ACCOUNTS (new accounts opened), DISPLAYS (how many product displays the salesperson set up), and SELL TO PRICE (how much discount the salesperson gave away). Obviously these are simple examples, and might vary from situation to situation. The actual performance on each of the activities of importance is shown in the third column. Actual as a percentage of the quota for each activity is calculated in column four. In the fifth column, a relative importance weighting is assigned to each activity (these weightings must obviously add up to 1). This can be done by the sales manager, or by the sales manager in consultation with the salesperson. Finally, the weighted performance on each activity is calculated in column six, and these are added to obtain an overall performance against quota.

Figure 11.1: A simple weighted quota performance system for a salesforce

REP:	THOMAS	SMITH			
ACTIVITY	QUOTA	ACTUAL	ACTUAL/QUOTA%	WEIGHT	WEIGHTED %
VOLUME	500	500	100%	0.65	65.00%
NEW ACCS	25	25	100%	0.20	20.00%
DISPLAYS	10	10	100%	0.05	5.00%
SELL TO PRICE	90	90	100%	0.10	10.00%
				1.00	100.00%

REP:	HARRY	CASUAL			
ACTIVITY	QUOTA	ACTUAL	ACTUAL/QUOTA%	WEIGHT	WEIGHTED %
VOLUME	400	450	113%	0.65	73.13%
NEW ACCS	15	11	73%	0.20	14.67%
DISPLAYS	8	15	188%	0.05	9.38%
SELL TO PRICE	80	90	113%	0.11	1.25%
				1.00	108.42%

REP:	MARY	WILSON			
ACTIVITY	QUOTA	ACTUAL	ACTUAL/QUOTA%	WEIGHT	WEIGHTED %
VOLUME	600	500	83%	0.50	41.67%
NEW ACC.S	30	25	83%	0.30	25.00%
DISPLAYS	12	10	83%	0.10	8.33%
SELL TO PRICE	92	90	98%	0.10	9.78%
				1.00	84.78%

If we look at each of the fictitious salespeople, we can see the following: Thomas Smith is our most simple example case, and shows how the numbers fit together. His actual achieves quota on each activity, and so his performance matches quota, at 100%. Harry Casual achieves 108, 42% of quota. He has achieved this by selling volume (presumably by discounting, for he under-achieves here), and by not putting up displays. He makes up for this by opening more than the targeted new accounts. Mary Wilson is far under her quota, achieving only around 84%. This is because she is far below her volume quota, and she also under-achieves on new accounts and displays. Part of her volume problem might be due to the fact that she is reluctant to give discounts. She sells at an average of 92% of list price, although the target is 90. This might not be a bad thing, and is why the firm actually sets a quota in this regard. However, it will also be noticed that the sales manager has changed the weightings in Mary's case. Volume is relatively less important, weighted only ,5, and new business is more important, weighted ,3. This might be because the area does not have a lot of potential, or the company might want a lot more new business in that area, or it might be easy to achieve volume in the area.

Whatever the reason, what is valuable from this simple analysis is that the sales manager can use the system to motivate and control salespeople. The system can force the individual to focus on those activities which the sales manager deems important, reward them for those activities for which they put in above-quota performance and penalise them for those on which they fall short of target. The sales manager can also use it to give attention to particular activities for particular salespeople, by varying the quota, the weighting, or both. Note that running a system such as this on a computer spreadsheet is reasonably simple.

11.6 CONCLUSION

The focus in this chapter has been on marketing communication, both one-way and two-way. Under one-way communication we looked at advertising, particularly in terms of what it can achieve for the marketer: awareness, persuasion and reminding. Two-way communication focused on the role of the sales manager, and his or her responsibilities with regard to the various aspects of sales management.

References

Mayer, David & Greenberg, Herbert M. 1964. What makes a good salesman? *Harvard Business Review*, July–August: 119–125.

12

The marketing of services: different or not?

Introduction

What makes services different?

Services are not different!

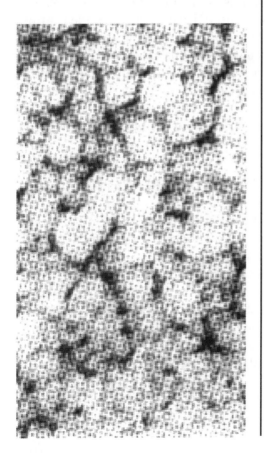

12.1 INTRODUCTION

In many economies today the role of services has grown to the extent that they comprise a greater proportion of gross national product than manufactured goods. Yet it is only in recent years that marketing academics, practitioners and indeed service firms have begun to give attention to the marketing of services as distinct from products. The question that we wish to address in this chapter is whether the marketing of services is different from the marketing of goods, and, if so, what makes it different. To do this, we need to look at whether services are different from products. The answer to this question is ambiguous: yes, and no. We will take both of these perspectives and see what we can learn from them. Answering 'yes' provides important insights to service firms, highlighting particular problems in marketing services, but also emphasising that there are many opportunities arising from the differences. Answering 'no' offers insights not only to services marketers, but to goods marketers as well, and exploring this should therefore be useful to most firms. We begin with the view that services are different from products.

12.2 WHAT MAKES SERVICES DIFFERENT?

What makes services different from products, in other words, what unique characteristics do services possess that products do not? What makes our purchases of things such as banking, airlines, telephone services, hotels, rental cars, restaurants, accounting, dental care and corporate consulting distinct from our purchases of items such as soft drinks, canned peas, cars, dishwashing liquid, computers, milling machines and toothpaste? Services possess four unique characteristics that products do not, and we need to understand them to anticipate problems and exploit opportunities facing services marketers. The unique characteristics of services are intangibility, simultaneity, heterogeneity and perishability. Let us look at each of these in a little more detail.

12.2.1 Intangibility

Services are intangible. Whereas you can see, touch and hold a product, you cannot do these with a service. This is the most fundamental difference between products and services. Whereas products are things, services are performances or experiences. This characteristic creates problems for services marketers which product marketers never experience. Intangibility means that you have nothing really to show customers, for them to feel the quality of or to try out. For customers, intangibility means that they cannot see what it is they are buying, and will have nothing much to show in exchange for their money once they have bought the service and used it.

Thus, a challenge facing services marketers is to overcome the problems created by intangibility. Most successful services marketers overcome intangibility problems by 'managing' them. Some of the things that can be managed are evidence, tangibles, sampling and memories:

12.2.1.1 Evidence

Because customers cannot see the service, we have to give them evidence of what it is they will get when purchasing it. If we think of a life assurance policy as a service, it is actually very difficult for the customer to understand what it is, and even more difficult to try the service out, since most policies pay out only on the death of the policyholder! So how do good life assurance companies overcome this problem? By the effective management of evidence in their communication. Advertisements feature individuals and families similar to the customer who have purchased the service, and illustrate the benefits they have enjoyed from it. They give references in the form of testimonials. Pension companies find it hard to communicate to their customers just how well their investments are doing, apart from dreary financial reports. How do you as a customer actually see your money growing? Some companies now put up signs on the billboards at major building sites in which they invest, saying, 'Our shareholders' funds at work'. Good hotels also manage evidence well. When you see the bed turned down when you return to the room after dinner, you begin to understand why you are paying the high room rates. It is the hotel's way of saying, 'Even while you were out of your room we didn't stop working to make you happy'.

12.2.1.2 Tangibles

Although we have said that services are intangible, effective services marketers do a fine job of managing the things that are tangible. There is a simple but critical reason for this: when you can't really see what it is that you are buying, you look for clues, or what psychologists call cues. If you don't really understand aeroplanes, airlines or flying, then tangible things become important. The appearance of the check-in counter, the appearance of check-in staff and even the simple airline ticket start to give you some information about what you might experience. The flight crew wear uniforms, although there is no good reason for this: this is an airline, not a military airforce! What it does, however, is convey a sense of security: here are important-looking people who certainly look as if you could trust them to do a good job of flying an aeroplane safely! The appearance of the aeroplane and its condition inside are also important. If it is shabby, untidy and perhaps even a little dirty, you might begin to wonder about crucial things such as how well they maintain the engines and train the flight crew.

Quite simply, in the absence of other clear information about the core service itself, customers of service firms place great emphasis on the tangible things they can see. Tangibles such as buildings, equipment, the appearance of people and of printed items such as brochures and business cards assume an importance they do not have in manufacturing firms.

12.2.1.3 Sampling

It is very difficult to sample a service. With products, for instance, the best way to convince people to purchase wine is to let them sample some. If they like it, they may buy a case, or at least a bottle. Wine estates realise this and provide tastings as a major element of promotional strategy. Similarly, car dealers arrange demo drives, and bookstores have their wares on display for customers to browse through before making a choice. This is far more difficult with services, because they are intangible. How do you sample a hospital's service without actually undergoing surgery, or an airline without actually flying on it? However creative services marketers do find innovative ways for customers to sample their services. Hotels invite secretaries for lunch, or have conference organisers to stay at a nice venue over a quiet weekend. Airlines arrange complimentary flights for travel agents or other important travel decision makers. Finding a clever way for customers to sample services presents a challenge, but a worthwhile one.

12.2.1.4 Memories

Because services are intangible, the customer frequently relies on the testimony of others (word of mouth) to a greater extent than in the case of products. In addition, whereas in the case of a product the customer actually has something to show for it, with services there is usually just a memory. Smart services marketers realise that these memories can be managed to their advantage — to increase word of mouth, first, and, second, to bring past customers back by reminding them just how good the service was.

If you want to observe good memory management in action, watch some of the better colleges and universities dealing with their alumni. Recent students who have had a successful period of study provide fertile word of mouth recommendations to future students. Those who graduated many years before are regularly solicited for financial support and also as parents of prospective students.

12.2.2 Simultaneity

Let us consider a product for a moment. Imagine drinking a can of soft drink. It was produced and canned in a factory somewhere, then stored, transported somewhere else, stored again, then arrived in the store or restaurant where you purchased it, and now you are going to consume it. The point is: production and consumption do not occur at the same time. Now, in the case of a service this is not the same. If you want your teeth fixed, you have to go to the dentist, and while the dentist is producing the service, you are consuming it. The dentist has to be there, and so do you, for the service to be produced and consumed. In this case, the production of the service and the consumption thereof are simultaneous. You did not have to be present when the soft drink manufacturer produced the can of beverage, nor did the manufacturer have to be there when you drank it. In the case of services this condition is generally true: producer and consumer both have to be present. This is probably the most exciting characteristic of services, for astute services marketers exploit it to create unique services or unique automation of services, to extract huge value from the market, and to innovate service concepts and service processes that capture whole new markets. Again, just as in the case of intangibility, to get the most out of simultaneity there are a number of issues which have to be managed. Some of the issues which can be managed are customisation, customer participation, innovation, service industrialisation, and the 'theatre' of service provision.

12.2.2.1 Customisation

Because services are produced and consumed simultaneously, the provider can customise the service. If this is done well, it can lead to giving the customer what he or she wants to a far greater extent than is the case with most products. A simple example of this occurring in a service is a hairdresser, who, while performing essentially the same work for each customer, customises each performance by styling suitably, according to what the customer wants. Thus there is in services the opportunity to create something unique for each customer. Where this can be managed, where it is appropriate and where the customer is willing to pay for this to the extent that it not only covers costs but creates superior margins, service customisation is worth pursuing. However, it might not always be worth while or necessary.

12.2.2.2 Managing the customer as a part-time employee

We distinguished above between products and services by saying that in the case of a can of soft drink the customer did not need to be there when it was produced, and the producer did not need to be there when it was consumed, yet in the case of a dental service, both parties had to be there. We can take these situations a little further. Most consumers of soft drinks have probably never been inside a canning plant, and would not wish to. The idea lacks interest value. Equally, it is unlikely that the soft drink factory would welcome a visit by a group of consumers. If a group of customers did want to visit, production staff in the factory would probably find them a nuisance!

Services are different. In order to get them the customer generally has to come into the factory, or the service provider has to take the factory to them. Furthermore, once inside the factory the customer has to do a bit of work, or even a substantial amount of work. If you use the services of an accountant to have your income tax return completed for you, you need to keep records, invoices and accounts, sign forms, file returns and so forth. If as a client you failed to do this, your accountant would probably tell you that he or she would not be able to give you the best service you need to minimise your tax liability. So, not only does the customer come inside a service factory and do some work, in many cases the quality of the service is almost as dependent on the customer as it is on the service provider. The customer can therefore be seen as a coproducer in service firms, and is in a substantial sense a 'part-time employee'.

Now, if the customer is a 'part-time employee' in a service firm, the firm will need to manage its customers if they are to receive the quality of service they demand and require. Without going into too much detail, this would make most of the things we know about managing employees equally relevant to the management of customers in a service business. Firms should think carefully about *recruiting screening and selecting* customers; customers might need to be *trained* in some ways; customers need to be *motivated* in order to achieve what the firm wants them to receive; customers certainly need to be *organised;* and, of course, customers need to be *controlled.* Even *firing* certain customers might be necessary if the firm is to achieve its broader objectives and act in the interests of the majority of profitable, paying customers.

12.2.2.3 *Innovation as part of customer participation*

If we understand that in service settings the customer is a necessary co-producer and participant in the service creation process, then we can think of many possible service innovations. If customers are willing to do some work, we can create enjoyable environments for them to do it in, and we can also devise service efficiencies that lead to significant cost reductions. A good example of getting the customer to do some work is the fast-food restaurant chain Taco Bell. Whereas in most fast-food restaurants a service person gets the soft drink from a machine for a customer, in Taco Bell customers serve themselves with soft drinks. After paying for the drink, the customer receives a paper cup, and fills it. Benefits to the restaurant are obvious: the chain works with one less crew member per shift, and as it has over 3 000 outlets, the savings in wages are considerable. However, the customer has to be motivated to do this work, so what is the reward? As many free refills as you want. Of course, Taco Bell knows that the average customer can manage only one container of a gassy cola drink, and so this reward goes largely unclaimed.

At a more advanced level of getting the customer to do some work and thereby creating an innovative service concept, an example is a chain of steakhouse restaurants in Australia in which customers cook their own steaks. You enter, go to the bar and order drinks. Then you go to a salad bar to help yourself to salad and baked potatoes. Next you proceed to a display of the finest prime beef steaks and select a steak, after which you move on to a large grill. Then, accompanied by a large group of other keen steak grillers, you grill your own steak. You retire to your table to eat and drink. The benefits to the customer come exclusively from participating in the production process: it is fun, entertaining and congenial. The benefits to the restaurant are considerable, the most fundamental of which include a very low kitchen and serving staff requirement, and a very small kitchen, with more space for productive dining. Even more important, though, are the benefits that come from allowing customers themselves to manage the quality of what they receive. As a result there are very few complaints.

12.2.2.4 Service industrialisation

A page or two back we referred to the fact that unlike goods producers, service firms have to put up with the customer coming inside the factory. However, this is not always true, and we could say that a fundamental dilemma facing services marketers is to decide on the extent to which they want the customer to come inside the factory or not.

Some years ago, Ted Levitt, in a wonderful article called 'The industrialisation of service', argued that service firms would be more successful not if they provided more service, but if they provided less of it. They should, he said, industrialise themselves and become more like mass producers of goods than benevolent panderers to the whims of individuals. Rather than try to solve the problems which arise in service firms, they should try to eliminate them; rather than try to fix the system, change the system. In doing so they would be giving customers what they really want: not more service, but less service! A few simple examples can be used to illustrate Levitt's point:

- Consider how you would have telephoned New York twenty years ago. After waking to speak with an operator, who would then get the number for you and call you back, you would be connected through an exchange. Today, you dial directly. Which do you prefer?
- Twenty years ago, if you had wanted to withdraw cash from your bank account, you would have waited for the bank to

open and then stood in line until a teller was able to assist you. Nowadays you use an autoteller machine, on any day of the week and whenever it suits you. Which do you prefer?

There are many other similar examples. This seems to support Levitt's arguments: don't solve the problem, eliminate the problem; don't fix the system, change the system. Customers don't want more service, they want less. In both of the examples the problem for the customers was waiting — for an operator or a teller. Solving the problem or fixing the system and giving the customer more service would have involved employing more people as operators and tellers. Eliminating the problem or changing the system and giving the customer less service, not more, actually gave customers what they wanted.

The problem with Levitt's view if it is taken to the extreme is that the world may end up being a very bleak place, where people interact only with machines or faceless screens! Services marketers should think carefully about industrialisation, and manage it where they can. They should also conceive of their service operations as being either a factory . . . or a theatre.

12.2.2.5 *The service business as a factory or a theatre*

Along the lines of Schmenner (1986), we can think of most service businesses along two key dimensions. The first is the extent of customisation. As we have already pointed out, customisation of services is made possible by the fact that they all tend to be produced and consumed simultaneously. What this means is that the service provider is able to customise the service: rather than produce a standard haircut, the hairdresser is able to produce one just for that customer; a little longer in front perhaps, more off the sides, square at the back. The second is whether the various activities are visible to the customer ('front office'), or invisible ('back office'). Thus, in a conventional hospital, for example, there are activities which are front office (nursing, admissions, food service and so on) and those which are back office (food preparation, the operating theatre, because the patient does not see the operation if it is under general anaesthetic).

If we construct a grid along these two dimensions we are able to classify the activities which occur in any service firm into four categories.

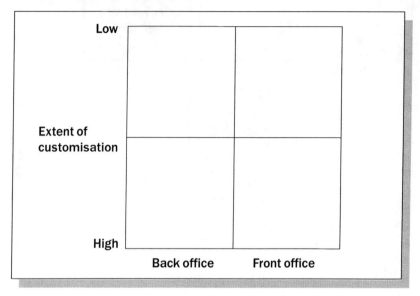

What is the point of this? Well, first, it is useful to speculate in which of the four quadrants most problems occur in service firms. The answer is actually easy: top right, or in the front office, where customisation is low. This is because the service firm is not doing anything special for anyone, but all of these activities are visible to the customer. For example, in a restaurant, the most common problems are issues such as poor table service, waiting for a table and reception, wrong orders and wrong accounts. Now, what is the problem with the highly customised back office? The problem here is that the service firm might be doing something which requires a high degree of skill, but no one sees this being performed. Thus a skilled chef might be preparing a creative meal for the individual, but no one sees this happening. The situations are best summarised by the following diagram.

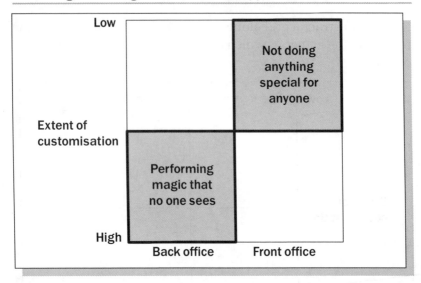

One solution to these two issues therefore seems to be to concentrate on the diagonal *away* from these two cells; that is, either to shift all the front office activities where customisation is low to the left, or down; and to shift the back office activities where customisation is high to the right, or up, as this next diagram shows.

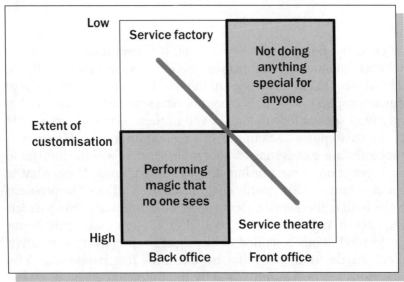

In the restaurant example, front office activities with low customisation can be shifted to the back office. There will then be no reception, no table service, and customers will pay a cashier at a cash register on ordering. Or they can be highly customised. Customers can be met personally, by name, table service is by a dedicated waiter or waitress, and the bill is presented, handwritten, in a leather-bound folder. Similarly, back office activities that are highly customised can be shifted to low customisation. The chef will no longer cook meals for individual diners, but merely prepare a limited selection of meals with little opportunity for the customer to have more of this and less of that. Alternatively, these activities can be shifted to the front office, taking much of the drama of a kitchen into the dining room to entertain the customers. It really is exciting to watch a good chef prepare a flambéed steak, or crêpes suzettes.

The point of this analysis is that service firms can look for opportunities along the diagonal, and that there is room in the market for both kinds of firms. Of course, they end up being very different kinds of firms. The kind of firm where activities tend to be concentrated in the back office, with low customisation, is characterised by low costs, mass production, efficiency, in fact all of the things that make one think of a factory, which is why this type of firm is called a service factory. In the restaurant business, McDonald's fits this category very well. There is no table service, payment is up front, patrons seat themselves, and limited menus are mass-prepared. The firm where most of the activities are front office and highly customised evokes thoughts of being something special or out of the ordinary, somewhere a customer would go to be entertained as much as to purchase the core service, which is why it is also called a service theatre. Indeed, all the metaphors of a theatre are appropriate in this situation, with props rather than equipment, costumes rather than uniforms, sets and decor rather than premises, and so forth.

Again, most service firms can be analysed along these lines, and surprising opportunities emerge when this is done. Banking can either be theatre or factory (personalised banking versus autotellers), so can hospitals (the Mayo Clinic, with its highly skilled experts, versus the Shouldice Hospital in Toronto, which performs only inguinal hernia surgery on a factory line basis). So can business schools (the small, taught programmes at a school such as the Graduate School of Business at the University of Cape Town, versus the very large distance education and learning programmes of the Open University in the UK, or Unisa in South Africa).

12.2.3 Heterogeneity

If you look carefully at most products, such as cans of cola drink, you will notice their sameness; each can is exactly the same as each other can, and would also taste the same. This is known as homogeneity, and is not achieved by accident. Rather, producers set up manufacturing lines in such a way that they produce homogeneous products. Furthermore, good producers have procedures in place to test products as they come off the line to ensure that defective products do not actually reach the market. This is known as quality control.

Because services are intangible, and are produced and consumed simultaneously by people, it means that one cannot set up production lines to deliver an identical service each time. Nor can one control the quality. By the time the customer has received the poor service, it is already too late. Thus, services have the characteristic of heterogeneity; in other words, they vary in output. This creates a number of marketing challenges for the services marketer. Once more, there are a few things which the services marketer can manage in order to overcome the problems caused by service heterogeneity.

12.2.3.1 Standardisation

Some services marketers are reluctant to standardise service activities because they feel that this tends to mechanise an interaction between individuals. In some circumstances this is true, but this does not mean that managers should not look for opportunities to produce service activities in as uniform a way as possible. Many people are cynical about the sincerity of the greeting, thanks and farewell that one receives in a McDonald's restaurant. However, by standardising something as simple as this the company at least has ensured that everyone is greeted, thanked and bade farewell. They have succeeded in eliminating much of the unpredictability that customers face in so many other similar restaurant settings: surliness or complete indifference, or, alternatively, service which is gushingly insincere. The real skills of a services marketer become apparent in the ability to decide what should be standardised and what should not.

12.2.3.2 Variability

Along with standardisation, shrewd services marketers overcome the problems of heterogeneity by managing variability, and even by reducing it. The use of machines is one way of achieving it. Another is by giving service personnel as little discretion as possible, and no room to make mistakes. Alternatively, by empowering service personnel to correct problems on the spot, problems caused by service variability can be remedied immediately.

12.2.3.3 Service quality

Quality is more difficult to control with services because of heterogeneity. Thus service quality needs to be carefully managed (Zeithaml, Parasuraman & Berry, 1990). In order for it to be managed it needs to be measured. In the last ten years, tremendous progress has been made in the measurement of service quality. The development of the Gaps model of service quality, and the use of an instrument called SERVQUAL, has contributed significantly to this. Similarly, the procedures available within the Gaps approach to service quality measurement and management make it possible for services marketers not only to measure their shortfalls in service quality, but also to examine the barriers within the firm that obstruct their efforts to deliver better service.

12.2.4 Perishability

Because products are produced before they are consumed, they can be stored until needed. Services cannot, for they are produced and consumed simultaneously. This gives them the characteristic of perishability: services cannot be inventorised. If there are twenty empty seats on an aeroplane, the airline cannot say, 'Don't worry, stick them in the store. We'll certainly be able to sell them over the Easter weekend'. They are lost forever. The same is true for many other kinds of service firms. Hotels and hospitals have rooms and beds that perish; car rental companies have unrented vehicles that perish; consulting firms have consultants' time that dies the moment it is not used; insurance companies have idle financial capacity. This is not to say that some products do not perish too. Produce such as fish, meat, vegetables and fruit do deteriorate. However, sophisticated technology enables prolonged storage periods.

It does not take a gifted marketer to fill a resort hotel in Cape Town in the summer holidays, just as it does not take a lot of talent to fill a ski resort in the Swiss Alps in March. Services marketing really becomes skilled when it can put backs on beds in Cape Town hotels in July and August, or hikers on Swiss ski slopes in July and August, or tourists in downtown business hotels and in the driving seats of rental cars on quiet weekends. To understand and minimise the effects of service perishability, astute services marketers manage two things: supply and demand.

12.2.4.1 Supply

Managing supply in a service setting requires organising all those factors of service production which affect the customer's ability to acquire and use the service. Thus, it includes attention to such things as opening and closing hours, staffing, and decisions as to how many customers will be enabled to use the service at any particular time. Opening hours can be extended in peak season, or shortened in the off-season, or facilities can be closed altogether. Additional part-time staff can be employed in peak season, or permanent staff can work longer hours. Staff with multiple skills can be employed in order for them to do different types of work depending on the season, or staff can be required only to take vacations when demand for the service is at its lowest. Service firms have developed sophisticated yield management systems, which enable them to forecast demand more accurately. Airlines frequenily follow a practice of overbooking on certain flights as a result of their careful study of so-called no show patterns. Thus, while there may be 400 seats on a particular flight, the airline overbooks it by 80 seats, or 20%, based on the system's experience that around 20% of passengers with reserved seats do not turn up for that flight. On days when everyone does arrive, the airline begins to trade in its own seats, and offers to buy back seats at a given price, with an additional promise of accommodation and a guaranteed seat on the next flight. When this does not work either, airlines may point to the fine print in the ticket contract, and eventually inform some passengers that despite having a valid ticket, they are just not going to make that flight home this evening. This is why it is wise to try to be first in line when you really want to fly, and why there is good reason for that hour or two before check-in on international flights!

A final way to manage supply is to get the customer to take control of it, or to 'own' it. Certain service firms in recent years have been very successful at this. They sell customers the service for years in advance so that if customers then do not use it, it is their problem and not the service firm's. Health clubs sell life memberships, video rental ouilets sell annual memberships, restaurants sell ten meals in advance at discounted prices, and resorts sell time-sharing holiday accommodation. In effect, the service firm is passing ownership of the service inventory on to the customer. If customers choose not to exercise their rights of ownership by exercising regularly, watching a video every night, eating all the meals or visiting the resort each year, that is their problem and not the service provider's. In many cases the service provider can still sell the service. Visitors can use a gymnasium' s idle exercise equipment, casual renters can view videos and casual diners can eat in restaurants. Most time-share resorts still require 'owners' to confirm they will use their accommodation at the time they 'own' well ahead of time. This means that if they do not use it, it can be 'resold'.

12.2.4.2 *Demand*

Services marketers also cope with service perishability by managing demand. This means they use aspects of the services marketing mix, such as promotions, pricing and service bundling, to stimulate or dampen demand for the service. Demand for the service in the off-season can be stimulated by emphasising the attractiveness of other features. For example, Cape tourism promotion some years ago emphasised the attractions of visiting the Cape in the 'green season', between June and September. Of course, the reason the Cape is green during that period is that it is quite liable to rain most of the time. Similarly, ski resorts may promote the attractions of hiking in the mountains and enjoying the scenery.

Alternatively, pricing strategy can encourage demand in off-peak periods. Business restaurants offer low-price, all-inclusive lunches over weekends, car rental companies offer lower weekend rates, and resort hotels offer special deals during the week. Airlines and telephone companies have become particularly astute at pricing services by understanding who is sensitive to price and who is not, as discussed in our chapter on pricing strategy. Most service businesses are characterised by a high fixed cost component as a proportion of the total cost structure, so in many situations even low prices for those last few seats or rooms is preferable. Getting 20 or 30% of list price is still better than nothing when the service would perish anyway. Pricing can also be used to discourage the use of a service at certain times. Plumbers, electricians and certain medical practitioners have weekend charge-out rates which discourage people from interfering with their private time.

Finally, some services marketers make good use of service bundling, putting together inclusive packages of services in a way that allows value to the customer to far exceed what the customer would have spent purchasing each component of the bundle individually. For example, Air New Zealand offers a 'mystery weekend' on its internal flights, where the mystery is one's destination. The airline, of course, is aware of your destination: anywhere there are empty seats available. Your accommodation is also part of the mystery to you, but rest assured it will be a good hotel. Downtown business hotels in the destination town offer the rooms they usually have difficulty selling over a weekend. You will not know where you will dine, but it will be a fine restaurant: again, a downtown restaurant normally frequented by business people during the week. And, of course you don't know what rental car you're going to drive . . . . The possibilities for service bundling in this situation are almost endless. The attraction to the customer is a top-class combination of travel opportunities with the excitement of a little mystery, at very good prices. The advantage to the service providers involved in putting together this bundle is that they are selling capacity that would otherwise have stood idle.

12.3 SERVICES ARE NOT DIFFERENT!

So far we have taken the view that services are different from products because they possess the four characteristics of intangibility, simultaneity, heterogeneity and perishability. By discussing these characteristics and how they can be managed, we have identified a number of ways of dealing with the problems that these cause, as well as exploiting the opportunities they offer. However, an alternative perspective on services which may be useful to both services and goods marketers alike is that products and services are not different. After all, customers do not really purchase products and services: they buy want satisfaction or needs satisfaction, solutions to problems, performances and experiences. So many of the things on which we spend our money have both a product and a service component that it is often difficult to distinguish where one ends and the other begins. We now take the view that products and services are not different, and that all purchasing and consumption really occur along a spectrum of tangibility, ranging from very tangible at one extreme, to very intangible at the other.

An astute services marketing expert called Lynne Shostack gave us a powerful tool for examining the spectrum of tangibility back in 1977. Her thinking is shown in Figure 12.1 on the next page. We can place any product or service on this spectrum, as is shown with the five basic categories in the diagram. At the extreme left side we find relatively pure products. These products are almost entirely tangible, with virtually no service attached to them. Many of the products we buy in supermarkets fit this category: cans of beans, frozen peas, cartons of milk, prepacked beef steak (in a styrofoam tray, shrink-wrapped in plastic, which is the example we will use). There is very little service attached to this type of product. A producer has delivered them to a supermarket, and that is about all. At the other end of the spectrum, we find the most intangible products: services which have almost nothing tangible about them. No special buildings, no identifiable equipment or vehicles, no special way of dress for the providers, no business cards, brochures, letterheads or information packs. Nowadays, surprisingly, very few services fit this category. A good example is baby sitting. He or she wears no uniform, and we don't see the service being performed.

In the middle of the spectrum is that 50/50 mix of product and service, the hybrid. This category contains almost equal amounts of tangibility and intangibility. The best examples are restaurants, especially fast-food restaurants. What you receive is tangible: a burger, or a pizza, in a box, with some drinks in a can or paper cup. However, there has been some service as well. The restaurant has prepared the food for you, given you a choice, served it to you perhaps, or at least have cleared up after you, and maybe even delivered it to your door. This represents a 50/50 mix of product and service.

Figure 12.1: Shostack's spectrum

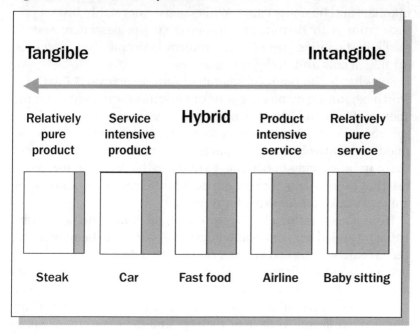

Between the relatively pure product and the hybrid on the spectrum we find the service-intensive product. This is a purchase which is essentially tangible (the customer takes something tangible away from the purchase encounter), but to which a number of services are attached. The most simple example of this is a car. The customer buys something physical: an engine, wheels, seats, steering wheel, doors and so forth, but also a considerable amount of service as well: finance, warranty, repairs, maintenance insurance, membership of the AA, etc. Similarly, between the relatively pure service and the hybrid on the spectrum, we find the product-intensive service. Most common services today tend to be product-intensive. While what the customer buys is an intangible effort, experience or performance, this is accompanied by many tangibles. Banks look like banks for a reason, airline pilots dress in military style uniforms for a reason, car rental companies generally have clean new cars, and most service providers have professionally designed brochures, letterheads, manuals and business cards. While a customer really buys a passage from A to B from an airline, what the passenger sees is check-in facilities, people in uniforms, aircraft, seats, meals, drinks, tickets and in-flight magazines.

So, what is the point of this rather simple analysis? First, it is worth beginning by placing your organisation somewhere on the spectrum. Second, there is merit in considering an increasingly common phenomenon: a movement from the ends towards the middle. Relatively pure products and relatively pure services seem to be striving to become hybrids. Why? Because firms realise that there is much to be gained by differentiation and adding value. Let us consider this for a moment.

How does a relatively pure product, such as a steak, acquire value by added service? Some might say that it can be marinated, the fat can be trimmed off, or a sauce added. Not bad ideas, but to become a hybrid from this side of the spectrum we have to add *service.* How do you add service to a piece of steak? One can print nutritional information or provide recipes and cooking instructions. What if you went over the top, and delivered the steak to the door? Some butchers still do this. In fact, one of the fastest-growing forms of distribution of fresh beef today is home delivery. There is a firm in the USA called Omaha Steak that does prime US beef steak by mail order. You call up, place your order on the telephone, and the choicest cuts of beef arrive on your doorstep the next day. Not by mail of course, but by an express courier such as Federal Express. Of course, this is steak of a superior quality, and that is precisely the point. Omaha Steak doesn't compete against supermarkets, and has profit margins that reflect this. Similarly, in the UK, one can order smoked Scottish salmon in much the same way. In South Africa, the Wine of the Month Club delivers wine to one's door in a little van shaped like a wine vat. it is exactly the same wine that you could buy in a liquor store or a supermarket. Or is it? It comes packaged specially for you, and is the result of a tasting by people who really know wine and have selected the best just for you. It comes accompanied by their tasting notes, comments from the wine maker, and recipes and suggestions for meals to complement the wine. It is no longer a product, but a hybrid.

Similarly, a relatively pure service such as babysitting can be turned into a hybrid by making it more tangible, that is, by adding tangibles. While it might be a good idea for the babysitter to do the housework while one is out, this would be just service bundling, similar to adding sauce to the steak. It would be preferable to add tangible things, so that the babysitter can differentiate himself or herself from all the other teenagers. Nowadays smart babysitters come dressed for the role, as clowns or nurses, and bring interesting toys, videos, games, food or bags of goodies. Many parents are prepared to pay a little more for a babysitter who is more appealing to their children.

So, there is value to be gained by moving towards the middle of the spectrum. However there is also strategic perspective to be gained in considering moving towards the outside. What would a fast-food restaurant look like if, in addition to being a hybrid, it moved towards becoming a relatively pure product? It could use the brand equity generated by being in the restaurant business to sell products on supermarket shelves. Customers would recognise the restaurant brand and purchase it for home consumption.

Similarly, if we take a typical product-intensive service, such as a hotel, we can explore movement in both directions along the spectrum. If a conventional hotel was moving in the direction of the relatively pure product, it would take most aspects of service out of the operation and become much more of a tangible product. No reception, no porters, no bars, no restaurants, no room service, in fact, as little of the human touch as possible. What kind of hotel would we have? Probably something like the Formule 1 concept which was created in France, spread through much of Western Europe and is now also well established in South Africa. Not the most delightful, warm accommodation in the world, but functional, and very inexpensive. However, by moving in the other direction on the spectrum, a hotel takes out all the physical trappings of a conventional establishment and concentrates on service. Signs come down, rooms no longer all look identical, no one wears a uniform, menus disappear from the dining room, and guests are greeted by name. What kind of hotel is this? A guest house. And why is it attractive? Because it is just like home. Both segments of the hotel market, the hotel as product (Formule 1) and the hotel as relatively pure service (the guest house) have grown in recent years, which supports our argument that it is worth considering movement along the spectrum to explore strategic opportunities for all businesses, whether one is in products or in services.

12.4 CONCLUSION

In this chapter we have taken two opposing views on services from a marketing perspective. One is that because they possess the unique characteristics of intangibility, simultaneity, heterogeneity and perishability they are different from products. The other is that there is no real difference between services and products, because customers do not buy services or products: they buy needs satisfaction Any offering of a firm can be placed along a fundamental spectrum of tangibility, and the astute manager is always alert to the opportunities to be provided by movement along this spectrum in either direction. So which view is right? As the question of services difference is ambiguous, we could say it deserves two ambiguous answers, both of which have their merits. Each of these views offers useful strategic insights, not only to services marketers, but to goods marketers as well.

References

Levitt, Theodore. 1976. The industrialization of service. *Harvard Business Review*, September–October: 63–74.

Schmenner, Richard W. 1986. How can service business survive and prosper? *Sloan Management Review*, 3(2): 1–32.

Shostack, G Lynn. 1977. Breaking free from product marketing. *Journal of Marketing*, April: 73–80.

Zeithaml, V, Parasuraman, A & Berry, LL. 1990. *Delivering Quality Service: Balancing Customer Perceptions and Expectations*. New York, NY: Free Press.

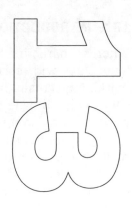

Introduction

The effects of the Internet on communication with and between stakeholders

The Integrated Internet Stakeholder Communication Matrix (I²SCM)

Case examples

13

Broadening the management of relationships[1]

---

[1] Based on De Bussy, NM, Watson, RT, Pitt, LF & Ewing, MT. 2000. Stakeholder communication management on the Internet: An Integrated matrix for the Identification of opportunities. *Journal of Communication Management*, 5(2): 138–146.

13.1 INTRODUCTION

Whereas marketing has been defined as the management of relationships with customers, many observers have argued that marketing actually has to do with the management of relationships with a broader range of parties. Marketing to a firm's employees, for example, is referred to as 'internal marketing'. Supply chain management contends that firms need to manage relationships with their suppliers and distributors. Other stakeholders, such as government and the public, are also seen as critical to the attainment of overall corporate and marketing objectives. This is a daunting task. However, technology may be coming to the aid of marketers, in the form of the Internet. In this chapter, we look at a simple model of stakeholder management – online.

At the heart of managing relationships is communication, for it is through communication with stakeholders that the organisation shapes and forms it relationships with them. Organisations inform customers of new products and prices, remind them of their existing offerings, and attempt to favourably influence their perceptions using various communication tools. Similarly, organisations communicate with various other stakeholders, such as employees, government, suppliers, intermediaries and investors, in their attempts to manage these relationships for mutual benefit. Until recently, the nature of this communication has tended to be:

- unidirectional (i.e. the organisation generally communicates to, rather than with a stakeholder); and

- simple – the organisation is at the centre of the communication structure and communicates to stakeholders at the periphery, with little communication between stakeholder groups.

The Internet is changing the nature of an organisation's communication with its stakeholders in ways that are unprecedented. Stakeholder communication will no longer be unidirectional, and as stakeholders increasingly communicate with one another (either about or not about the organisation), this communication becomes infinitely more complex. Marketing becomes more than managing communication with stakeholders – it evolves to become the management of communication between stakeholders too. Unfortunately, many of the tools and models of marketing were developed and refined in a pre-Internet world, and are of little assistance in dealing with stakeholder communication that is increasingly complex and multi-directional. We address these issues in this chapter.

First, we expand on the effects of the Internet on communication with and between stakeholders. Then, we introduce an Integrated Internet Stakeholder Communication Matrix (I^2SCM), and explain its use in identifying issues that need to be managed with regard to the Internet and marketing. We illustrate the use of the matrix through a number of cases of organisations using the Internet to successfully manage stakeholder communication. We conclude by speculating on how these issues may evolve, and how organisations will need to change their management of the marketing function to deal with this evolution.

13.2 THE EFFECTS OF THE INTERNET ON COMMUNICATION WITH AND BETWEEN STAKEHOLDERS

The rapid growth and adoption of the Internet, and the World Wide Web in particular, has constituted not only a fundamental change in the nature of business, most markedly by killing physical distance (Cairncross, 1997), but also because it has revolutionised the way in which firms communicate with their stakeholders. Organisations are increasingly using the Internet to market products and services to customers, transact with suppliers and intermediaries, communicate with employees, deal with government and inform investors. In a very short period, the Internet has emerged as an all-purpose communication medium for interacting with stakeholders. Organisations now need to be concerned with how they manage their corporate image (a net effect of the communication between its publics) in cyberspace (Quelch & Klein, 1996). As organisations stampede to the Internet, they find that there is no systematic way to examine communication opportunities and relate them to both available Internet tools and stakeholder communication behaviour. What is absent is an integrated approach to managing communication with and between stakeholders in the era of the Internet.

These issues are perhaps best conceptualised in Figure 13.1.

Figure 13.1: How stakeholder communication has evolved on the Internet

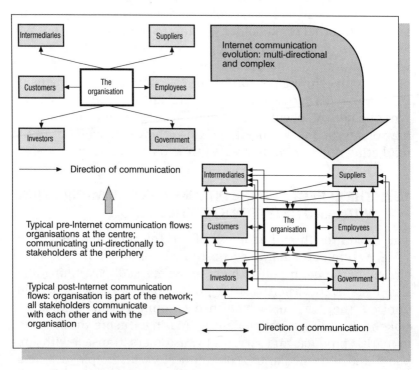

Hoffman & Novak (1996) examine the effects of computer-mediated communication between the organisation and its customers (although the implications will be similar for other stakeholders). They argue that the real effects of inter-stakeholder communication on the Internet will be that, rather than the organisation communicating *to* the stakeholder, it will now communicate *with* stakeholders. This has been referred to as interactivity (Blattberg & Deighton, 1991), and rather than resembling 'shouting', the communication between the organisation and its stakeholders is now similar to a conversation. Rather than this communication being *relatively simple*, it now occurs in a *complex network*, with stakeholders able to use the Internet to communicate with one another as well as, and even independently of, the organisation. This may take place with the knowledge, approval and support of the organisation, or it may not. Either way, it can, and inevitably will, occur. Customers can talk not only with a firm but also among themselves. They can also communicate other stakeholders, such as employees, government, suppliers, intermediaries and investors. Similarly, all the other stakeholders can communicate with the organisation, with each other, and among themselves. For example, a government department can communicate with a firm, with the firm's customers or suppliers, and with another government department about the firm or its industry. Similarly, a firm's suppliers can talk with the firm, amongst each other, or directly with the firm's intermediaries. The fundamental principle of this new network communication is that it can and will occur, regardless of the organisation's approval. Therefore, it is better for the organisation to take cognisance of this and manage it.

13.3 THE INTEGRATED INTERNET STAKEHOLDER COMMUNICATION MATRIX (I²SCM)

The I²SCM is illustrated in Figure 13.2. It is constructed by identifying the major stakeholders an organisation and mapping all the possible communication links between them. For the sake of completeness, the matrix includes the organisation itself. In Figure 13.2, we have included customers, suppliers, investors, intermediaries, government and employees as stakeholders, although individual managers may identify others as relevant and wish to include these – for example, a local community, educational institutions, pressure groups, and the like. This is not problematic, for the matrix can be expanded. It also becomes immediately obvious that additional stakeholders can and will use the Internet for communication with the firm, with each other and with the already-incorporated stakeholders in the I^2SCM. However, for purpose of brevity, we suffice with the stakeholders identified in Figure 13.2.

The I^2SCM can be used by organisations to search systematically for opportunities to use the Internet to support marketing strategies. The concept is that each cell of the matrix is a focal point for brainstorming. An interactive version of the matrix, constructed by and for an organisation's managers, can be used to stimulate thinking by highlighting how other organisations use a particular cell. Thus, clicking on the cell at the intersection of Employees (the talkers) and Customers (the talked to), for example, could jump to a page containing links to situations where an organisation's employees use the Internet to communicate (either favourably or unfavourably) with that organisation's customers. Similarly, clicking on the cell at the intersection of Investors (the talkers) and Investors (the talked to) could jump to a page containing links that the marketing department has collected of situations where potential investors in a firm use the Internet to communicate (either favourably or unfavourably) with other potential investors. The idea is that, by studying and thinking carefully about these links, managers should be able to identify and either exploit or manage similar situations within their own organisation and among its stakeholders.

We often learn by modelling the behaviour of others, or what Bandura (1977) has termed vicarious learning. Linking I^2SCM cells to existing Web examples should assist managers to identify opportunities for their organisation. By identifying and studying case studies of the situations in other organisations, managers will be able to ask and hopefully answer the question: How might this work in our stakeholder environment? This would lead to other strategic questions, such as: How can we influence the situation, become part of it, and manage it to mutual benefit – or at least minimise the threat it poses? Furthermore, by providing a variety of examples for each cell, creative behaviour should

Figure 13.2: The Integrated Internet Stakeholder Communication Matrix (I^{2}SCM)

Talks to →: Talker ↓:	Organisation	Customers	Suppliers	Employees	Inter-mediaries	Government	Investors
Organisation			Caterpillar				
Customers		Third Voice		Ford servicing		Passenger-rights.com	
Suppliers			GE				
Employees		Untied		Intranets			
Inter-mediaries							
Government							
Investors							

be aroused, because each example can be a different stimulus (Watson, Pitt & Zinkhan, 2000). In the following section, we present case examples of stakeholders, including the organisation, using the Internet to communicate with one another. Ideally, the organisation should strive to find appropriate examples in all relevant stakeholder-exchange cells in the I^2SCM; those we provide are not meant to be exhaustive, merely illustrative. Furthermore, in the interests of brevity, we do not give examples for each of the cells in Figure 13.2. To help the reader track the examples, we have entered each one into the appropriate cell in Figure 13.2.

13.4 CASE EXAMPLES

An organisation talking to its suppliers: Caterpillar (www.caterpilar. com)

Caterpillar made its first attempt at serious on-line purchasing on 24 June 1997, when it invited pre-approved suppliers to bid on a $2.4 million order for hydraulic fittings – simple plastic parts that cost less than a dollar but can bring a $2 million dollar bulldozer to a standstill when they go wrong. Twenty-three suppliers elected to make bids in an on-line process on Caterpillar's website (Woolley, 1998). The first bids came in high, but by lunchtime, only nine were still revising offers. By the time the session closed at the end of the day, the lowest bid was 22 cents. The previous price paid on the component by Caterpillar had been 30cents. Caterpillar now attains an average savings of 6% through its website supplier bidding system.

Customers talking to customers: Third Voice (www.thirdvoice.com)

Software from Third Voice allows consumers to post comments – in the form of virtual sticky notes – on any web site. It thus empowers users to hold online public discussions and weave their opinions with existing content. Posting comments with Third Voice is in no way hacking, since they are stored elsewhere and visible only to browsers with the Third Voice software. The consequence of this innovation is that individuals can comment on the mass advertising and publicity afforded by a company's web site. For example, a claim on a company's web site of a maximum 1-hour turnaround of consumers' queries can be publicly questioned or confirmed by users who have experienced the service. Such software will empower customers to an unprecedented degree. Suddenly the once-private communications of disaffected customers will be broadcast in public to many consumers. The once-asymmetrical dialogue between company and customer is set to change – in the customer's favour. Companies will be forced to become more circumspect about their advertising and public relations claims, and more proactive in the handling of consumer feedback.

Customers talking to employees: Ford Servicing

An innovative Ford dealer has installed live video cameras in its service bays, and relays a live feed to its web site. In this way, customers are able to 'visit' the service centre and check on the progress of their car's service. By opening up the service centre for continuous customer inspection, the dealer is not only making the quality of its service evident, it is also enabling customers to talk with employees while the job is being done (Watson, Berthon, Pitt & Zinkhan, 1999: 111).

Customers talking to government: Passenger Rights
(www.passengerrights.com)

Travellers who experience problems with airlines, hotels, car rental companies or tour operators can now research and exert their rights via the web site www.passengerrights.com. This site enables consumers to research their rights online, concerning a range of travel issues, such as ticket refunds, airline overbooking, insurance claims, and lost or damaged luggage. Consumers are guided through a comprehensive complaining process if they wish to make a complaint. They are also advised to whom they should complain, and passengerrights.com forwards the complaint electronically on their behalf. Passengers can use the site to communicate with government; as a formality, the site assists by copying every complaint to the US Department of

Transportation. The service also enables follow-up, so that if no response is received, the consumer can complain again. The site also summarises complaints by type and by industry, offers travel secrets, offers subscription to a newsletter, and gives prizes for the best travel horror stories. The site also encourages word-of-mouth communication among travel consumers.

Suppliers talking to suppliers: General Electric (www.GE.com)

General Electric (GE) was one of the first major companies to exploit the web's potential, purchasing to the amount of $1 billion over the net as far back as 1996 (Pitt, Berthon & Berthon, 1999). The company encourages suppliers to link their web pages on the GE web site, so that they can 'see' each other, and more importantly, talk to one another. Whereas there is some danger of collusion by suppliers, GE believes that it is ultimately in the firm's interest if suppliers communicate, hopefully solving some of GE's problems, and identifying mutually beneficial opportunities.

Employees talking to customers: Untied (www.untied.com)

A site set up by disgruntled United Airlines passenger, Jeremy R Cooperstock, called, not unsurprisingly, Untied.com, has been described as 'the place that allows frustrated former United Airlines passengers a chance to speak out'. The site includes hundreds of passenger complaints, and there is a complaints form for irate passengers to fill out that automatically puts the complaint on the web site and copies it to United's director of customer relations and president. The site keeps a daily tally of complaints submitted (many) and responses received from United (very few). There is also a summary of employee lawsuits against the airline and links to any stories in the general media that show United in a less than favourable light. Many disgruntled United employees use the site to talk anonymously with one another, but, more importantly, with the firm's customers. Some merely sound off about the company, but others take the opportunity to explain things to customers, giving useful tips on how to deal more effectively with the giant airline.

Employees talking to employees: Intranets

Many companies are now using internal Internets, or 'intranets' to facilitate communication among employees. Cisco is the world's largest manufacturer and distributor of routers and switches. In order to achieve this position, it has adopted an aggressive growth strategy, acquiring companies, their employees, and new employees at a rate of 250 to 300 employees per month. Obviously, it is important that new employees are able to communicate not only with one another but also with those who have had longer tenure with the firm. The Cisco Employee Connection (CEC), a corporate intranet, is the primary means by which new employees are absorbed and acculturated. The CEC is also the principal means of interaction for the multi-functional work team approach Cisco employs.

Similarly, Nortel Networks, a Canadian firm that employs over 70 000 people worldwide, uses an intranet as an 'agent of disruption', to push critical information to individual desktops and to build feedback loops (Raffoni, 2000). The intranet uses chat rooms to discuss topics, and the forum enables employees in different business units and business functions to engage in a free exchange of ideas and issues. The chats are then used to create newspaper articles. Nortel's public relations department used to print a monthly newsletter for the company, but now these are published only periodically and focus on a particular topic, as the company relies on the intranet for employee communication.

13.5 CONCLUSION

As communications are increasingly conducted electronically, an organistion's web sites (both external and internal) will be its defining image and focus of interaction with its stakeholders. Consequently, organisations must ensure that they take full advantage of the technology available to maximise their impact. A systematic approach, using the I^2SCM and modelling the behaviour of others through cases, provides a framework for designing and implementing effective web sites that take full advantage of Internet tools. Integrated use of this technology, however, is not enough. An enterprise with a jumble of page layouts and icons communicates disorganisation. The collective image of the web site must communicate the overall integration and message of the organisation, as an aggregation of the communication with and among its stakeholders. A firm's web presence must be cohesive in order to communicate a consistent message to stakeholders.

The I^2SCM may be a precursor of a new form of publication. If advertising and public relations are succumbing to the problems of traditional media, maybe the same fate awaits paper journals. The reason for this is that we cannot adequately represent some ideas in a purely print medium. The concepts of integrated communication apply to all forms of communication, not just that between communicator and audience. Viewing the I^2SCM as an electronic publication will enable the organisation to communicate in an integrative way with its stakeholders, and enable opportunities to be identified.

References

Bandura, A. 1977. *Social Learning Theory*, Englewood Cliffs, NJ: Prentice-Hall.

Berthon, PR, Pitt, LF & Watson, RT. 1996. Marketing communication and the World Wide Web. *Business Horizons*, 39, 5 (September-October): 24–32.

Blattberg, RC & Deighton, J. 1991. Interactive marketing: Exploring the age of addressability. *Sloan Management Review*, Fall: 5–14.

Cairncross, F. 1997. *The Death of Distance*, Boston, MA: Harvard Business School Press.

Ellsworth, JH & Ellsworth, MV. 1995. *Marketing on the Internet: Multimedia Strategies for the World Wide Web*, New York, NY: John Wiley and Sons.

Hoffman, DL & Novak, TP. 1996. Marketing in computer mediated environments: Conceptual foundations. *Journal of Marketing*, 60 (July): 50–68.

Pitt, LF, Berthon, PR & Berthon, JP. 1999. Changing channels: The impact of the Internet on distribution strategy. *Business Horizons*, 42, 2 (March–April): 19–28.

Pitt, LF, Berthon, PR & Watson, RT. 1996. Conversion and efficiency on the World Wide Web: What marketing managers might want to know. *Journal of General Management*, 22, 1 (Autumn): 1–13.

Quelch, JA & Klein, LR. 1996. The Internet and international marketing. *Sloan Management Review*, 37 (Spring): 60–75.

Raffoni, M. 2000. Managing your virtual company: Create a communication plan. *Harvard Management Communication Letter*, Reprint no. C0004d: 3–4.

Watson, RT, Berthon, PR, Pitt, LF & Zinkhan, CM. 1999. *Electronic Commerce: The Strategic Perspective*, Fort Worth, TX: The Dryden Press.

Watson, RT, Pitt, LF & Zinkhan, G. 2000. Integrated Internet marketing. *Communications of the ACM*, June, (in print)

Woolley, S. 1998. Industrial buyers are getting more out of on-line comparison shopping than consumers are. Why? *Forbes*, 9 March: 32.

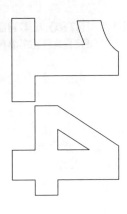

14

Marketing and the Internet[1]

Introduction

Convergence, disruptive technologies and killer apps

Five new forces

Something happened in the music business

---

[1] Based on Pitt, LF. 2001. Total E-clipse: Five New Forces for Strategy in the Digital Age. *Journal of General Management*, 26, 4 (Summer): 1–15.

14.1 INTRODUCTION: TOTAL ECLIPSES, TRADITIONAL STRATEGY AND KILLER APPLICATIONS

An eclipse of the sun takes place when the moon comes between Earth and the sun, so that the moon's shadow sweeps over the face of the Earth. To an observer within the umbra or total shadow, the sun's disk appears completely covered by the disk of the moon. This is known as a total eclipse. In ancient and medieval times, eclipses of both the sun and the moon were often regarded as portents; hence, it is not surprising that many of these events are mentioned in history and in literature, as well as in astronomical writings. It is almost as if, 'when the lights come back on', the world is a changed place, which needs to be seen through new eyes, and for which new tools are appropriate.

Disruptive technologies have similar effects to total eclipses. They come between our comfortable worlds and us, and as their shadows sweep overhead, the landscape beneath them changes. Our old models for dealing with our environments are then less useful, and don't point the way as they used to. Disruptive technologies have always had this effect. However, until recently, disruptive technologies had the decency to appear at reasonable intervals, so that we had time to adjust to them. Now they emerge in a licentious manner, and not only disrupt (as their name suggests) but interrupt, as they cut short our thinking on how to cope with one by presenting us with another.

A leading influence on strategic thinking throughout the 1980s and 1990s was Harvard Business School strategy professor, Michael Porter. Practitioners, academics and consultants alike have used his 'Five Forces' model to evaluate industry attractiveness and strategic positioning. Porter's model (Porter, 1998; 1980) is orderly and structured – in fact, very applicable to the 1980s, which was a far less fragmented era than the late 1990s and into the new millennium. It explains neatly why some industries are more attractive than others in a way that at least gave managers confidence in their judgment, even if it didn't make them feel better about being in a dead-loss market.

Similarly, the forces were about business and management issues – customers and suppliers, barriers to entry and substitute products, and firm-to-firm competition. Small wonder then that practitioners, consultants and academics adopted the model, for it gave reasonable predictability in a reasonably predictable world.

The traditional view of strategy in organisations has been that it is possible to understand the environment in which the organisation functions, and to plan for the firm's future accordingly. This view might be acceptable when the environment changes slowly and the future is reasonably predictable. However, some observers have noted that the environment is changing so swiftly that it is impossible to plan strategically (Downes & Mui, 1998). Indeed, the effect has been similar to that of a total eclipse – warm, comfortable light suddenly disappears, and the world that reappears just a short time later seems different. We might refer to the changes currently occurring in the business environment as a total e-clipse. The changes that occur rapidly are not so much in the political or legal, economic, or social and cultural environments – rather, they emerge as the result of phenomenal changes in technology and the effects these have on society.

Many of the existing models used by firms, applied by consultants and taught by business schools are less useful because they were developed in and for a time of less turbulent change. Readily following Porter, I suggest there are five new forces for strategy in the digital age that managers may find constructive in attempting to cope with the challenges of disruptive technologies. Unfortunately, these new forces and their implications are not as neatly assembled as Porter's. However, by asking what each force will do to his or her firm and industry, or indeed to him or her, the manager may at least anticipate the shifts prompted by these forces. We will also look at a newsworthy case example of how these forces disembowel one of the world's most profitable industries. This should prompt managers to anticipate when disruptive technologies will do similar things in their own markets.

14.2 CONVERGENCE, DISRUPTIVE TECHNOLOGIES AND KILLER APPS

Most of us have used television sets, telephones and computers as separate and distinct devices. The television set is a box on which to watch news, entertainment and sport in the comfort of our living rooms, while the telephone is a device used to call friends, family or business associates. The computer has been a device on which to do word processing and spreadsheets, send emails, play games and make overhead slides. In recent times, these three technologies have converged. Digital television enables interaction and communication, cellular telephones have become devices for being entertained and informed, and the computer is as easily able to perform the function of a television set as it communicates with other computers.

The rate at which technological change occurs over time is prominent. During the Middle Ages, for example, significant innovations appeared at a very slow rate – sometimes as infrequently as 200 or 300 years apart. During the time of the Renaissance, new technologies materialised slightly more rapidly – for example the invention of movable type by Gutenberg in the fifteenth century. During the Industrial Revolution, inventions began to emerge far more frequently, at the rate of one every 10 or 15 years. Entering the twentieth century, we see innovations surface every five or ten years, until we get to the 1980s, and they arrive at least annually. Indeed, towards the end of 1999, CNN featured on its web site (www.cnn.com) a poll asking viewers to vote on the 'Top 10 new technologies of 1999'!

These innovations are not simple enhancements of the 'new and improved' variety – rather they have become known as 'killer applications'. A killer application or 'killer app' (Downes & Mui, 1998) is not merely an innovation that improves the way something is done. It is not even something that changes a market or an industry. Rather, it is something that changes the way society works and functions. The motorcar was a 'killer app' because it didn't just simply replace horse-drawn carriages, or transform the way people travelled – it changed the way we live, shop, work, and spend our leisure time. It also altered the appearance of the physical environment in most countries.

Over the past 10 to 15 years, we have seen killer applications arise at a rate of more than one a year, and this frequency is increasing exponentially due to 'spreading' technologies such as the Internet. Consequently, strategy that attempts to plan five years ahead is befuddled by the fact that society and the way the world works may change at the rate of one, two or even more killer applications a year. The more traditional strategic planning models, such as Porter's, are less effective at dealing with the kind of strategic planning problems that killer applications and rapid or disruptive technological changes cause.

14.3 FIVE NEW FORCES

We need to develop a perspective on the new forces that impact on strategy and the way organisations deal with the future. One possibility is that, in the spirit of Porter's model, we consider five new forces that will affect the way the business and management environment works. The effect of these forces on individuals and organisations is illustrated in Figure 14.1.

Figure 14.1: The Five Forces

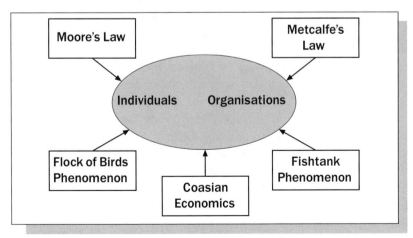

14.3.1 Moore's Law

In 1965, Gordon Moore, an engineer at Fairchild Semiconductor, noted that the number of transistors on a computer chip doubled every 18 to 24 months. A corollary to 'Moore's Law' (as the observation became known) is that the speed of microprocessors, at a constant cost, also doubles every 18 to 24 months. Moore's Law has upheld for more than 30 years. It worked in 1969, when Moore's start-up, Intel Corporation, put its first processor chip – the 4-bit, 104-KHz 4004 – into a Japanese calculator. Moreover, it still works today for Intel's 32-bit, 1000-MHz Pentium III processor, which has 15 million transistors and is 466 000 times faster than the 2 300-transistor 4004. Intel says it will have a 1-billion-transistor powerhouse performing at 100 000 MIPS in 2011.

For users ranging from vast organisations to children playing computer games, Moore's Law has been experienced as a fast, fun and mostly free ride. But can it last? Although observers have been saying for decades that exponential gains in chip performance would slow in a few years, experts today generally agree that Moore's Law will continue to govern the industry for at least another 15 years.

The implications of Moore's Law are that computing power becomes ever faster, ever cheaper. This not only means that just about everyone can have affordable access to powerful computing, but that the power of computers can be built into other devices. Moore's Law also drives convergence by placing computer chips into objects that previously had nothing to do with them. For example, today there is more processing power in the average cellular telephone or digital television set than NASA had access to when Neil Armstrong landed on the moon in 1969. Computers are used in products as diverse as vehicles, surgical equipment and elevators, enabling these machines to operate efficiently, predictably and safely. In the not too distant future, we can expect to see computer chips in disposable products, such as packaging, as the costs continue to decline. They become ubiquitous; they are everywhere, but we don't consciously think of them or notice them.

The primary question that Moore's Law should prompt in strategic planners is: What will our industry or market be like when computers or chips are literally everywhere – in every product we make or part of every service we deliver? Some managers may think this is irrelevant, simply because it may be difficult for them to imagine a computer or chip in their product or service. Yet there are countless products or services being delivered today that have computers as an integral part, that the same reasoning would have been applied to just ten years ago: hotel doors with chips that facilitate card access, and record entry and exit; cellular telephones; and digital television.

14.3.2 Metcalfe's Law

How useful is a piece of technology? The answer depends on how many other users of the technology there are and on how easily they can be interconnected. For example, the first organisation with a facsimile machine had no one to fax to, and no one to receive faxes from! One telephone is useless; a few telephones have limited value. Many millions of telephones create a vast network. These effects are known as Metcalfe's Law. Robert Metcalfe, founder of Novell, 3COM Corporation, and the designer of the robust Ethernet protocol for computer networks, observed that new technologies are valuable only if many people use them. Roughly, the usefulness or utility of the network equals the square of the number of users – the function known as Metcalfe's Law.

The more people who use software, a network, a particular standard, a game, or a book, the more valuable it becomes and the more new users it will attract, increasing both its utility and speed of adoption by still more users. The Internet is perhaps the best illustration of Metcalfe's Law. Whereas it began in the 1960s, it is only in recent years that it has gained momentum; as more users joined the medium, it became more useful to even more users, thus accelerating its growth. Now its potential to spread new ideas, products and services is remarkable. Other good examples of Metcalfe's Law in recent years have been cellular telephones and the Palm digital assistant. In the case of the latter, most early adopters recommended the product to friends and colleagues, and the Palm succeeded not because of a large advertising budget but because of word-of-mouth. The early adopters insisted that others buy the product not only because it was good, but also because it increased the size of their network, which made their own Palms more useful. One of the key factors in this success was the Palm's ability to 'beam' to other Palms via a built-in infrared device.

Networks are important because they create short cuts. Anyone who is part of a network can contact anyone else who is part of it, bypassing traditional channels and structures. This is important for planners, who should consider what the effects of technology will be that enables their customers to talk to each other, suppliers to talk to each other, and customers to talk directly with suppliers, wherever they may be in the world. According to Metcalfe's Law, as networks grow, their utility increases; this is true for those who are part of the network and for those who choose to join it.

14.3.3 Coasian Economics

Nobel Prize winner in economics, Ronald Coase, made a discovery about market behaviour that he published in a 1937 article 'The nature of the firm' (Coase, 1937). Coase introduced the notion of 'transaction costs' – a set of inefficiencies in the market that add or should be added to the price of a good or service in order to measure the performance of the market relative to the non-market behaviour in firms. They include the costs of searching, contracting and enforcing. Transaction cost economics gives us a way of explaining which activities a firm will choose to perform within its hierarchy, and which it will rely on the market to perform for it. One important application of transaction cost economics has been as a useful way to explain outsourcing decisions – for example, whether the firm should do its own cleaning, catering or security, or pay someone else to do this.

The effect of communication technology on the size of firms in the past has been to make them larger. Communication technologies allow transaction costs to be lowered to the extent that firms can subsume many activities within themselves, and are thus able to operate as larger entities even across continents. This has enabled multi-nationals such as General Motors, Sony and Unilever to operate as global enterprises. Communication technology such as telephones, facsimile machines and telex machines enabled these operators to communicate as easily between Detroit and Sydney as between Detroit and Chicago. Smaller firms found this more difficult and expensive. Large firms brought more activities within the firm (or the 'hierarchy' in transaction cost terms), for it was cheaper to do this than to rely on the market.

What strategic planners overlook at their peril in the age of the Internet, is that these same communication capabilities are now in the hands of individuals, who can pass messages worldwide at as low a cost as the biggest players. The effect of the new communication technologies, accelerated by Moore's Law and Metcalfe's Law, will be to reduce the costs of the hierarchy – and of the market itself. As the market becomes more efficient, the size of firms might be considerably reduced. More pertinently, as the costs of communication in the market approach zero, so does the size of a firm, which can now rely on the market for most of the activities and functions that need to be performed. This is a very thorny strategic issue indeed!

Coasian economics prompts many strategic questions in the age of the Internet. However, what should top the agendas of many strategic planners is what functions the Internet will permit them to outsource. Allied to this is the matter of responding to competitors who do not carry the burden of infrastructure normally borne by traditional firms, having relied on technology to effectively place these in the market.

14.3.4 *The Flock of Birds Phenomenon*

A feature of the new communication technologies has been that, in many cases, they do not 'belong' to any one institution or are controlled by any particular authority. The Internet is a case in point. This has been referred to as the 'Flock of Birds Phenomenon'. When one observes a flock of birds flying in formation, or fish schooling in a distinct pattern, one is tempted to speculate whether there could be a 'bird in charge' or a 'head fish'. Naturalists will explain that flocking is a natural phenomenon and that there are no 'head' fishes or birds. The network becomes the processor.

We have been conditioned to seek a controlling body or authority for most of the phenomena we experience, because that is how most modern societies have been organised. The response to the questions: 'Who is in charge?, Who controls this?' or 'Who owns it? is generally 'some large firm', 'the government', a government department or ruling institution. For many phenomena, such as the Internet and the World Wide Web, there is no one in charge. They are like giant flocks of birds or schools of fish. The response to questions such as Who owns them? or Who is in charge? is either 'we all do' or 'no one does'. These are great mechanisms for democracy, but their effects can also be anarchic. Society may have to develop new ways to deal with such liberating effects.

The effect of the Flock of Birds Phenomenon is that access is equalised, unlike what occurs in traditional media. In a very real sense, no one has a 'better right of access' and no one, not even the largest corporation, can shout louder. The smallest player, the individual, has a right and the opportunity to be seen and heard. Furthermore, many laws designed to regulate a physical world do not work as effectively when no one owns or controls the medium.

14.3.5 The Fish Tank Phenomenon

Moore's Law and Metcalfe's Law combine to give individuals inexpensive and easy access to new media such as the Internet. This means that anyone can set up a web site and, theoretically at least, be seen by the world. As a result, many have noticed the so-called Fish Tank Phenomenon. This phenomenon is named after the fact that, in the early days of web sites, people used to put a video camera on top of their tropical fish tank, so that when you logged-on to their site, this is what you saw. This added to the clutter on display; today there are thousands of futile, 'junk' sites that only do something silly – let the viewer build a cow, tickle Elvis Presley's tummy, cure their addiction to lip balm, or whatever. The question this prompts is: Would it be better if, instead of relying on individuals for their input on the Internet, we depended on the considerable resources of large institutions and corporations?

The answer to this question really lies in another: What is more profound? And the answer is that it is the creative inputs of millions of individuals, all over the world, who have the ability to show us what they can do. In other words, the creative outputs of millions of individuals will often beat the activities of large institutions. Every now and then, someone is going to produce something so revolutionary that it will change our world. For strategists, this means that many firms may find themselves threatened by small start-ups that were previously unable to access the market. It will no longer be good enough to merely observe close and known competitors, because in the future these competitors could be anyone and anywhere. They may be difficult to see before it is too late.

14.4 SOMETHING HAPPENED IN THE MUSIC BUSINESS: HOW THE FIVE FORCES WORK IN AN INDUSTRY

While technological changes have entered the recorded music industry over the years – in the form of improved recording techniques, hi-fidelity stereo, and the advent of the compact disk (CD) – essentially the industry has remained stable, with its structure largely unaffected by technological developments. Recording companies found and recorded talent and marketed it, and the products of the industry – essentially disks and cassette tapes – were distributed through record stores. Artists were re-munerated in the form of royalties, retailers in the form of margins, and the record companies kept the rest.

The fundamental distribution issue of assortment (Stern & El-Ansary, 1988) was, and in many ways still is, perhaps the most significant dilemma in the market for recorded music. The structure of the industry and the way the product was produced held an inherent problem for both the retailer and the consumer. The retailer's predicament is that of inventory – the need to hold very large stocks of records, in order to provide a selection to customers, and to make available to the customer the one that they will choose, when they want it. This means that a lot of capital is tied up in stock, much of which moves slowly, and often needs to be discounted to meet working capital requirements. The consumer is also in a quandary: Will the particular retailer stock the one album they are looking for? And, will they be able to find it among the thousands of other items? Once found, the consumer's problems aren't over. There may be 12 songs on the record, whereas the consumer may only really want three or four.

In early 1998, the application of technology created an online firm that seemed to answer all these quandaries. Music Maker (www.musicmaker.com) was a web site that allowed customers anywhere to create their own CDs by sorting through vast lists of recordings by various artists of every genre (Pitt, Berthon & Berthon, 1999). The website charged per song, and then allowed the customer to personalise the CD by designing, colouring and labelling it. The company then pressed the CD and delivered it to the customer by mail. Rather than compile a collection of music for the average customer, like a traditional recording company, or attempting to carry an acceptable inventory, like a conventional record store, Music Maker let customers do the sorting themselves. If a customer wanted Beethoven's Fifth and Guns 'n Roses on the same CD, they could have it.

In the latter half of 1998, however, the ground shifted again in the music business – MP3 arrived on the Web. MP3 is short for Moving Picture Experts Group Audio Layer III or 'MPEG3', and is a compression format that shrinks audio files with only a small sacrifice in sound quality. MP3 files can be compressed at different rates, but the more they are scrunched, the worse the sound quality. A standard MP3 compression is at a 10:1 ratio, and yields a file that is about 4 MB for a three-minute track. MP3 started life in the mid-1980s at the Fraunhofer Institut in Erlangen, Germany, which began work on a high quality, low bit-rate audio coding with the help of Dieter Seitzer, a professor at the University of Erlangen. In 1989, the Fraunhofer Institut was granted a patent for MP3 in Germany, and a few years later it was submitted to the International Standards Organization (ISO).

In 1997, a developer at Advanced Multimedia Products created the AMP MP3 Playback Engine (essentially a piece of software that plays MP3 recordings), which is regarded as the first serious MP3 player. Shortly after the AMP engine was made available on the Internet, two university students, Justin Frankel and Dmitry Boldyrev, took it, added a Windows interface and dubbed it 'Winamp'. In 1998, when Winamp was offered as a free music player, the MP3 craze began. Music enthusiasts all over the world started MP3 hubs, offering copyrighted music for free. Before long, other programmers also began to create an entire toolset for MP3 enthusiasts. Search engines made it even easier to find the specific MP3 files people wanted, and portable Walkman-size players like the Rio let them take MP3 tracks on the road after first downloading them to a computer hard drive and then transferring them across. MP3.com, a web site for down- and uploading MP3 content, became one of the most heavily trafficked sites on the Internet. Music Maker began to look a little ancient, only a few months after its inception.

The recording industry did not stand still and attempted to block technologies such as MP3 and Rio players in any way possible, including litigation and threats to sue for copyright infringement. These efforts met with mixed success.

Then came Napster. Napster is the application that has received more media attention than any other MP3-related software. In 1999, when Napster became available on the Internet, it allowed anyone with a connection to find and download just about any type of popular music they wanted, in minutes. By connecting users to other users' hard drives, Napster created a virtual community of music enthusiasts that has grown at an astonishing pace. Developed by a 20-year old student, Sean

Fanning, Napster boasted some 20 million members worldwide by the end of 2000 (*see* www.napster.com).

The Recording Industry Association of America (RIAA) has made extensive legal and political efforts to close Napster. It sued Napster, charging it with copyright law violations, and on 26 July 2000, won a decision in a US District Court that, in effect, ordered Napster shut down. However, the next day, a Court of Appeals halted the order and ruled that Napster could stay in business until completing its trial. In the meantime, Napster entered into a strategic alliance with giant German publishing firm Bertelsmann, which would see it distributing Bertelsmann's content for a fee through the Napster system.

As with many of the events in the short history of music on the Internet, Napster developments moved so rapidly that the ideas and technology behind it might not matter by the time the legal issues are resolved. Even if Napster is forced to shut down, MP3 has found many other ways to survive and thrive. The reason MP3 took off and became the audio standard on the Web is that the original patent holders made it freely available for anyone to develop a decoder or player for it. MP3 innovators worldwide have hacked around and developed players and other software that spreads fast and easily.

Among the popular file-trading applications are Gnutella and Freenet. Gnutella is a program that allows the user to share all types of files. What makes Gnutella special is that is it not centralised, meaning that no single computer is responsible for keeping the network up. This means that, unlike Napster, Gnutella doesn't have to hook up to a central server to communicate with other people running the client and share files. Both the client and server are in the same file execution mode, and a user is free to connect to any of the users running Gnutella. This method also provides for faster file transfers.

While the RIAA has been concentrating its efforts on web sites such as MP3.com and Napster, it appears that developments such as Gnutella have left it entirely flat-footed. Commenting on the RIAA's attempts to block Napster, Charles Nesson, professor at the Berkman Center for Internet and Society, Harvard Law

School, had this to say of Gnutella: 'The only way for the music industry to stop Gnutella is to turn off the Internet.' He added: 'There is a generation of young people out there who have already learnt that music is something you get on the Net, rather than buy.'

The case presented above illustrates the effect that the five new forces can have on an industry and a market very appropriately. These impacts are summarised in Table 14.1.

Table 14.1: The Five Forces and the music industry

New force	Its effect on the music industry
Moore's Law	Almost everyone can afford a relatively powerful computer, and use it as a device for recording and playing recorded sound. The cost of storage media has declined exponentially; multi-gigabyte hard drives that would have exceeded the storage capacity of entire countries just a few years ago are now so inexpensive that individuals can use them to store complete music collections.
Metcalfe's Law	Users no longer need to rely on centralised distribution or central servers for their music – the Internet is a huge network of distributed power, which connects anyone to anyone else in a very short time. Napster's 20 million users are a case in point; the fact that Gnutella does not rely on a central server amplifies the situation.
Coasian Economics	Hierarchies such as large music companies and their distribution networks are no longer able to achieve the lowest transaction costs in the record industry. The low costs of communication and distribution have made the market more efficient, and millions of individuals benefit as a result.
The Flock of Birds Phenomenon	The exchange and distribution of recorded music has become very difficult to legislate and control. While it might be possible for the RIAA to take action against Napster, it is unlikely that it can have the same results against millions of individuals worldwide. In addition, just because it may succeed in one country (e.g. the USA) does not mean it will succeed in another with a different legal system. Technologies like Gnutella make this even more unlikely and complex. As Professor Berkman says: '... to do so would mean switching off the Internet'. Since no one owns it or controls it, that is impossible.
The Fish Tank Phenomenon	While there is a lot of junk placed on the Internet by individuals, there are also an incredible number of good ideas developed by individuals that can come to the fore through this medium. A firm's next serious competitor might not be a multinational conglomerate, but an individual operating from home. This individual now has a unique mechanism for bringing good ideas to market.

14.5 CONCLUSION

In the future, firms may still need to consider five forces, but they will be a very different set of forces. There will be the technological effects of Moore's and Metcalfe's laws, hyper-accelerating change and spreading it like a virus. There will be the contradictory effects of transaction cost economics – not only making firms smaller, but virtual too. There will be the societal effects of the Flock of Birds Phenomenon bringing undreamt of democracy along with the threat of anarchy; and the Fish Tank Phenomenon bringing access to all.

Michael Porter argues that his Five Forces determine the attractiveness of an industry, which in turn influences the profitability of firms within that industry (Porter, 1980). The five new forces of the information age are more ethereal, and impact on firms and industries in ways that are far less predictable or structured. To use the new five forces astutely, the decision maker must depend on them not so much as guidelines and prescriptions, but as prods from behind to keep challenging oneself, one's firm and one's market.

The technological forces of Moore's Law and Metcalfe's Law accelerate change not only within a firm, but also within industries and markets, and this acceleration tends to be exponential. The decision maker must consider what will happen when computer chips are not just in computers, but also in every device and product, and what will happen when these computers, like all computers, become part of an exponentially growing network.

Transaction cost economics, and technology's effects on the efficiency of firms and markets, means that the manager must constantly reflect on what will happen to the shape and size of the firm. The decision maker must continually evaluate what activities the technology will enable in the market, and what functions may be brought back within the firm. In channels of distribution, managers will have to observe the constant tussle between disintermediation and reintermediation. In the former, many traditional intermediaries will disappear from channels as their roles are either usurped by technologies or performed more efficiently by other channel members. The Internet is having a profound effect on institutions such as travel agents and financial brokers, and the long-term impact of MP3 on conventional record stores is obviously of great concern to those institutions. In example after example of reintermediation, we are seeing new intermediaries enter channels using technology to improve its efficiency, while taking a share of the margins available in the channel for themselves. Online consolidators, such as Priceline.com in the travel industry and Autobytel.com in the channel for new and used cars, are prime examples of this.

The social forces of the Flock of Birds Phenomenon and the Fish Tank Phenomenon will require managers to work in a new environment, where control and governance are not as structured or as clear as they have been before. Managing in a world where significant issues are not really within the control of a government or a government department, or under the remit of a large organisation, will be a new and often scary experience for most managers. Not knowing where competition may come from, because it may not be up-front and visible, will also require a constant revisiting of strategy. When competition comes head on, or at least from the side or from behind, it can be seen and dealt with, even if slowly. When potential competition comes from a computer in the bedroom of a 17-year-old in another country, life becomes less predictable.

Many managers may take cold comfort from identifying the five new forces and what they will do to the business environment. They are not neat and structured, like Porter's Five Forces, nor do they seem to suggest much in terms of strategic direction, as do popular analysis tools such as the Boston Consulting Group grid. However, much of the recent writing on strategy emphasises the effects of these forces, and suggests that conventional approaches to strategy will at least be insufficient, if not ineffective, for coping with corporate survival. Many of these authors offer perspectives that are worth considering (Downes & Mui, 1998; Kelly, 1998; Shapiro & Varian, 1998; Schwartz, 1999). Whereas there is no absolute concurrence on their advice for strategy in the future, these authors do tend to agree on certain fundamentals.

In closing, it is worth summarising some of the basics. First, change is too rapid for anyone anywhere to feel comfortable; success has an anaesthetising effect that becomes its own enemy. Second, it may be a good idea to continually seek ways of destroying one's own firm's value chain and putting oneself out of business. If one doesn't, someone else will. Third, resources are less about tangible assets and more about knowledge and the ability to constantly innovate. Fourth, firms should constantly find and exploit ways to give the customer the opportunity to do as much of the work as possible. Technology offers great opportunities in this regard. Strangely, customers don't want more service, they want less. They want the control and the power to solve their own problems, and victory will go to those players who find ways for them to do this well (Berthon, Pitt, Katsikeas & Berthon, 1999). Finally, strategy is no longer long-term, as the half-life of ideas diminishes. The five-year plan or the long-term strategy is no longer viable, and the value of the annual strategic planning session should be questioned. Strategy becomes incremental rather than planned. It is revisited and revised not annually or even bi-annually, but monthly, probably weekly, and possibly daily. This is not to say that strategy should be eliminated. Rather, managers should consider that the strategy needed for the twenty-first century might be a new baby, born of five new forces in an age of convergence.

References

Berthon, PR., Pitt, LF, Katsikeas, C & Berthon, J-P. 1999. Virtual services go international: International services in the marketspace. *Journal of International Marketing*, 7, 3: 84–105.

Coase, RH. 1937. The nature of the firm. *Economica*, 4: 386–405.

Downes, L. & Mui, C. 1998. *Unleashing the Killer App*, Boston MA: Harvard Business School Press.

Kelly, K. 1998. *New Rules for the New Economy: 10 Radical Strategies for a Connected World*, London, UK: Fourth Estate.

Pitt, LF, Berthon, PR & Berthon, JP. 1999. Changing channels: The impact of the Internet on distribution strategy. *Business Horizons*, 42, 2 (March–April): 19–28.

Porter, ME. 1980. *Competitive Strategy: Techniques for Analyzing Industries and Competitors*. New York, NY: Free Press.

Porter, ME. 1998. *Competitive Advantage: Creating and Sustaining Superior Performance*, New York, NY: Free Press.

Schwartz, E. (Marino, L. (ed)) 1999. *Digital Darwinism: Seven Breakthrough Business Strategies for Surviving in the Cutthroat Web Economy*, New York, NY: Broadway Books.

Shapiro, C & Varian, HR. 1998. *Information Rules: A Strategic Guide to the Network Economy*, Boston MA: Harvard Business School Press.

Stern, L & El-Ansary, A. 1988. *Marketing Channels*, 3rd ed. Englewood Cliffs, NJ: Prentice-Hall.

The accidental superhighway. 1995. *The Economist*, 1 July, special supplement.

Introduction

What is planning?

**Different business plans —
marketing and the corporate
planning process**

**Writing the marketing plan —
getting down to it**

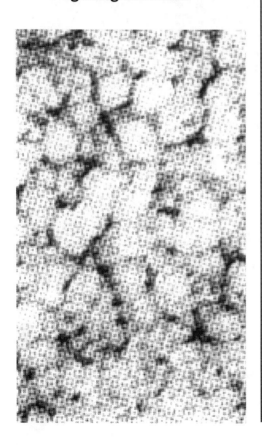

15

**A practical guide to
writing the marketing plan**

15.1 INTRODUCTION

Marketing executives are often required to develop marketing plans. The brief guide provided in this chapter is intended to serve as a modular approach to marketing planning for the marketing executive, regardless of level of academic expertise. Following the steps in the planning processes should result in useful, workable plans rather than clever ones.

15.2 WHAT IS PLANNING?

Planning is the process of using related fact and future assumptions to arrive at courses of action to be followed in seeking specific goals. Simply, planning is drawing from the past to help you decide in the present what you should do in the future.

Companies without plans tend to be like chickens with their heads chopped off. If one does not have a plan one cannot get anything done — because one does not know what needs to be done, or how to do it. Further, good plans can be adapted should circumstances change. Planning is also about learning the lessons that history teaches, which makes it as much about the past as the future. If you planned in the past and the plans went wrong and did not turn out as you had expected, at the very least you can learn from this. As Gabriel Garcia Marquez points out, 'Those who forget the lessons of the past are condemned to repeat them'.

15.3 DIFFERENT BUSINESS PLANS — MARKETING AND THE CORPORATE PLANNING PROCESS

All business plans have a heavy marketing input. Attention will be given here to two plans — the corporate (strategic or business) plan and the marketing plan (for the whole company, a division, a product line or an individual product).

15.3.1 The corporate plan

The corporate, business or strategic plan is an overall plan for a firm. It can be annual, intermediate or long-range. It deals with company missions; growth strategies; portfolio decisions; investment decisions; and current objectives and goals. It does not contain details on the activities of individual business units, but it does provide for the development of organisational structure as a logical outflow of strategy.

Figure 15.1: A simple model of corporate strategy

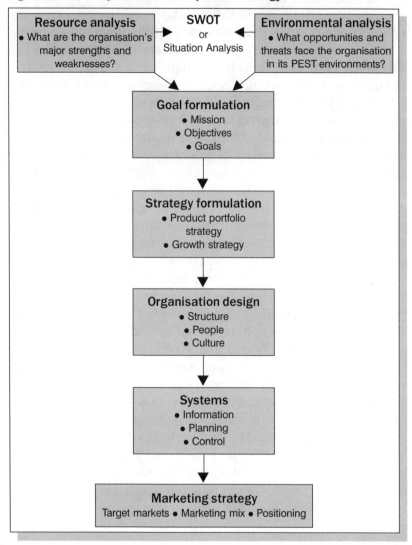

15.3.1.1 A model for the formulation of corporate strategy

The task of this guide is to develop a comprehensive, yet usable model for the formulation of corporate and marketing strategy. There are some requirements for such a model. Firstly, it should relate to decisions that affect the long-term competitive position and perhaps even the survival of the organisation. Secondly, it should relate to the routine, day-to-day operations necessary to carry out short-range programmes. Thirdly, it should be logical and easy to follow, and should stimulate obvious questions at each stage, almost in checklist fashion.

The process starts with a situation analysis, also known as a SWOT analysis. The organisation must analyse its resources to identify what its strengths and weaknesses are. At the same time the organisation must scan the environment in which it operates. This environment consists of political, legal, economic, socio-cultural and technological variables, which, although largely uncontrollable by the individual firm, will affect it in many ways. The environmental variables will mean opportunities for some firms and threats for others. It is important that the firm attempt to identify these and assess the impact they will have. The situation analysis (SWOT = strengths, weaknesses, opportunities, threats) will give the firm a clear picture of its current situation. The next step is to determine where the firm ought to go. This involves a process of goal formulation. The firm must formulate a mission statement or definition of its business; it must identify major objectives; and it must specify goals that it will strive to achieve.

Having defined where it is and where it wants to go, the organisation must formulate strategies that will enable it to get there. In the model above, strategy formulation is viewed as consisting of two phases. *Product portfolio strategy* involves asking the question, what products or major service lines does the organisation have now, and what will it do with them? This question focuses on the present situation. Answering the question moves it to the second phase: *growth strategy* requires that the organisation ask what it is going to do about new products and entering new markets.

Choosing a strategy requires that the organisation be designed in such a way as to be able to carry out this strategy. The organisation must have a structure, it must have people, and it must have a congruent culture if goal attainment through the chosen strategy is to be realised. If the strategic process is to be successful, it must be supported by three systems. Firstly, there must be a planning system, for the development of formal, disciplined plans. Secondly, there must be an information system which provides for a flow of relevant, timely information for decision making. Thirdly, there must be an adequate control system, which allows for the monitoring of plans, the measurement of results and the taking of corrective action.

This process of strategic market planning precedes the development of marketing strategy such as that outlined in the early chapters of this text. Stated broadly, marketing strategy consists of decisions in three areas.

- Target markets must be selected, which will be the focus of the organisation's marketing activities. This selection requires a process of market segmentation.
- The needs of the target markets chosen must be catered for by the development of a marketing mix for each of the target markets. The organisation needs to make decisions regarding the product or service, price, marketing communication and distribution, and how each of these four elements of the marketing mix will contribute toward the attainment of marketing goals.
- Finally, whether or not it is conscious of this, any organisation will be perceived as being something, or occupy some position in the market's mind. Far better that the organisation develop for itself a well-considered positioning strategy, in which how it wishes to be perceived is delineated, and meaningful points of difference between itself and its competitors are defined.

15.4 WRITING THE MARKETING PLAN — GETTING DOWN TO IT

Most marketing plans have the sections outlined in Table 15.1, and can be developed in the sequence presented in the Figure 15.2.

The sections shown in Table 15.1 are illustrated with a case study:

Smith's Chemicals is a small to medium-sized chemical company which produces and markets industrial anti-bacterial biocides. Major product lines are the responsibilities of product managers, who are required to plan for these lines so that Smith's financial objectives are attained.

Bill Jones is product manager of Smith's Tica-treat range. Tica-treat is a treatment for cooling water used on mines. The chemical on which the product is based is Trichloro Isocyanuric Acid (known as TICA). Smith's major goal for the product is to increase its market share and profitability in this market. As product manager, Bill is required to prepare a marketing plan for Tica-treat that will attain the established goals.

15.4.1 The executive summary

The written plan should begin with a short summary of the main thrusts, goals and recommendations to be found in the actual plan. This permits top management to gain rapid insight into the plan without first having to read the whole document. The summary should, of course, include a table of contents.

Here is Bill Jones's executive summary:

The 1998 marketing plan for the Tica-treat range aims at a marked increase in sales and profits over 1997. The profit target is R200 000 and the revenue objective is R2 000 000, an increase of 33.3% over 1997. I believe these increases to be feasible in terms of our improved pricing, more effective advertising, and the product improvements suggested. The required marketing budget will be R400 000, a 25% increase over last year.

15.4.2 The current marketing situation

The current marketing situation section requires a situational analysis that considers the current market situation, the product situation and the competitive situation, and various other variables.

15.4.2.1 The market situation

This section provides data on the current market situation. The size of and trends in the market in total and by segments are shown. Data on customer needs, perceptions and behaviour may be presented.

Table 15.1: Contents of the marketing plan

Section	What it is
I. Executive summary	An abbreviated summary of the main thrusts of the plan for management overview
II. Current marketing situation	Relevant background data on the market itself, the product, distribution, competition and the broader environment — 'What's happening?'
III. Opportunity and issue analysis	The strengths and weaknesses of the firm; the opportunities and threats facing it; the key issues that the plan must cope with
IV. Objectives	What the plan wants to reach, e.g. sales volume, market share, ROI
V. Marketing strategy	Who the target markets will be; what the blend of marketing mix elements (the 4 Ps) to reach them will be
VI. Action programmes	• What will be done? • Who will do it? • When will it be done? • How much will it cost
VII. Projected profit and loss statement	Summarises the potential financial payoff from the plan
Viii. Controls	How will the plan be supervised?

Figure 16: Contents of the marketing plan

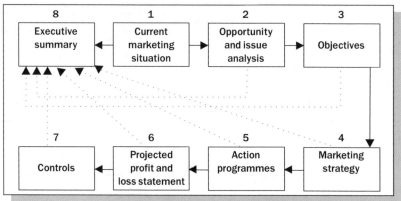

Bill Jones's plan reads in part:

The water treatment market is currently worth R20 000 000, has been relatively stable for some years, and is expected to remain so. Offshoot markets have tended to raise their heads, e g jacuzzi/spa treatments and factory water treatment.

15.4.2.2 The product situation

In this part of the plan, sales, prices, contribution margins and net profits are shown for several past years. The availability of computer spreadsheets such as Lotus 1-2-3 or Excel has greatly facilitated the manager's task in this regard. Not only is the preparation and display of topical data made that much easier, but projections, graphics and sensitivity analysis of future data can be achieved.

Bill Jones has used Excel to prepare his past product situation data. These figures are presented in the table below.

Table 15.2: Past product situation data — Tica-treat

		Rows	1996	1997	1998
1			5 000 000	8 000 000	10 000 000
2			0,05	0,1	0,1
3			1	1,4	1,5
4			0,8	0,9	1,0
5		(3–4)	0,2	0,5	0,5
6		(1×2)	250 000	800 000	1 000 000
7		(3×6)	250 000	1 120 000	150 000
8		(5×6)	5 000	400 000	500 000
9			30 000	40 000	50 000
10		(8–9)	20 000	360 000	450 000
11			40 000	80 000	100 000
12			20 000	80 000	100 000
13			30 000	80 000	100 000
14		(10–11–12–13)	−70 000	120 000	150 000

15.4.2.3 *The competitive situation*

Major competitors are identified and their postures in terms of size, product quality, market share and strategies described. Part of Bill Jones's plan was a market share analysis of major competitors for Tica-treat, which used the graph presented in Figure 15.3.

Figure 15.3: *Market share analysis: major competitors — Tica-treat*

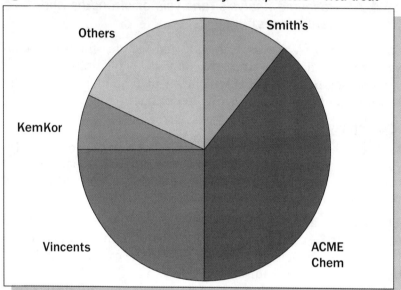

15.4.2.4 *The distribution situation*

This section presents data on the volume of products sold through each distribution channel, changes in the distribution situation, and the motivation of intermediaries. Bill Jones mentioned in his plan that 'mines exert considerable buying power due to their relative size and strong financial backing. For this reason distribution will require special attention.'

15.4.2.5 *The macroenvironment situation*

This section of the plan describes broad macroenvironmental trends which may have a bearing on the product — trends in the political, legal, economic, sociocultural and technological environments.

15.4.3 SWOT analysis

The analysis of the current marketing situation provides the basis of data for a SWOT analysis.

15.4.3.1 Resource analysis (analysis of strengths and weaknesses)

Strengths and weaknesses are internal factors which the manager should identify. Strengths may be capitalised on, while weaknesses point to areas which the plan should correct. The resource audit below allows one to do this.

a. Company resource analysis

Assess each of the following aspects of the organisation's resources. Do you believe it represents a strength to the company (i.e. the company is in a better position than its competitors) or a weakness (i.e. the company is in a worse position than its competitors)?

The resource audit form opposite is a very useful tool for a group of planners to use in assessing an organisation's strengths and weaknesses. Obviously the one shown in the example would not be suitable for all organisations.

It has been found that a planning team of between five and twelve managers can be used to complete a resource audit form. Each resource (and its critical dimensions) are rated according to whether the individual considers it to be a strength (low, medium or high), a weakness (low, medium or high) or a neutral point (neither a strength or a weakness). When each member in the group has completed the individual ratings, an aggregate is found and the results made available to the planning team during a discussion session. What generally happens is that there is a wide range of views, and different members of the planning team can then give and gain insight into the various organisational resources. Individuals are then again required to complete an audit form, and the process is repeated. The insights gained

RESOURCE	High	Medium	Low	Neutral	Low	Medium	High
PEOPLE							
Adequate							
Skilled							
Loyal							
Service-minded							
MONEY							
Adequate							
Flexible							
FACILITIES							
Adequate							
Flexible							
Location							
SYSTEMS							
Information							
Planning							
Control							
MARKET ASSETS							
Client base							
General reputation							

during the discussions, and re-evaluation of the resource profile eventually leads to conformity and congruence, as individuals begin to see an overall picture from each other's point of view. The resulting resource profile can be drawn as a plot along the means on the resource audit form, providing a snap-shot of the resource situation in the organisation.

Bill Jones has identified the following as Tica-treat's strengths:
- A high level of brand awareness
- Good relations with buyers (the mines)

and the following as weaknesses:
- Low advertising expenditure means that brand awareness has not resulted in brand loyalty (the buyer is willing to switch brands with minimal persuasion)

Threat matrix

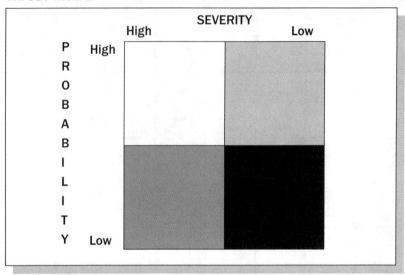

Opportunity matrix

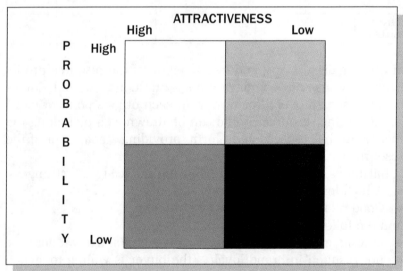

- Poor packaging in comparison to competitors (outdated package design)
- No defined positioning for the brand.

b. Environmental analysis (analysis of opportunities and threats)

Opportunities and threats refer to outside factors that can affect the future of business, and over which it has no control. Opportunities are observed trends or possible trends in the environment which are attractive to the firm. Threats are observed or possible trends in the environment that could be detrimental to the firm. Failure to identify opportunities and threats can lead to stagnation.

Many organisations are able to identify threats in the environment but then ignore them. The threat matrix offers a simple but powerful way of classifying and managing threats. To use it, the planning team simply needs to consider each of the threats identified and place them on the grid in the appropriate cell, evaluating each threat in terms of its severity and probability of occurrence. A serious threat is one that, if it materialised, could seriously hurt the company. If in addition it is highly likely to occur, it would be placed in the upper left quadrant. It would have to be managed constantly and contingency plans would probably be developed. A threat with low likelihood, or not a very serious threat, placed in the bottom right cell, could even be ignored. Threats in the other two quadrants could be monitored in terms of their movement along the axes.

Just as a planning team needs to consider the threats facing it, so too it must develop some facility of identifying, classifying and managing opportunities. An opportunity matrix can be used in very much the same way as a threat matrix. Attractive, probable opportunities should be managed and exploited; less attractive, less likely ones ignored; and opportunities in the bottom left to top right diagonal monitored for shifts in position. An opportunity matrix is illustrated opposite.

Bill Jones has identified the following opportunities facing Tica-treat:

- Mines using local products as they are cheaper than imported products, due to the weakness of the currency

- Changes in environmental legal requirements should increase the use of products such as Tica-treat

and the following as threats:

- Possible loss of the Japanese Tica suppliers as a result of poor relations with Smith's
- Major scientific advances by two American competitors.

15.4.3.2 Analysis of the competitive situation

Any appraisal of the strategic and marketing situation must include an analysis of the competitive situation. Too often, unfortunately, managers and academics alike misuse the term 'competitive advantage'. The cliché has been used and abused to the extent that its true meaning has become unclear. An excellent, simple model for understanding exactly what competitive advantage is and where it comes from is illustrated in Figure 15.4 below

Figure 15.4: The competitive advantage process model

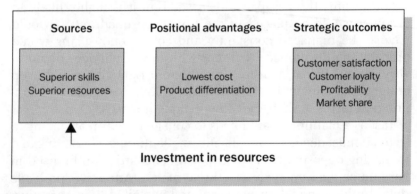

Briefly, what the process model tells us is:

Organisations have only two sources of competitive advantage. They either have superior skills (knowledge; ability; know-how) or they have superior resources (more money, more and better people, better plant, better facilities, better location, better information technology). Really fortunate organisations have both.

These sources of competitive advantage are used to gain a position of advantage. This positional advantage can be either the ability to be the lowest cost producer, or the ability to offer superior customer value. The ability to be the lowest cost producer means that the organisation can command a pricing advantage (sell at a lower price than competitors while making similar or higher margins). Alternatively, the company can sell at the same price as competitors and command higher margins. If the organisation cannot command a position of lower cost, it must compete on the basis of offering superior customer value. It must differentiate its product to the market in such a way that customers demand that product in particular, and may even pay more for it. This differentiation may take the form of better quality, more features, better service, longer warranty, bigger range, added convenience — whatever it is, it is something that makes the company's product different from that of its competitors.

If the organisation does command a positional advantage, a number of things will result, all of which should be important to management. The company will have customers who are so satisfied that they will support the company loyally. In addition the company will be profitable, and will maintain and even increase its share of the market. Theoretically, the financial results of competitive advantage are then ploughed back into what created the competitive advantage in the first place: superior skills and/or superior resources.

Most organisations give more attention to outcomes such as market share and profitability, than satisfaction and loyalty. The reason appears flawed when one considers that profitability and market share are transitory measures, taken at a point in time. Financial statements, for example, are really a company's history, and say little of its strategic future. Measures of satisfaction and loyalty are undoubtedly more effective indicators of strategic health.

15.4.4 Objectives

At this point in the plan the objectives must be outlined. Having defined where it is, the business must specify where it wants to

go to. An objective must be:
- measurable;
- time-constrained; and
- should allocate responsibility.

A marketing plan will probably include both financial and marketing objectives.

Bill Jones, in conjunction with Smith's financial team, has formulated the following financial objectives for Tica-treat:
- An average return on investment for the next three years of 25%
- Net profits for 1998 of R200 000
- A cash flow of R1 000 000 for 1998.

He has also formulated the following marketing objectives for Tica-treat:
- Attain sales of R2 000 000 for 1998, an increase of 33.3% over 1997
- Expand customer brand awareness from 50% to 60%, and top-of-mind awareness from 35% to 50% by the end of the year
- Increase market share from 10% to 16% by end 1998.

All the above objectives will be the primary responsibility of Bill Jones.

Objectives should also be stated in order of importance, and be reasonably challenging.

15.4.5 Marketing strategy

Having stated where the firm is and where it wants to go, the marketing plan should state how it is going to get there. The problems confronting most marketing planners is how to integrate marketing mix elements into the marketing planning process.

15.4.5.1 Integrating marketing mix elements into the marketing planning process

When writing a marketing plan, managers are often not sure exactly what to 'say' about the various marketing mix elements in the written marketing plan. We will attempt to highlight the important issues in the written marketing plan by discussing each mix element briefly, and then referring to a set of questions on the mix element. Answer these questions carefully and you'll find that you have a lot of the body of the marketing strategy section of your marketing plan.

a. The product plan

The strategy which an organisation adopts towards its product or service is the most important factor in its long-term success, but continued success will also depend on the ability to adjust to changes in the market place.

Products make profits for an organisation by effectively providing customers with the benefits they seek, within carefully controlled cost and revenue parameters. Here the concept of the product life cycle is useful, for it can be used to assess just where a product is in terms of growth, maturity or decline. This allows for the development of appropriate marketing strategies.

Decisions on product-market strategy should aim to maintain a product portfolio with a balance of growth products, mature products and declining products. This will provide a sound base on which to plan for future development, particularly the development of new products.

Try to answer these questions about the product, in writing:

- *What needs do our products/services satisfy?*
- *Who are our current markets?*
- *Will these groups be similar demographically, attitudinally or in behaviour?*
- *What are the sales trends for our products/services and the industry?*
- *What are our competitors' strengths in similar products/services?*
- *What marketing mix elements are important to the sale of our product/service?*
- *What changes will we make to existing products/services, in terms of such issues as quality, features, packaging, range and branding?*
- *What new products/services will we launch in the planning period?*

b. The distribution plan

The outlets available determine where customers buy products or services. Distribution planning should be based on a careful assessment of the market requirements and the ability of the organisation to meet them. The marketing channel through which products or services move is a network of institutions which themselves are linked by a series of mutually beneficial relationships. The marketing channel itself is dynamic, as are the markets it serves. Decisions regarding the choice of channel should be seen as an integral part of the organisation's marketing strategy, subject to adjustment in the light of circumstances.

Getting the product or service to the customer cannot be viewed by marketing management as the concern of others. The distribution activity of the organisation is as much a part of its marketing mix as are pricing, promotion and product decisions. The key to the successful development of the organisation's distribution is the adoption of a total systems approach, in which an integrative view is taken of the various activities involved in distribution.

The output of such an integrated system is customer service. The task implicit in the management of customer service is to achieve a balance between the cost of service and direct customer benefits. The appropriate level of availability, which is the principal component of customer service, depends not only on profitability, but also on the product-market competition and the channels used. Try to answer these questions about distribution:

- *What types of intermediaries are available for products/services similar to ours? What services do they perform?*
- *How broad is the market coverage of the different types of intermediaries?*
- *What are the financial and technical capabilities of current intermediaries?*
- *Who has the power within current distribution channels? What is their basis of power? How do they exercise their power?*
- *How are intermediaries motivated to cooperate with each other and with manufacturers for products/services similar to ours?*

- *What amount of communication is needed to keep distribution tasks running smoothly for similar products/services?*
- *Are there standard margins or pricing techniques for resellers of products/services similar to ours?If so are they sufficient to motivate our intermediaries?*
- *What is the average time for products/services to move from producers to customers in this market? How will this affect product design and distribution of our products/services?*
- *What intensity of market exposure do WE want?*
- *What are the channels of distribution and types of resellers used by our competitors?*
- *What types of intermediaries and how many do we want to get adequate market coverage given our sales and market share goals?*
- *What form of support can we expect from our intermediaries? How will we supplement this support?*
- *What factors will motivate intermediaries to buy and support our products/services?*
- *What margins will be expected by intermediaries and will these be sufficient to compensate them for service we expect them to perform?*
- *How will these margins affect our competitiveness in the market?*
- *Who will be in charge of distribution?*

Five areas, namely facilities, inventory, transport, communications and unitisation, constitute the *total cost* of distribution within an organisation.

- Decisions about facilities involve the number and location of warehouse and plant.
- Decisions about inventory involve how much inventory to hold in view of the problems of interest charges, deterioration, shrinkage, insurance and administration bearing in mind that the idea is to provide optimum availability.
- Decisions about transport involve owning or leasing vehicles, delivery schedules and so forth.
- Decisions about communications in the distribution system involve ensuring optimum customer support, which depends on optimum communications support.

- Unitisation concerns the way in which products and packages are grouped for handling.

There are **FOUR BASIC SETS OF OBJECTIVES in a distribution plan:**

1. Objectives related to outlet penetration
2. Objectives related to inventory
3. Objectives related to distributor sales and promotional activities
4. Objectives related to customer-development programmes (e.g. incentives for distributors).

c. The pricing plan

Pricing decisions are the most important part of marketing strategy. The price should always be related to the achievement of corporate and marketing objectives. The role of price must therefore be established in relation to such factors as the product life cycle; the requirements of the total product portfolio; and sales and market share objectives.

The methods used to achieve these goals are as dependent on the market and competitive circumstances as they are on costs. Indeed, the market-oriented approach to pricing sees costs as a constraint which may determine a lower limit to price, rather than as a basis from which price is determined.

Getting the price right has a direct effect on revenue and profits. Almost by definition, the price of a product determines the profit margin, that is, the difference between the cost of producing an item and the price at which it is sold. But price also affects the quantity of product sold, since a higher price may reduce demand, while a low price can lead to increased sales. The margins given to intermediaries in the marketing channel should be viewed in terms of the value added by them. In return for various functions necessary to the completion of the exchange process, the organisation will be willing to share some of the total channel margin available to it. The various types of margins commonly encountered are trade, quantity, promotional and cash discounts.

The price of a product depends on costs, on its perceived value and on the method of distribution. Pricing should never be done in isolation from other products.

Try to answer these questions about pricing:

- *What will our overall pricing objectives be?*
- *What are our costs?*
- *What are competitor prices for similar products?*
- *What is the perceived relationship between our prices and product quality?*
- *Are there any legal restrictions on our pricing policies?*
- *What control do we have or do we want over final prices that customers pay?*
- *What ability do we have to react to competitors' price changes?*

d. The communication plan: advertising and sales promotion

Communication with customers can be personal or impersonal. A salesperson's call is an example of the personal approach; a mass advertising campaign is an example of the impersonal approach. The mix between the two is known as the communication mix.

In the case of advertising, a vital element in devising persuasive appeals is an understanding of how purchase decisions are reached. The process of persuasion can be analysed as a series of steps up which a potential customer climbs, covering awareness, interest, attitude formation and the decision to act. If an organisation's offer has been correctly matched with customer needs, the customer should be persuaded to want the organisation's particular offer in preference to any other. This can often be accomplished by developing a psychologically unique appeal for the product or service (possibly through branding), correctly judging the price, and making the product or service available in a convenient way.

Managers can also utilise sales promotions. These must be used with precisely the same attention to objectives, testing and evaluation as in advertising. The cost effectiveness of any sales promotion must be established, and it must be integrated into the overall marketing plan. Sales promotions can be undertaken as a marketing tactic for any of the 4 Ps.

Finally, the manager must plan for the integration of information technology into marketing strategy, particularly as an aid to communication. Managers should learn to take advantage of new media such as the Internet and the World Wide Web.

Answer these questions about advertising and sales promotion:

- *What will the split be between personal and nonpersonal communication?*
- *Who is/are our target audience?*
- *What behavioural effects do we require of our advertising? Interest? Awareness? Conviction? Desire? Action?*
- *What are our advertising objectives? How will we measure them?*
- *How will we ensure that our advertising strategy fits the characteristics of each customer group?*
- *What will the advertising message be?*
- *What media will we use?*
- *How much will we spend on advertising?*
- *What will our sales promotion objectives be?*
- *What will our sales promotion strategy be?*
- *What will we spend on sales promotion?*

e. The communication plan: sales

Personal selling is often neglected by marketing management, yet personal selling is a crucial part of the marketing process and must be managed as carefully as any other aspect. Personal selling can be seen as a component element of the communication mix. A decision as to the role of personal selling in this mix can only emerge from an organisation's thorough understanding of the buying process which operates in its markets.

Particularly in industrial marketing, personal selling has a number of advantages over other forms of marketing communication. There are three basic issues that must be resolved if the salesforce is to operate efficiently. The first issue concerns the number of salespeople needed. The organisation should first establish the present pattern of work and then consider alternative ways of undertaking the tasks performed by salespeople. The next stage is to analyse the desired workload for each salesperson and determine how the work, once measured, can best be allocated in terms of territory and time.

The second issue is concerned with the objectives of the job of the salesperson. Sales objectives can be either quantitative or qualitative. Quantitative objectives are mainly concerned with what the salesperson sells, to whom he or she sells it, and at what cost. Qualitative objectives are related to the salesperson's performance on the job.

The third issue is overall management of the salesforce. Supportive modes of management are superior to repressive modes.

Try to answer these questions about sales management:

- *What is the required size of our salesforce?*
- *Where and how will we recruit our salespeople?*
- *How will they be selected?*
- *What plans do we have for sales training? How will we develop knowledge? How will we develop skills?*
- *How will our salesforce be organised?*
- *How will our salesforce be controlled?*
- *How will we develop, design and implement quotas?*
- *How will our salesforce be compensated? How will they be motivated?*
- *What will the responsibilities be in addition to product selling?*
- *What support can we expect from our intermediaries? How will we supplement this support? What factors will motivate intermediaries to buy and support our products? What margins will be expected by intermediaries?*

Try to answer these questions about the new media:

- *How will we use the World Wide Web in our marketing mix? What will we want to achieve with it?*
- *Who will design our web site, and how much will we spend on this?*
- *How will we ensure that our web site is continually updated and serviced?*
- *How will we measure the efficiency and effectiveness of our web site?*

Marketing strategy consists of the selection of a target market, the choice of a competitive position, and the development of an effective marketing mix to reach and serve customers. Bill Jones must decide specifically how he will attain his financial and marketing objectives. For example, his increased sales objective may be attained by increasing advertising, decreasing his prices, or pushing more salespeople into the field.

It is suggested that a strategy statement be presented in list form to cover major marketing areas and tools. Bill's strategy statement serves as an example. Here is the strategy statement for Tica-treat, prepared by Bill Jones:

Target market: All mines, with primary emphasis on coal mines; secondary emphasis on gold mines

Positioning: a cheap, effective treatment for cooling

Product line: redesign package

Price: somewhat below major competitors

Distribution: through Smith's salesforce only

Salesforce: to call more on mines with special 'deals'; relook at areas; incentive scheme

Service: technical advice and 24-hour service to be upgraded

Advertising: increase trade press advertising

Sales promotion: increase budget by 15% to allow for mass sampling at trade shows

Web site to feature an easy-to-use product specification tool whereby after the customer enters his or her information, he or she can identify the product in our range with the right specification to solve the problem

Research and development: increase expenditure by 20% to allow for conclusive research to be performed by the newly acquired expert

Marketing research: increase expenditure by 10%

15.4.6 Action programme

While the strategy statement represents the broad thrust that the marketing manager will use to achieve his or her objectives, each element of the strategy must answer the following questions:
- *What will be done?*
- *When will it be done?*

- *Who will do it?*
- *How much will it cost?*

After some thought, Bill Jones has decided that a project-scheduling type of action programme will best suit his needs. He has started to work on this and an example (incomplete, of course) of his action programme appears in Figure 15.5.

Figure 15.5: Part of Bill Jones's action programme

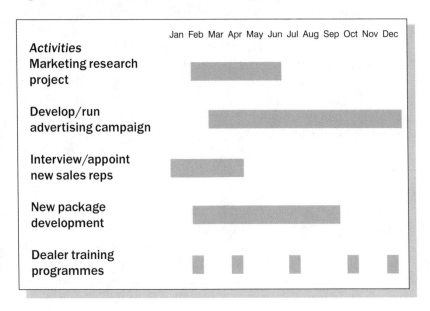

15.4.7 Projected profit and loss statement

The action plans should allow the manager to assemble a supporting budget that is actually a projected profit and loss statement. On the revenue side it shows forecasted sales, both in units and rands, at an average price. The expense side shows production costs, physical distribution and marketing costs, and these can be broken down into further categories. The difference is projected profit.

Once approved, the budget becomes the basis for developing material procurement plans and schedules, production schedules, recruitment plans and marketing operations.

15.4.8 Controls

The budget sets standards that should be achieved. A comparison of these standards with the actual results achieved, and the taking of corrective action, are essential parts of the control process. This last section of the plan outlines the control procedures to be applied to monitor the plan's progress.

The possibility of contingency plans should also be considered. A contingency plan outlines how the main plan will change if certain unexpected events occur, such as major competitor price changes. The purpose of contingency planning is to encourage managers to give prior thought to some difficulties that might be ahead.

15.5 CONCLUSION

There is no such thing as a perfect marketing plan. Most marketing plans are developed, redeveloped, altered, and then changed again over a planning period. By far the most important thing is that a group of individuals get together and talk about the future of a company, and where they want it to go in the future. The. procedures used and the document produced are far less important than the fact that they take the time to think carefully about where they are, where they might go, and where they would actually like to go. In addition, planning is as much about the past as it is about the future. Paradoxical as this may sound, planning is also about learning from the mistakes made in the past.

Introduction

The marketing concept and marketing departments

Creating competitive advantage: The ultimate challenge

Creating the future: Marketing capability without a marketing function

The task ahead

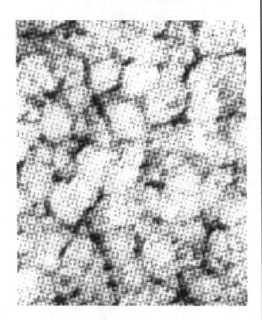

This chapter is based to some extent on: Hulbert, J.R., and Pitt, L.F. (1996) Exit Left Centre Stage? The Future of Functional Marketing, invited paper, *European Management Journal*, 14, 1 (February), 47-60.

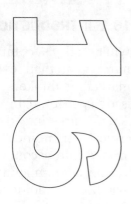

16 Does functional marketing have a future?

16.1 INTRODUCTION

While today's competitive climate means that marketing is more vital than ever to the success of corporations, many marketing thinkers are concluding that functional marketing is dying. How can organisations be simultaneously marginalising marketing departments and proclaiming marketing's critical importance? Our answer to that question will need to take into account both the competitive challenge presented by the contemporary market place and the unwillingness or inability of traditional marketers to cope with that challenge. The major focus in this final chapter is on how to manage the process of change in marketing itself.

16.2 THE MARKETING CONCEPT AND MARKETING DEPARTMENTS

Although marketing, and brand management in particular, had its birth in the 1920s or 1930s, it was not until the late 1950s that the concept of marketing was well articulated. Visionary thinkers such as Peter Drucker (1954) and Jack McKitterick (1957) predicted that the world would move over time from conditions of relative scarcity (sellers' markets) to relative abundance (buyers' markets), which would lead to the primacy of the customer. They also argued convincingly that a dramatic change in the way firms organised and managed themselves would be required to deal with this new reality. Many chief executives took notice, and the marketing practices of consulting firms such as McKinsey grew significantly as senior management adopted a traditional approach to such a challenge: delegation.

Thus began the functionalisation of marketing in many organisations, following both the example of fast moving consumer goods (FMCG) firms and the suggestions of some management theorists. Marketing became a 'function' of business, along with other functions such as operations, finance, administration and personnel management. In many non-FMCG companies marketing was a staff function, with responsibility in the hands of

someone commonly referred to as a 'marketing services manager'. However, specialised departments were the usual organisational response. In many instances, such departments were
perfectly adequate to meet the marketing challenges of the
1960s and 1970s. By the mid- to late 1980s, however, it had
become apparent that over the long term, functionalisation could
be viewed as no more than a stop-gap solution. Drucker's vision
of the 1950s was clearly coming to pass: a function that had
evolved to manage marketplace change was instead becoming
its victim.

16.2.1 Changing markets: marketing's death knell?

What is driving metamorphosis in the nature of marketing?
Figure 16.1 shows three related forces contributing to the death
of functional marketing.

Figure 16.1: *The marketing force field*

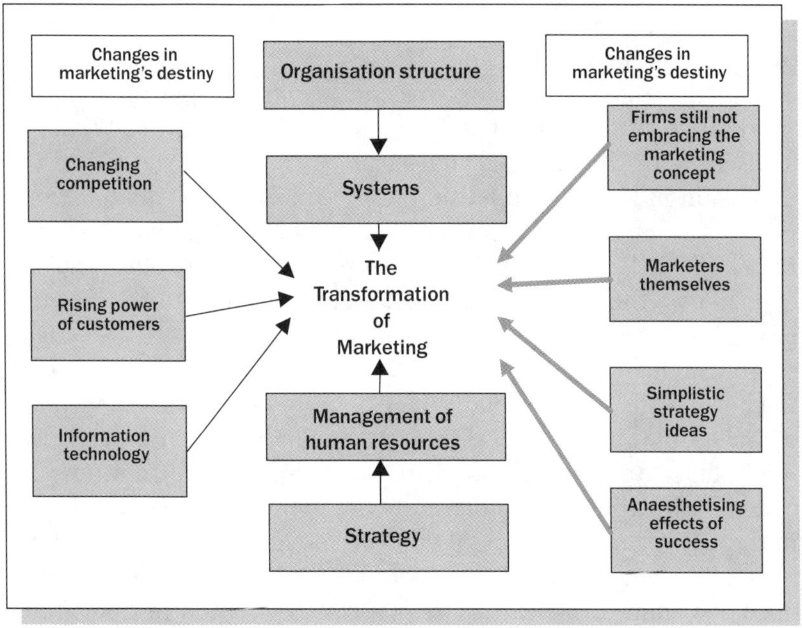

- changes in the nature of competition
- changes in the nature of customers (both intermediaries and final consumers)
- changes in technology (especially information technology).

16.2.1.1 Changing competition

World economies are becoming more competitive as business becomes globalised and industrial capacity increases accordingly. Current capacity levels and competition are such that supply will lead demand in most industries for the foreseeable future (Shapiro, 1994). The implications for marketing communication, branding and particularly pricing strategies will be profound. In the United Kingdom, for example, Coke and Pepsi, two brands formerly regarded as unassailable, came under such vicious attack in 1994–1995 that their market shares in supermarket sales have declined by 27% (Coke) and 28% (Pepsi) respectively, as shown in Figure 16.2. Other branded cola drinks have seen their share of the same market completely decimated. While it might be comforting to argue that no real threat has been presented to brand-name recognition and prestige, and that only supermarket soft drink sales have been affected, such complacency is the marketing equivalent of fiddling while Rome burns. What we are seeing in the UK cola market is simply one example of the explosion in global competition. Cott, an obscure Canadian company, has been competing very successfully against Coke and Pepsi, in markets ranging from Europe to Africa, by putting whatever names their customers want on its products. In the UK, this name has varied from Sainsbury's Cola (which looked and tasted so suspiciously like Coca-Cola that Cott was taken to court by Coca-Cola), to Virgin Cola (which is now being served in place of Coca-Cola on Virgin Atlantic Airline). Current brand leaders might take some consolation from the fact that supermarket sales of cola beverages do not constitute the major portion of total sales in the UK, where the bulk of volume moves through other channels. However, it will also be noted from Figure 16.2 that supermarkets' share of sales has grown by 18% in the period under consideration. If a successful but relatively small airline is able to have its own brand of cola, what is to stop the giants of the hamburger business or, indeed, the corner convenience store, from doing the same?

What is happening in the cola market is also occurring in other branded convenience goods markets, as chains go on making room for their own brands next to market leaders on their shelves. Nor is this by any means the only market affected, anywhere in the world. The Korean automaker Daewoo entered the UK car market in 1995, selling cars at fixed prices with three-year unlimited warranties, having no dealer network, and employing used car salespeople on a noncommission basis. This strategy seemed to fly in the face of all conventional wisdom in the auto industry. Yet the company took more than 2% of the British market within a year. When one considers that the better known brands such as Volvo and Saab have never achieved 2%, then the achievement is quite remarkable. Furthermore, as if the forces of global competition were not enough in themselves, the decline of barriers traditionally created by regulation and technology has accelerated the rate at which traditionally protected players in the media, financial services, telecommunications and power utilities have been battered and bruised by change.

Figure 16.2: UK supermarket cola shares

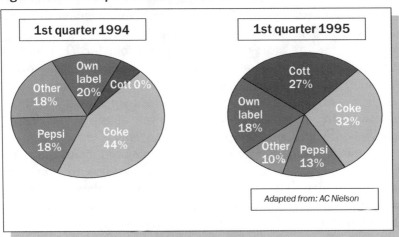

16.2.1.2 Rising power of customers

While astute marketers have always respected the power of the customer, in recent years this power has grown exponentially, until every business has been forced to acknowledge it. As Dickson's (1992) theory of competitive rationality suggests, aggressive competition has led to increased choices for customers, who at the same time are becoming ever more sophisticated. Thus, achieving effective differentiation grows more difficult all the time, while accelerating imitation means that even a high level of innovation is not enough to protect a business from its competitors. Paradoxically, then, while innovation becomes ever more essential, its advantages seem to dissipate just as rapidly.

The Industrial Revolution put scale into manufacturing, and for a hundred years or more manufacturers were at the helm. The last twenty years have witnessed a distinct erosion of the dominance of manufacturers. In many markets one can date the decline of manufacturers almost to the moment the first retailer scanned the barcode on the first product. Within some of these countries, we find great asymmetry in bargaining power, as measured by ratios of domestic sales revenues of suppliers to retailers. So it is not surprising that some manufacturers have chosen to restructure themselves in order better to serve their retail customers: 'At Procter and Gamble, there is now a marketing manager in charge of A&P and another one in charge of Giant Food Stores. These managers see their jobs in terms of solving problems for the stores they are responsible for' (Peppers & Rogers, 1993). For business-to-business marketers, the rationalisation of many industries has reduced the number of traditional buyers, even where new customers have appeared. Defence, pharmaceuticals and foods are just three of the industries in which significant consolidation has occurred.

Obviously, not all industries have been concentrating. In newer industries, small and medium-size start-ups are common while deregulation has increased the number of players in industries such as telecommunications. The fact remains, however, that thanks to GATT and now WTO agreements, large powerful buyers have global selection of competing vendors. In addition, technology and deregulation have made for quite dramatic increases in buyer power, which further changes the relationship between purchasers and vendors. The procurement functions of many large companies have begun trying to develop partnerships with fewer vendors, using systems such as just-in-time manufacturing (JIT) and electronic data interchange (EDI) to achieve precise integration.

As already indicated, however, it is unwise in a discussion of buyer power to overlook the position occupied by the consumer. First, the driving forces alluded to (globalisation, technology and deregulation) will affect consumers as much as business-to-business customers. And even more fundamental forces are at work, driven by demographic shifts. It is well known that slowing birthrates are rapidly ageing the populations of countries such as Germany, Japan and the US, where median population ages in the 30s are common. What is not so widely recognised is that the great progress on the population front in the '70s and '80s has produced a global shift of huge proportions.

Age distribution forecasts for the world's population in the first part of the 21st century, based on currently available data, show the ageing of the population is becoming a global phenomenon, with enormous consequences for marketers. An ever-growing proportion of future markets will be composed of experienced buyers who are more self-assured, more able to judge the relationship between quality and price, more sceptical of superficial blandishments and more confident of being courted with ardour by a multitude of sellers. Much better attuned to what value is, they will seek it out avidly, aided in their search by technology. It is both interesting and a little frightening for marketers to speculate on what this might mean for brand marketing. Will it make strong brands even stronger, or will consumers increasingly turn to house brands as they search for value? Will the corporate brand become as important in consumer goods as it is in services, with shoppers seeking to buy 'baskets' of products from a reputable company?

Where discretionary purchasing power rises, many different industries will be vying for affluent consumers' money. At the same time, the information resources consumers will be able to draw on when making their choices are set to expand dramatically. For those suppliers who create and deliver real value, prospects are brighter than ever (Gale, 1994), but for the fly-by-night, short-term seller they will become increasingly gloomy.

It is not only in so-called first-world markets that the major international players are being challenged. As trends such as rapid urbanisation intensify, consumer marketers realise that even having well-established rural markets cannot protect them against competition. When companies such as Unilever and Colgate Palmolive were the only firms with a marketing presence in many African villages, for example, their brands became generic: synonyms for the products they represented. As the descendants of consumers of these products move to the cities, however, they quickly learn that there are other kinds of 'Sunlight' (soap) and other kinds of 'Colgate' (toothpaste).

16.2.1.3 The effects of information technology

The market place of the future will be driven by technology to a far greater extent than it is today: interactive television, consensual databases, electronic couponing, fax machines in the home and a broad range of opportunities for electronic interactions with consumers, including the Internet and the World Wide Web, will become the norm (Peppers & Rogers, 1995). The revolution in information technology has already brought about radical change in the core capabilities on which competitive advantage in some industries rests.

Developments in information technology are also radically reshaping the nature of the organisation's interaction with its customers, with one-way communication increasingly being replaced by two-way interactions. As more and more information is exchanged back and forth, the infrastructure of many firms and the competitive environment in which they do business are being revolutionised. Already, many marketers are operating in what Rayport and Sviokla (1994) call the 'marketspace'. When traditional marketplace interaction is replaced by marketspace interaction, the wisdom of separating marketing (what the customer wants) from strategy (what the firm does) becomes more questionable than ever (Morris & Pitt, 1994).

The capacity to address the customer as an individual — what Peppers and Rogers (1993) refer to as one-to-one marketing, and what Blattberg and Deighton (1991) call 'interactive' marketing or addressability — could render many of marketing's most cherished assumptions obsolete.

- *Would it not be preferable to be able to address the customer as an individual rather than as a member of a target market however creatively defined?* Existing technology makes it possible to identify individual customers and to remember the history of each of their transactions with a firm. This, in turn, makes it feasible to tailor each part of the marketing offering to that individual. The customer transaction database becomes the most valuable asset for most firms (and the only asset for some). Businesses can now segment customers as precisely as they can segment markets.

- *Is share of customer not more strategically important than share of market?* Even knowing that a company has a 20% share of a given market is not that helpful strategically (nor is increasing that share a clear strategic objective). Does the figure mean that one in every five customers purchases the brand all the time, or that everyone purchases the brand once for roughly five purchases in the product category? Would it not be preferable to know an individual customer by name, and know that this customer would spend a certain amount of money on a product or service over his or her lifetime? Now the objective can be to obtain a particular, or increased, share of those specific purchases. Information technology is already making this both feasible and measurable.

- *Once we begin to think in terms of segmenting individual customers, and of customer share rather than market share, is there not a more effective financial measure of marketing performance than indicators such as ROI, or similar profitability measures?* If a firm is able to remember all the transactions it has with a particular customer, and uses these to predict future business with that customer based on likely reaction to marketing efforts, it can calculate the lifetime value of that customer. This means that marketing performance can be assessed by its impact on customer lifetime value. The lifetime values of the customer base can be thought of as customer equity. Customer equity may be a better measure of financial performance than ROI or similar indicators, and tracking changes in this a more efficient diagnostic of the strategic health of a firm.

Information technology is not the only technology that affects marketing and strategy. There are so many other exciting kinds of technology that are changing the world as we know it. Some observers are predicting, for example, that genetic engineering will be the next quantum leap forward. Emergent biotechnology makes it likely that the food, pharmaceutical and medical industries will increasingly be competing with each other, a trend we are already witnessing in skin and beauty care. A clash between the traditional values of the health care industry and the consumer-oriented (patient-oriented) strategies of some of the new players seems inevitable.

16.3 CREATING COMPETITIVE ADVANTAGE: THE ULTIMATE CHALLENGE

If markets are more competitive, customers more powerful and technology more pervasive, it must follow that the task of creating and maintaining competitive advantage becomes at the same time both more critical and more difficult. Indeed, various writers on the subject have speculated that sustaining advantage may be impossible in what is termed a hypercompetitive world (D'Aveni, 1994). Even those who believe it can be achieved, however, are unlikely to argue that functional marketing is capable of creating such an advantage in today's climate.

Marketers are increasingly accustomed to distinguishing between 'qualifying' attributes (those necessary to be in the customer's consideration set) and 'determinant' attributes (those that in fact determine which alternative will be chosen). In many cases increased competitive intensity will result in parity on some of the most important attributes, leading to the paradox of choice resting upon distinctions in relatively minor attributes.

Levitt addressed many of these issues with his concept of the augmented product and success via 'the differentiation of anything' (Levitt, 1980). Noncore product attributes not only afford the opportunity to differentiate, but in many cases bring the suppller closer to an understanding of the customer's reality. Misdirected quality efforts are likely to lead to a perfect 'tangible' product, delivered at the wrong time or place, or imposing intolerable cost on the customer. (See Gale, 1994, for a discussion of conformance quality.) In today's market place, price and product quality are insufficient, for the premium on speed, reliability, service support, reduced downtime and similar attributes is substantial. Increasingly time saved, effort spared and risk eliminated must take pride of place (along with price) in customers' trade-off decisions. As competition intensifies, then, marketers will increasingly need to identify new or shifting sources of value that can create advantage.

Unfortunately, however, identification alone is not enough, for once identified, value must be delivered. In brand management structures, traditionally, marketing had some control over the product, but as the basis of competition moves beyond the product and the brand this tenuous influence will almost certainly prove insufficient to control all the elements that will be necessary to satisfy the customer. In staff-oriented marketing organisations, even this limited degree of influence was rarely attained. In both cases, the expansion of bases of competition beyond the traditional domain poses enormous difficulty. If customer satisfaction increasingly depends on to-the-minute delivery performance, seamless IT interfaces, codesign of subsystems and macrosystems, multilevel multifunction supplier–customer partnering and other such (increasingly common) arrangements, what hope of solution is there with current structures? Creating and delivering this kind of customer value requires cross-functional cooperation of the highest order. Such cooperation can most probably not be achieved with traditional functional marketing departments, most of which lack the technical expertise, imagination and organisational clout to pull it off. In that sense, they are incapable of creating the kind of differential advantage that will be needed for survival as competition intensifies, and thus their demise seems ensured.

16.4 CREATING THE FUTURE: MARKETING CAPABILITY WITHOUT A MARKETING FUNCTION

16.4.1 Barriers to the transformation of marketing

One of the biggest barriers to defunctionalisation is management's failure to recognise the need for a marketing philosophy to permeate their companies (as shown in Figure 16.1). This is particularly true in the high technology and commodity industries: industries characterised, perhaps not coincidentally, by high failure rates and low returns respectively! Without agreement on the need for change, prospects for successful transformation are very low.

In other instances, the source of resistance is marketers themselves. When their function is politically powerful within their firms, they are frequently inclined to defend what they have rather than helping to create a broader future. Many marketing departments have, for example, seen tools such as Total Quality Management (TQM) as problems rather than as opportunities and have been slow to embrace information technology.

For all these reasons marketers are frequently seen as defenders of old strategies (particularly channel arrangements), rather than creators of the new. It is often the sales function that has collaborated with logistics and IT to lead in the new reality; as a result, many sales functions have been revitalised. The movement to capability-based marketing shifts decisions away from the marketing function, even where the function persists structurally. Either functional marketers must adapt to this reality and build their technical skills, or they will find themselves increasingly bypassed, until they have no role at all to play in the organisation.

Although sales may enjoy a new lease of life because of change, in some companies the 'lock' of sales on customers has had stifling consequences. Since the sales function may derive siguiflcant power from its ownership of the customer interface, there can easily be resistance to opening up that interface to participation by other functions. Encouraging sales to lead in this area can prove effective in 'debottlenecking', for partnering will typically demand orchestration, not control, from the sales function.

In other cases, a firm's preference for simplistic strategic ideas may block change. Many firms have invested immense amounts of energy in misguided attempts to define 'competencies' (Prahalad & Hamel, 1990, but see Quinn, 1992, for additional perspective). Vast amounts of time and money have been expended on defining competencies that have nothing to do with meeting customer needs, or that may have been useful in the past but are irrelevant for the future.

Perhaps an overemphasis on Porter's dichotomy of differentiation' and 'cost leadership' leads to a similar waste of resources. While simultaneously achieving high value and low cost is not easy, it is, as David Sainsbury of the UK supermarket group Sainsbury's has pointed out (Sainsbury, 1988), the target at which to aim. On another front, the US fast-food chain Taco Bell has achieved differentiation at low cost, enabling it to deliver the promise which makes it live in the customer's mind: value. The company has successfully positioned itself against hamburger giants such as Burger King and McDonald's by offering an alternative form of fast food in a different setting, while at the same time lowering its cost structure in such a way that it is able to provide inexpensive yet wholesome food.

Finally, there is the anaesthetising effect of success. The more successful a company has been, the more easily complacency can set in: firms become so successful that they fall asleep. There is in most organisations some inherent resistance to change, which success often reinforces. While failure may make it clear that it is necessary to change, the real test of leadership is the ability to see the need to change before failure occurs. Too few marketers successfully act as heralds for this kind of change, even though terms such as reinvention and managed change may permeate their vocabulary.

16.4.2 Managing marketing transformation

There is considerable cultural resistance to change in large companies (Kotter & Heskett, 1992). In order to succeed, change efforts must be preceded by a perceived need for change (Tichy & Devanna, 1986). Keeping organisations open to information from the outside and ready to act on it is therefore a key leadership task, for external inputs from customers, competitors, benchmarks and other key constituencies provide powerful stimulants. Further, change cannot typically be accomplished by a small oligarchy. Gaining the commitment of others is essential. Beyond creating a perception of the need to change and enlisting others in the cause, however, what have we learned about successful change management? Another key insight is the need for a holistic approach to change. Both McKinsey's seven Ss approach (Pascale & Athos, 1981) and the congruence model of Nadler and Tushman (1979) emphasise the need for the change effort to permeate all the structures of an organisation; attempts to change only one element in a complex organisation will inevitably risk being subverted by the other elements, so powerful (though often hard to observe) are the forces of stasis in most large firms.

Figure 16.3 provides a comprehensive view of the elements which can contribute to making marketing a true capability rather than merely a function. For organisational transformation to succeed, all these elements must reflect and reinforce the commitment to change. Most transformation programmes have focused on developing (or reworking) mission statements. While not wishing to be dismissive of these efforts, our experience has been that they are often defeated by deep-seated characteristics of the organisation, which have been grouped together in 'supporting' requirements. Let us therefore commence with these.

Figure 16.3: A holistic view of marketing transformation

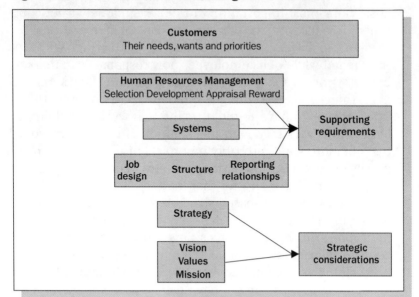

16.4.2.1 Organisation structure

Postfunctional marketing will undoubtedly require a core group of technical marketing specialists, ideally with a conceptually broad strategic focus within which these specialists can use their skills. Such a group of technical experts will almost certainly fit today's model of a staff function, for most traditional marketing activities, strategic and operational, are likely to be conducted elsewhere in the organisation. Any of the structural models described below seems capable of accommodating the changes one can anticipate.

1. An inclusion model. In the early days of the marketing concept, Pillsbury described how virtually all activities had been grouped under the heading of Marketing (Keith, 1960). Although at first glance this appears to be a brute-force approach, and was subsequently found unsatisfactory, British Airways has more recently found this approach, which one

might dub inclusion, very effective. Recoguising that two of customers' most important requirements, namely safety and schedule reliability, were under the control of operations, BA resolved to have operations report to marketing. With approximately 80% of its employees now responsible to marketing, BA comes close to McKenna's dictum, 'Marketing is everything and everything is marketing' (McKenna, 1991). They appear to have found a recipe that works for them, at least at this stage! Though this solution is not for everyone, the situation would probably be typical of most service businesses, where it is difficult to say where marketing starts and operations ends (or HR, for that matter).

2. Market and customer-based structures have a long history in marketing (Hanan, 1974). They have not often developed fully; powerful internal forces have ensured that structures were formed around products, technologies or even plants. As customer power has grown, however, structures focused on markets and customers have gained ascendancy. Procter and Gamble's catering to supermarkets, described earlier, is a case in point. As vertical partnerships become more common, more companies will reorganise in this manner. What may appear initially to be merely a salesforce change will, in an era of total competition, increasingly revolutionise many businesses, as more activities in IT, logistics, operational marketing and ultimately, perhaps, packaging and production, become grouped under customer or market banners.

3. Process-based organisation is a structural approach with many proponents. Although the company retains a classical function-based structure, the work is actually performed by cross-functional process teams. Much operational marketing is not within the domain of the marketers, who do, however, play the key strategic role in the brand development process.

Teamwork and integration are key parts of all the above, as they must be in any sensible restructuring of the marketing effort. Indeed, interfunctional coordination has traditionally played an important part in the marketing concept, as reaffirmed in recent research regarding what constitutes 'market orientation' (Jaworski & Kohli, 1993). But as intense competition makes factors such as billing, credit approval, fast delivery and customer service, crucial variables in more and more markets, such co-operation becomes vital. The satisfaction of customer needs in these areas demands teamwork of a high order. Appropriate organisational structure can provide a firmer foundation on which to build change efforts.

16.4.2.2 Systems

The technological power of systems, when used creatively, can contribute enormously to marketing effectiveness, but few companies have capitalised on their potential. The perspective on systems is usually that of the computer analyst or the operations expert; systems are therefore mostly used only to reduce costs, rather than to add value.

Yet merely by making information on customers more available and more widely distributed, systems can have a significant impact on the firm's orientation (Barabba & Zaltinan, 1991). More sophisticated systems applications can reduce the time, effort and risk involved in making a purchase.

Apart from user-friendliness, systems can also provide a means for companies to attack the soulless anonymity of trans-action-based markets. By providing customer records, systems permit even the largest companies to begin to emulate, the historically high personal service strategies of small local firms. The local grocer, who met and knew each and every one of his or her customers by name, and built a business on this knowledge, was a case in point. An example is the vendor-managed inventory pioneered by American Hospital Supply. More examples are well-designed loyalty programmes that various airlines have established and certain credit card companies have started to emulate. These are beginning to infiltrate even supermarket retailing. Data-based systems will increasingly support so-called segment-of-one or one-to-one marketing (Peppers & Rogers,

1995), and, combined with future interactivity, presage major changes in marketing, with more and more proactivity towards customers. Outsourcing partnerships might be especially relevant. A recent UK newspaper report (Lascelles & Adonis, 1995) has offered the following scenario:

'In your back kitchen, where you used to have your central heating boiler, a small gas-fired electricity generator whirs quietly It produces your power and uses the waste heat for central heating. It is controlled by an intelligent meter which works out every half hour whether it is cheaper to generate electricity or buy it from the grid. If it senses that the grid is heavily loaded, it can even pump surplus electricity back up the wire and sell it for you.'

The key to the changes is a view of the utility, not as a service, but as a marketing route into the home. Companies in the vanguard of these changes are those which appreciate the crucial importance of the firm's relationship with its customers.

Planning systems can also make an important contribution to developing an outward orientation. How, then, can planning and budgeting contribute to the transformation process? Firstly, good planning is externally driven and commences with a full review of the external environment, focusing particularly on customers and competitors. Secondly, good planning focuses on strategic development. On the other hand, preoccupation with financial budgets erodes the quality of strategic thinking which should be part of the planning process. Recoguising that the budgets show only our best estimates of the consequences of decisions and do not have an independent life is an important step in controlling this tendency. Thirdly, good planning is generally participative, involving not only line management but also those who will be responsible for implementing plans. This is not a new lesson, but one frequently disregarded in practice. Fourthly, planning should be an explicit process, in which assumptions and decisions are shared and critically reviewed. In the absence of such a process, quality of plans diminishes and learning is unlikely. Finally, good planning must rest upon a shared basis of good information. Political gamesmanship, involving withholding of information, inevitably defeats effective planning.

A final but vital impact of systems is in the area of measurement and control. When even accountants begin to attack the validity and usefulness of accounting data, surely marketers should take notice. A veritable furore has shaken up the field, as witnessed by multiple critiques of conventional approaches. Rappaport, for example, pointed out the gulf which separates accounting data from economic reality (Rappaport, 1987). Kaplan and others allege that many companies are saddled with archaic and irrelevant cost accounting systems (Johnson & Kaplan, 1987). Leading thinkers on accounting and finance are increasingly moving toward measures that look outward and forward rather than inward and back. Activity-based costing is making a siguiflcant dent in traditional costing approaches, while Kaplan has made a positive contribution by calling for measures which include stock market, operations and customer data (Kaplan & Norton, 1992 and 1993).

Meanwhile, in the field of marketing itself, advancing theoretical and empirical knowledge is beginning to have an impact. Theory on brand equity (Aaker, 1991) is being translated into formal brand health checks in leading packaged goods companies. An evolving alternative to brand equity is the concept of customer equity, whereby the financial worth of an organisation is calculated in terms of the net lifetime values of its customer base. Strategies could then be evaluated in terms of their ability to add to or detract from customer equity. Brands are thus viewed as important, but also do not have a life of their own. They are significant only as surrogates for the firm's customer equity. Movement in this direction is already underway, for in some companies measures of customer satisfaction have become routine. When properly used, these can be shown to have significant impact (*see* Liswood, 1989 and Anderson, Fornell & Lehmann, 1994). An emerging body of research based on the data from the PIMS project also has siguificant implications for measurement and control, and should lead total-quality committed companies to the realisation that the customer is central in defining value. In a recent book summarising much of this work, Gale re-emphasises the strong relationship between superior financial performance and providing the values customers seek at competitive prices (Gale, 1994).

There is an old but wise saying that 'managers do what is inspected, not what is expected'. As marketing becomes transformed into an organisation-wide activity, we expect to see major changes in systems for measuring and controlling business activity, which in themselves will help reinforce the changes of which they may be a consequence.

16.4.2.3 *Management of human resources*

If we review the traditional tools of human resource management, we see many examples of how they might be used to facilitate change. Recruitment and selection afford excellent examples. Some companies regularly recruit from their own customers to expand their insights into customers' needs. Likewise, many companies try to select employees who are customer-responsive. Southwest Airlines even uses frequent flyers as part of the selection team that interviews prospective customer-contact employees. That these attitudes and values penetrate the firm as a whole, rather than just marketing and sales, will be essential to the success of post-functional marketing.

Slater and Narver (1991) regard employee education as a precondition for developing market orientation. Certainly training and development present marvellous opportunities for both attitude change and knowledge and skill acquisition. Firstly, more companies are modifying their training courses to include greater customer participation, either as speakers or as participants and facilitators in the training process. Periods of customer contact work can be built into all career paths, preferably early in the employee's experience. Following the pioneering example of Townsend at Avis (Townsend, 1970), many service companies require periodic re-exposure. Going beyond the basics, other companies are becoming especially creative in seeking to obtain new insights into their customers' lives. In certain Unilever companies, cross-functional teams are pioneering new approaches to market research, whereby employees from a variety of functions are simultaneously exposed to customer input. Gessy-Lever of Brazil has experimented with ethnographic market research, with company employees living for a few weeks at a time in the *favellas* of Rio de Janeiro, in attempts to better understand these consumers' reality. At BHP, a large Australian resources company, teams of executives regularly engage in such activities as interviewing customers, visiting new country markets and developing market entry recommendations as part of advanced management development courses. In state-of-the-art companies, action learning of various kinds (Revans, 1971) is breaking down traditional bafflers both between learning and action and between firm and customer, and a stream of publications is beginning to advance such innovative approaches. (*See*, for example, *Business Week* (1992), also Fortini-Campbell (1992), and Gouillart & Sturdivant (1994).)

A final, vital opportunity lies in recognition and reward systems. Capability-based marketing rests on a shared understanding of the role of customers, and just as measurement and control systems should evolve, so must those pertaining to recognition and reward. At Xerox and AT&T, customer satisfaction measurement plays an important role in managers' incentive systems. At British Airways, where a change in management practices was viewed as an essential precondition to service excellence, employee-based assessments of management style became a central feature of managerial incentive systems. In a recent interview a well-known thorn in BA's side, Richard Branson, goes even further, as quoted before (Sheft 1995): 'I am convinced that companies should put their staff first, customers second and shareholders third — ultimately that's in the best interests of customers and shareholders.' In other companies, rewards based on teamwork rather than individual performance have helped to reinforce the message that cooperation is key to success.

When Dupont faced the challenge of improving its marketing competence, the company not only trained over twenty thousand (marketing and non-marketing) employees, they also instituted a marketing excellence programme which deliberately included extrafunctional considerations, such as demonstrating intra- and interbusiness marketing excellence. In the postfunctional era, cross-functional career paths will become more common, but capability-based marketing will mandate both direct and indirect strategies for moving the whole firm closer to the customer.

16.4.2.4 Strategy

A strategic approach to marketing is the final and very powerful means of restoring its effectiveness. It should be clear by now that in today's climate of intense global competition, the buyer, and not the supplier, rules. Consequently, firms have no choice but to focus great attention on customers. Such attention must entail more than the traditional type of responsiveness, however. Only through having real insight into customers' problems and being able to identify latent, not just expressed, needs and wants can market leadership be achieved. Clearly, firms need to nurture and develop appropriate capabilities and selectively match these to key opportunities; equally clearly, they may need to find new capabilities, whether by internal development, acquisition or alliance, in order to succeed in the future. Beyond any doubt, however, they need to beat competitors in creating and delivering value to targeted customers. The outlook for firms which fail in this central task is dismal indeed.

Self-renewal is ultimately necessary if transformation is to be successful. We argued earlier that success often breeds complacency. There is, in fact, considerable evidence that large organisations in particular are at their best when dealing with incremental change (e g 'continuous improvement'), but cope quite poorly with discontinuities (Tushman & Romanelli 1985). Indeed, large organisations need a modicum of predictability in order to function, even though this may sometimes result in rigidity via programmed 'standard operating procedures' (March & Simon, 1958). For that reason, there is an entrenched preference for the status quo in many companies that creates a powerful barrier to change.

Unfortunately for those reluctant to change, the firm's external environment is undergoing dramatic and rapid change. The need to adapt and evolve is therefore clear, yet runs contrary to a natural organisational predisposition. How can this final paradox be resolved? How can we ensure that we do not accomplish one change process, only to arrive at an end state already outdated by changing events (an outcome that is all too likely, given the rate at which large organisations change)?

The answer lies in defining an end-state which itself has an inherent capacity to adapt and evolve — hence the choice of the term 'self-renewing'. Truly strategic marketing plays a vital role in this renewal process. Self-renewing organisations are open to their environments, seeking inputs and learning from them (Devanna & Tichy, 1990). Of the various inputs, those from customers and competitors are key, those from other benchmarks invaluable. Marketing as a capability may ease the classic trap into which so many marketers fall: charged with responsibility for defending what is, while also embracing what will be. How can we defend mainframes while simultaneously marketing PCs? Tom Bonoma (1990) has suggested, with only a bit of tongue in cheek, that it is marketers' job to self-destruct, by making themselves unnecessary, because they have succeeded in making the whole organisation market oriented. As Drucker (1954) pointed out long ago, marketing is too important to be viewed as a specialised activity. And it may well be that only by sowing the seeds of our own destruction can we reap the benefits of long-term survival.

16.5 THE TASK AHEAD

Traditional marketers will increasingly face early retirement, unable to cope with, let alone contribute to, the change process. For forward thinkers, however, the ultimate victory is in sight. We write for the latter group, with a few suggestions for getting the process under way.

Leadership can play a crucial role. One of strategic marketing's key roles is to initiate change (Simmonds, 1986), and *carpe diem* (seize the day) is a good maxim for marketers. Weilbacher (1993) argues that too few marketers are advocates for their own customers ran uncomfortable but vital role in the transformation process.

Starting small also has much to recommend it. Some authors argue for a more bottom-up approach to organisational change, based on providing success models for promotion and emulation (Beer, Eisenstat & Spector, 1990). Some of the structural changes discussed earlier, like the customer-based reorganisation within Procter and Gamble, began on a small scale with the need to give special attention to important customers, and then broadened to include others, rather than emerging fully fledged. Grandiose schemes are not only sometimes overpromoted, raising unrealistic expectations, but are also dangerous, since the underlying assumption is that someone has all the answers beforehand. Such is rarely the case, and to operate on that premise tends to inhibit learning by doing, a 'cut and try' approach that often produces the best results. Lots of small successes can add up to a very big one, as long as those successes are communicated and recognised, rather than being ignored or viewed as exceptions.

The bottom-up approach was shown to be highly effective in research on achieving market orientation sponsored by the Marketing Science Institute (Slater & Narver, 1991). Market-back approaches, which involve exposing more of the organisation directly to customer feedback, with continuous evolutionary change in structures and systems, proved to be even more successful. Thus, broadening customer interfaces via multilevel, multifunctional contact for business-to-business firms, initiating free-phone talkback lines for consumers, eliminating intermediaries and interlocutors wherever possible, spending a day in the life of customers, and many of the approaches advocated in this paper do not just improve the way in which the organisation 'hears the market'. The evidence suggests that this is the most helpful way to promote a more fundamental shift of cultural values for the firm as a whole — to help it move further toward a market orientation.

Above all, change efforts should retain a practical focus. Not only is an overly intellectual approach likely to be less effective, it will almost certainly prove more expensive. Overt emphasis on such concepts as Vision, Mission and Values may prove helpful, but the obstacles to change are often deeply embedded in the firm's formal organisation, systems and human resource management practices. The prevalence of practices such as sampling and trialling indicates that marketers are well aware that it is sometimes more effective to change behaviour first, and trust that attitudes will follow. This looks to be both the simplest and most effective way to rid marketing of its functional heritage and place it squarely where its early proponents always intended it to be: at the heart of the enterprise, driving the actions of all of a company's employees.

References

Aaker, D. 1991. *Managing Brand Equity.* New York, NY: Free Press.

Anderson, E, Fornell c & Lehmann, DR 1994. customer satisfaction, market share, and profitability. *Journal of Marketing,* 58 (July): 53–66.

Barabba, VP & Zaltman, G. 1991. *Hearing the Voice of the Market.* Boston, MA: Harvard Business School Press.

Barwise, P. 1995. Marketing today and tomorrow. *Business Strategy Review* 6(1) (Spring): 45–59.

Beer, M, Eisenstat, RA & Spector, B. 1990. Why change programs don't produce change. *Harvard Business Review,* November–December: 158–166.

Blattberg, RR & Deighton, J. 1991. Interactive marketing: Exploiting the age of addressability. *Sloan Management Review,* 33(1) (Fall): 5–14.

Bonoma, T. 1990. A marketer's job is to self-destruct. *Marketing News,* June: 24: 10.

Business Week. 1992. Car dealers with souls. April 6: 66.

Capon, N, Farley JU & Hulbert, JM. 1988. *Corporate Strategic Planning.* New York: Columbia University Press.

Chartered Institute of Marketing. 1994. *Marketing — The Challenge of Change. UK: Cookham, Berks.*

D'Aveni, R. 1994. *Hypercompetition.* New York, NY: Free Press.

Devanna, MA & Tichy, NM. 1990. Creating the competitive organization of the 21st century: The boundaryless corporation. *Human Resource Management,* 29(4) (Winter): 455–471.

Dickson, PR 1992. Toward a general theory of competitive rationality. *Journal of Marketing,* 56 (January): 69–83.

Drucker, PF. 1954. *The Practice of Management.* New York, NY: Harper & Row.

Fayol, H (Storrs, C, trans). 1971. *General and Industrial Management.* London, UK: Pitman Paperbacks, Pitman Publishing.

Financial World. 1994. What's hot and what's not. August 2: 40.

Ford Motor Company: Dealer Sales and Service (Harvard Business School Case, 9-690-030). Boston, MA: Harvard Business School Publishing.

Fortini-Campbell, L. 1992. *Hitting the Sweet Spot.* Chicago, IL: The Copy Workshop.

Gale, B. 1994. *Managing Customer Value.* New York, NY: Free Press.

General Electric. 1990 Annual Report.

Gouillart, FJ & Sturdivant, FD. 1994. Spend a day in the life of your customer. *Harvard Business Review,* January–February: 116–125.

Hanan, Mack. 1974. Reorganize your company around its markets. *Harvard Business Review,* November–December: 63–74.

Jaworski, BJ & Kohli, AJ. 1993. Market orientation: antecedents and consequences. *Journal of Marketing,* 57 (July): 53–70.

Johnson, HT & Kaplan, RS. 1987. *Relevance Lost: The Rise and Fall of Management Accounting.* Boston, MA: Harvard Business School Press.

Kaplan, RS & Norton, DP. 1992. The balanced scorecard — Measures that drive performance. *Harvard Business Review,* January–February: 71–79.

Kaplan, KS & Norton, DP. 1993. Putting the balanced scorecard to work. *Harvard Business Review,* September–October: 134–147.

Keith, RI. 1960. The marketing revolution. *Journal of Marketing,* 24(1) (January): 35–38.

Kotter, J & Heskett, JL. 1992. *Corporate Culture and Performance.* New York, NY: Free Press.

Lascelles, D & Adonis, A. 1995. Highways into your home. *Financial Times.* April 8/9.

Levitt, T. 1980. Marketing success through differentiation — of anything. *Harvard Business Review,* January–February: 83–91.

Liswood, LA. 1989. A new system for rating service quality. *Journal of Business Strategy,* July–August: 42–45.

March, JG & Simon, HA. 1958. *Organizations.* New York, NY: John Wiley and Sons.

McKenna, R. 1991. Marketing is everything. *Harvard Business Review,* January–February: 65–79.

McKitterick, lB. 1957. What is the marketing management concept? In Bass, FM (ed). *The Frontiers of Marketing Thought and Science.* Chicago, IL: American Marketing Association, 71–82.

Morris, MH & Pitt, LF. 1994. The organization of the future: Unity of marketing and strategy. *Journal of Marketing Management,* 10: 553–560.

Nadler, D & Tushman, ML. 1979. A congruence model for diagnosing organizational behavior. In Kolb, D, Rubin I & McIntyre, J (eds). *Organizational Psychology.* Englewood Cliffs, NJ: Prentice-Hall, 443–458.